WRONG SIDE OUT

WRONG SIDE OUT

MADNESS MISDIAGNOSED

BENTON SAVAGE

Auctorem House
276 5th Ave, Ste 704-2591
New York, NY 10001
www.auctoremhouse.com
Phone: 1 888-332-7718

Published by Auctorem House: 02/24/2026

ISBN: 978-1-968059-32-3(sc)
ISBN: 978-1-968059-33-0(e)

Because of the dynamic nature of the Internet, any web addresses or links contained in this book may have changed since publication and may no longer be valid. The views expressed in this work are solely those of the author and do not necessarily reflect the views of the publisher, and the publisher hereby disclaims any responsibility for them.

CONTENTS

For my mother, Rachel, and
sister, Emily, for obvious reasons.

INTRODUCTION

Before I was diagnosed, I thought manic depression meant someone was a depressed maniac. I have since learned that the term describes the cycles between the polar opposites, mania and depression, that are separated by symptom-free intervals. The term "manic depression" was replaced with "bipolar disorder" by the medical establishment in 1980. The best reason I can uncover for this metamorphosis is that many people were confused by the term "manic depression," which led to the negative stigma perpetuated by such popular phrases as "manic Monday" or "homicidal maniac." The term "bipolar disorder" is believed to describe the condition more clearly.

I was diagnosed with bipolar disorder when I was twenty-five, the average age of onset, though many people are not diagnosed until years later. In fact, seventy-five percent of people with bipolar disorder have been misdiagnosed at least once, and many struggle for years not knowing what is wrong but knowing full well that something isn't right. Many are initially diagnosed with depression and are given antidepressants like Prozac or Paxil rather than mood stabilizers. This mistreatment exacerbates the condition by thrusting them into a dangerous mania.

The next ten years were marked by chaotic behavior and psychotic thoughts so bizarre I can't fathom how they happened to me, and nobody can believe I can recall those years in such detail. I really am lucky to be alive and fortunate I'm not in prison. There is no exaggeration or hyperbole in this book. If anything, I've toned it down, because some things I must bear on my own and take to the grave with me.

When I was released from the mental hospital in 2008, for what I believed would be my last time, I decided to write *Wrong Side Out: The Bipolar Experience* with total honesty, no matter how embarrassing the events were. My primary goal at the time was to prove to people that mental illness is real, because for ten years I had heard people say I was weak for taking medication. These people, often friends, would say, "I'm bipolar too. I just don't take medication. I deal with it on my own." If I had a nickel for every time I heard that . . . After collecting five dollars' worth of nickels and finally doing well again because I was taking my medication daily, I eventually would believe the naysayers and try once again to live medication free. The results were disastrous each time, growing worse and worse, because severely mentally ill patients cannot be reasoned with if they have been off their medication for a couple of months. At a certain point, they simply won't believe a word you say.

There are three types of mood episodes in bipolar disorder: mania, depression, and mixed. While I think most everyone understands what depression means, mania and mixed states are more complex and often difficult to identify, especially for the patient. Reasoning with a person who is manic is next to impossible. It is an alluring condition, and many sufferers long for those fleeting moments when they believed themselves omnipotent, invincible, and destined for greatness. To this day, I still look back on my manic days as some of the happiest in my life. Don't get me wrong: I don't want to return to that irrational thinking. But at the time, my optimism about my life was off the charts, and it was difficult to accept that I am simply human like everyone else.

A mixed bipolar episode is the worst and most confusing, not only for the sufferer, but also for those close to that person. It is defined by symptoms of mania and depression occurring at the same time, which doesn't make sense; but I have learned through experience that very little concerning mental illness does make sense. For example, a person in a mixed episode may refuse to eat because he believes he will live forever if he doesn't pollute his body with toxins. Not wanting food is a symptom of depression, while feelings of immortality are characteristic of someone in a manic phase.

Most patients who have mixed episodes are diagnosed with Bipolar I, characterized by inflated self-image, hypersexuality, and, more than likely, substance abuse. These individuals are hard to reach in their manic phases, which can last anywhere from a few weeks to several months, until they cycle into depression. In the depressive phase, they feel remorse and embarrassment over their past indiscretions. Bipolar I patients can't miss medication for even a single day without risking a venture into mania, and the longer the person is off his medication, the more manic he becomes, usually believing that he is "chosen" or "on a mission from God."

Bipolar II is more difficult to diagnose for a couple of reasons. First, Bipolar II patients tend to spend more time in a depressive state and are often misdiagnosed. Though Bipolar II is more manageable on a day-to-day basis, the excessive time spent in depression results in a higher suicide rate. It is speculated that as many as 50 percent of Bipolar II patients will attempt suicide in their lifetime.

Secondly, Bipolar II patients don't experience full-blown manic states but instead the lesser form, known as hypomania. Because this person is functioning at a high level and is exciting to be around, the life of the party, some people claim this condition is an advantage, particularly for the artist. Ernest Hemingway is considered to have had Bipolar II and obviously used the condition to his benefit for much of his life until his death by suicide. Although medicine wasn't available at the time, Hemingway probably wouldn't have taken it anyway, opting instead for alcohol.

I can't find any clear scientific evidence that having a family member who is or was alcoholic contributes genetically to a person being bipolar, but many doctors speculate that it does. One of the first questions a doctor asks a patient is whether there is a family history of illness. When I reply "No," the next question is inevitably whether there is alcoholism, to which I reply, "Yes. On both sides." This is followed by a nod of the psychiatrist's head and a checkmark on the chart.

While there may be no genetic evidence linking family alcoholism to bipolar offspring, more than sixty percent of people with bipolar disorder have drug and alcohol issues. With so many people misdiagnosed for a large part of their lives, many turn to alcohol and drugs to self-medicate, which only worsens the symptoms. Besides Hemingway, other heavy drinkers who are considered to have been bipolar include Vincent van Gogh and Winston Churchill.

Lithium is the most prevalent drug used to treat bipolar disorder. Although lithium was recognized in the late 1800s for its mood-stabilizing attributes, it wasn't until 1949, when John Cade published the first paper on its use in treating acute mania, that it came into wide use. For almost fifty years, medical experts didn't know why it worked. Then, in 1998, researchers at the University of Wisconsin discovered that lithium kept cells in the neurotransmitter glutamate at a healthy and stable level.

While lithium, just a salt, is hailed as a savior for many bipolar patients, I experienced tremendous side effects, including hand tremors, increased thirst, increased urination, weight gain, impaired memory, and poor concentration, the last two of which were especially troublesome for an aspiring writer.

Of course, we are living in the Golden Age of mental health pharmaceuticals; today there are many other drug options. But it is important to find the right fit, which can entail extended periods of trial and error. I took everything from lithium to Depakote, Lamictal, Paxil, Haldol, and Lexapro. Some worked better than others, but at no time in the last ten years did I feel stronger than I do now. Currently, I am taking 30 milligrams of Zyprexa Zydis, 40 milligrams of Celexa, and 300 milligrams of Wellbutrin. While this combination is working well for me, every bipolar patient is different. If your medication does not have you or someone you love fully functional, I recommend continuing to try different medications until the right mix is found. Unfortunately, some people with bipolar disorder do not respond to any medication. I am not one of those. But if this is your situation, keep faith, more drugs are on the way.

I believe a person is born bipolar. The disorder may lie dormant until a crisis arises, such as the death of a family member or the breakup of a relationship, but it was always there. Whether a person is fifteen or fifty when it first emerges, the most important treatment is medication. Although a good therapist can help you come to terms with the illness, therapy without medication will not suffice.

Why did I come to accept my illness when I did? Certainly, timing had something to do with it. A bipolar person must understand that he is powerless over the disease. I could no longer argue that I was not bipolar. There were no more loopholes left. I could no longer see ways to make a stab at life on my own. The only weapons I have are my medication and my support group.

I can't emphasize enough how essential it is to find the right medicine for your body chemistry. For nine of the last ten years, I was on lithium. There was never any discussion about my ever getting off it. I never questioned my doctor's decision. That is not their fault. I should have taken a more active role in my recovery. The madness we experience is as much a mystery to them as it is to everyone else.

My advice to those suffering: stay involved in your treatment. Talk honestly with your doctor. If you or someone you love is suffering from bipolar disorder, join an organization like the National Alliance on Mental Illness (NAMI). At the very least, educate yourself about the disease. There are many books on the subject and abundant information online.

Which brings us to the big question: Would I rather have the life of a bipolar person or the relative safety of being a "normal" person? My advice to those who are bipolar: don't bother thinking about it. It's never going to happen. Untreated, bipolar disorder leads to repeated "episodes" that can include arrests, hospitalizations, and suicide attempts, sometimes successful ones. Treated, you can enjoy a productive, satisfying, and "normal" life, but not necessarily as a "normal" person. Even with medication, I think about my illness all the time. It makes me question my own judgment. I don't fully trust myself to do the right thing anymore. I recognize that relapses are possible. And that is where I'm at: not only working to regain the trust of my friends and family but also striving to regain trust in myself.

I hope that Wrong Side Out: The Bipolar Experience aids those affected by bipolar disorder in understanding and accepting their condition and provides valuable insights for their friends and loved ones, who are undoubtedly impacted as well. By delving into the internal workings of my mind and presenting an honest account, I believe this memoir will be beneficial not only to individuals personally navigating this disorder but also to therapists, social workers, psychologists, educators, counselors, law enforcement officers, EMTs, ER doctors and nurses, other first responders, psychology and medical students, and anyone with an interest in mental health. In my experience, many people know someone with bipolar disorder, and nearly everyone has a perspective on this transformative condition. This memoir offers a genuine depiction of living with it.

New York City
Summer 2009

PROLOGUE

I don't know exactly how long I was locked in the trunk of my car, but it must have been two or three hours before I realized that I was being ridiculous. I had locked myself in the trunk because I thought that I was being spied on with hidden cameras by my lost love. A girl that I hadn't seen or spoken to in over a year. I had lived with this paranoia for close to two months, roughly the same amount of time that I had been off my medication. Figuring there was no way anyone could video me in the trunk of my car, I pulled the door closed and waited. I thought for sure this woman would open the trunk, and we would begin our life together. I thought that my plan was genius.

It was dark, and I felt confined, but I adjusted and eventually relaxed enough so that I was comfortable. I listened to the voices of unsuspecting people as they walked by my car. More time passed. I began to have second thoughts. I wasn't dehydrated, but I had enough sense to know that soon I would be. Finally, I began to thrust my hips up to the trunk in an attempt to crash my way out of there. I did it again and again. Bang. Bang. Bang. *Slowly I made a dent. A sliver of light snuck through the newly formed crack.*

I rested. Then bang, bang, bang *once again. My body was getting sore, and though a light, refreshing breeze now filtered through the opening, I was getting the general feeling that the trunk was idiot proof. I needed someone to get me out of there.*

Luckily, I was on a busy downtown street. Looking back, it is surprising that no one noticed me earlier. Maybe they did and were just afraid of what they might find inside. It's not every day that someone locks himself in the trunk. Finally, I heard the static of a two-way radio, followed by the deep voices of policemen.

"Who's in there?" one of them called out.

"Benton Savage."

"Are you all right?"

"Get me out of here."

A moment later a crowbar came through the crack as the policemen jimmied the trunk open. I shielded my eyes from the light. Besides the two policemen, a crowd of ten or twelve people had gathered around the car.

"Thanks a lot," I said, hopping out.

"What were you doing in there?" asked one of the policemen.

"I locked myself in."

"Why?"

"I'm bipolar. I haven't been taking my medicine."

"Were you trying to kill yourself?"

"No. I knew I would get out eventually."

"Really?"

"Yeah. Listen. I really need to get something to drink."

"We need to take you to the hospital."

"No. Believe me. I'm going to take my medicine."

"Just the same. We need to have you checked out."

The policemen took me to the psychiatric ward of the local hospital. I guess I was in shock because for the life of me, I don't remember one detail about my visit except that they released me the next day. I can't imagine what I must have said to be granted that luxury.

CHAPTER 1

I never saw it coming. No one wants to believe he is completely unhinged. Maybe I should have taken the hint when, throughout my life, friends referred to me as "Crazy Benton." Of course, I took it as a compliment—a label for someone who liked to have fun at any cost. That's where I'm going with this. As a rule, people with bipolar disorder are drawn more intensely to pleasure than the average person, let alone a cocky kid fresh out of college.

Everything shifted in my mid-twenties, when I experienced my first "episode," as it's called in psychiatric circles. The buildup was slow and agonizing. In the early days of grappling with my diagnosis, I tried to pinpoint when it began, but the truth is it started at birth. There was nothing I could have done to prevent it. It was part of me from day one.

Sometimes I regret my past behavior, the wasted time, the lost opportunities. I think of college days when, after a night of heavy drinking, I would spend the next day sprawled on the couch watching reruns of *Saved by the Bell*, too lazy even to smoke pot. Or my childhood, when I cried like an infant after losing a YMCA basketball game. I think of the fact that I had only one serious girlfriend until I was thirty-five. These might sound like the typical pitfalls of growing up; after all, no one is perfect, I tell myself. We all have problems. But more likely it was this strange illness, already wreaking havoc in my life.

It wasn't until 1998, when I was living in Atlanta and working as a commercial real estate agent, that the real theatrics began. An untreated bipolar woman might become promiscuous, but most women are repelled by the advances of a manic man, and I was no exception. I would get fixated on women who wanted nothing to do with me. I had always been a little awkward around women, but I had never crossed boundaries—until then. That changed quickly, and I was powerless to stop it. I began doing things I knew were wrong but couldn't restrain myself. If a woman gave me the slightest hint of interest, I pursued her to the gates of hell, humiliating myself in the process. I wasn't exactly a stalker, but I was on the fringe.

By then, my first wave of friends were marrying their college sweethearts, and I didn't want to be left behind. I was desperately unhappy, convinced that marriage, and only marriage, could redeem my life and lift me from the downward spiral. I pursued that goal with a reckless abandon I had never known before.

This was no small task. Even on my sanest days, I wasn't remotely a womanizer, not even in my wildest dreams. I could talk to women, but I never seemed to say the right things, though they didn't always walk away. With Lane Johnson, however, things were different.

I had dated Lane two years earlier, back when I was still relatively normal. She was on summer break from college, while I was lingering in our hometown of Cleveland, Tennessee, trying to launch the brilliant career I was certain awaited me. On our first date, we shared a bottle of wine at an outdoor café in Chattanooga and spoke with a candor I had never experienced with another human being. Lane was younger than any woman I had ever dated, yet despite the age difference, she made me feel naïve in a strangely endearing way. She questioned my belief in an Almighty God and challenged the contradictions in my conservative political views, for example, how could a far-right Republican advocate the death penalty but prohibit abortion? We laughed and listened as each of us talked about the things that mattered most, mainly our families. By the time I dropped her off at the end of the night, I was hopelessly caught in her web.

When Lane returned to college at the end of summer, we stayed in touch for the next two years through long-distance phone calls and handwritten letters. They weren't love letters, just thoughtful notes about our daily lives. She studied abroad in Leeds, England, while I was in Atlanta, trying to do my thing. Around her, I tried hard to act normal. I didn't want to ruin whatever chance I might still have. I knew she was dating other men, and meanwhile, I was making a fool of myself chasing after any girl who showed me the slightest kindness. Yet in the back of my mind, Lane was always there. She was the only woman I had ever met whom I would have married without hesitation and never regretted it. Then one thought struck me: Why don't I just ask?

It wasn't going to be easy. Lane and I had drifted out of touch, and we hadn't spoken much in the past six months. But suddenly, with this revelation, that maybe all I had to do was ask her to marry me and she would be mine, I couldn't wait. Tomorrow wasn't soon enough. I was sitting at my real estate office, staring blankly at my computer screen, when the idea hit. Without calling, I left work and drove straight to Nashville, where she was attending Vanderbilt. I bought a map, found her address, and showed up at her apartment without even packing a change of clothes. I was completely out of control.

Unfortunately, Lane wasn't home. Her roommate invited me in, and I sat nervously on the couch while she called Lane. I hadn't been this anxious about seeing a girl since the day I lost my virginity. After a few minutes, I couldn't sit still. My restless legs carried me around the apartment. On the refrigerator, magnet letters spelled out Rufus. Though I had never met him, I knew Rufus was Lane's dog. The silence pressed in on me, so I felt compelled to make conversation with her roommate.

"That's the good thing about dogs, they always come back home," I said.

"If they're smart, that is," she replied.

Her words echoed in my head. *Was I the dog, returning home to Lane, hoping to prove myself smart for doing so?* Everything felt off, as if the walls were closing in. I couldn't decide if I was happy or sad. If I had been a spiritual person, I might have called it an enlightened moment.

Lane showed up about a half hour later, looking like hell. She was one of the most beautiful women I had ever known, but something was wrong. Her hair was a mess, her clothes were shabby, and she looked like she hadn't showered in days. A burly guy with a beard walked in behind her. This was not how I had pictured the moment.

"What are you doing here, Crazy?" Lane's eyes widened as she walked over and hugged me.

I asked if we could talk in private, and she led me into her bedroom. That was the room I wanted to be in, but again, something felt off. Clothes were strewn everywhere, and when I ducked into the bathroom for a nervous piss, the toilet hadn't been flushed. I didn't know what to make of it. Were these signs? Could she have known I was coming?

We sat on the edge of her bed. After the four-hour drive from Atlanta to Nashville, I was wound so tightly I thought I might hyperventilate.

"Calm down, Benton. What do you want to say?"

Her deep voice soothed me, and without hesitation I blurted, "Lane, I love you."

"I love you too."

She smiled, but it wasn't enough. I don't know what I expected, but I had hoped we'd start tearing off our clothes right there. A simple I love you too felt inadequate. So I pressed forward with brutal honesty, as if that had ever worked for me before.

"You don't understand. I want to spend the rest of my life with you."

Her eyes and mouth sagged. "I can't commit to something like that. I'm going to Scotland next semester. You'd have to go with me."

Hoping the third try would be the charm, I said, "I want to marry you. Right now."

"You're crazy. You know that?"

"I'm serious."

"I know you are."

"Is it because of that guy?" I nodded toward Paul Bunyan out in the living room. The whole time, I half expected him to burst in with an axe and chop me to pieces. I'm not exaggerating—that's the beauty and the curse of the untreated manic mind. Anything feels possible.

"It's not about him," Lane said.

"Then what is it?"

"I just can't. I'm not ready. I don't even know if I believe in marriage."

"Trust me, Lane. I've grown up a lot in the two years since we dated. I'm ready for this."

"I can tell you've grown up, and I know you're ready but I'm not. Please try to understand. I don't want to hurt you. I'm just not ready."

"I'll get a ring. What size do you wear?"

"A five. But you're not listening to me. I'm not ready to start a family. We haven't even talked about whether you want children or if I want them."

"I always figured you'd want a whole football team of boys," I said.

"Maybe. But not now."

Lane stopped and fixed her gaze on me. She was clearly taking this proposal seriously.

"Can I kiss you?" I asked.

When we kissed, Lane bit my lip. I pulled away. She smiled slyly. What did the bite mean? Was she being playful, or spiteful? With Lane, it was impossible to tell. She was almost as unpredictable as I was which was one of the reasons I loved her.

"I need to go," I said.

"Right now?"

Of course I didn't want to leave, but I hoped she might come to her senses and stop me as if one kiss could be as powerful as Prince Charming's.

"I've asked you what I wanted to ask. I need to get back to Atlanta. I have to work tomorrow."

"That's one of the reasons I love you so much. You're so spontaneous. Don't be mad at me because I'm not. I wish I were, but I'm not made that way," Lane said.

I saw the disappointment in her eyes. I wanted her to understand that I was just as disappointed, but I also needed to show strength that my life would continue at the same pace, with or without her.

"I know we're different, but that's what could make it wonderful. I don't want my wife to be a mirror image of me," I said.

"I understand. But what's the rush?"

"I'm not going to live forever. Time is precious, and I want to spend mine with people I love, and with people who love me. If you don't feel the same way, then I'd best go on my way."

"I'm still in college, Benton. You know that, don't you? I know you wouldn't trade your college years for anything."

"Listen, I understand. I really do. I just didn't want something to happen and you not know exactly how I feel."

Though I was heartbroken, I felt a certain satisfaction in believing I had done my best. And really, what did I expect? That she'd leap into my arms and we'd ride into the proverbial sunset? No. I knew better. She was still in college, and I had no intention of quitting my job and moving to Nashville, much less Scotland, for Chrissakes. All I wanted was to get her thinking. Maybe she'd change her mind tomorrow, or next week, or even next year. There was no harm in professing my love, and I planned to never tell a soul what I had done. It would remain just between Lane and me.

But my mind wouldn't slow down. I replayed our conversation backward and forward, trying to decode every word Lane had said. By the time I reached Atlanta, four lonely hours later, everything had changed. I was no longer satisfied that I had done my best. I was no longer willing to wait until tomorrow, next week, or next year. I wanted Lane right then, and I wasn't taking no for an answer. I was pulling out the trump card: I was going to buy a ring.

There were a few reasons I thought this was reasonable behavior. The most obvious was how readily Lane had disclosed her ring size. Unlike me, she wasn't the type to speak without thinking. She wouldn't have told me that unless she expected me to act on it.

But the deeper reason went back two years, when I was courting her like a European prince. I had tossed off a line about how I planned to raise my kids, that I'd guide them, but let them learn lessons for themselves instead of dictating conclusions. I thought autonomy was the best way to raise emotionally responsible children.

Of course, it was pure bullshit. I hadn't given a second's thought to how I'd raise kids. I don't think I had ever even held a baby at that point. I was just fishing for a flattering response, that one zinger to crumble any walls still standing between us. Apparently it worked, because Lane replied with the most flattering words I'd ever heard: "I want your genes."

I took it as a monumental compliment, and I never forgot it. I have a knack for remembering past conversations, but with Lane, I especially clung to every word. So when I crept back into my apartment in the middle of the night, my head was not just in the clouds, it was orbiting the sun with the other planets.

When I woke the next morning, the first thought in my head was buying the ring. My credit cards had low limits, so I gathered my financial records to prove to the jeweler that I could cover a large check. Then I sped out of Atlanta, heading back to Nashville, feeling like Dustin Hoffman in *The Graduate*, racing to Santa Barbara to stop the wedding in the final scene. Simon and Garfunkel echoed in my mind as I hummed, "Oh, where have you gone, Joe DiMaggio? Our nation turns its *lonely* eyes to you."

There was a jewelry store not far from Lane's neighborhood. I don't think I had ever set foot in one before, but its proximity was good enough. I walked in like a man on a mission. I didn't wander the aisles or gawk at the glittering cases, none of that interested me.

"I want to buy an engagement ring," I told the jeweler.

He eyed me with suspicion. Only then did I realize the gravity of the moment. This wasn't just a purchase; it was a negotiation—an activity I had never excelled at and certainly didn't want to attempt now. I was far too impatient to be a good bargainer, as I had already proven many times. Still, I steeled myself not to let this professional drain my bank account.

"How much do you want to spend?" he asked.

I'd heard that a man should spend ten percent of his annual salary on a ring. As a first-year commercial real estate agent working solely on commission, that formula would've landed me at a two-hundred-dollar ring. I'd seen on late-night shopping networks that two hundred bucks could get you a "diamelle"—whatever the hell that was, but of course, that wouldn't do. Luckily, I was a trust-fund kid living off money earned by generations before me.

I settled on a six-thousand-dollar ring. I could have gone higher, but I didn't want Lane to think I was trying to buy her love. The jeweler launched into a lecture on shape, clarity, cut, carat weight, and color. I barely listened. I was in a hurry, and none of that babble meant anything to me. All I wanted was to buy the rock and get the hell out of there. That was the only way I could stomach handing over six grand.

"What happens if she doesn't accept? Can I return it?"

The jeweler lowered his goggles and gave me a strange look. He wanted the sale, but he clearly didn't know what to make of me. In half an hour, I had walked in, picked out a diamond, and bought it, now I was asking about the refund policy.

"It's funny, young man. No one has ever asked me that," he said. "Men have returned engagement rings, but none have asked beforehand if they could."

I picked up the ring the next day at five o'clock. The store closed at seven. If Lane said no, I'd have only a narrow window to return it, or else I'd have to spend another night in Nashville. I needed to get back to Atlanta, I had a job, or at least I thought I still did. For all I knew, I'd been fired already. I hadn't even called in sick after walking out of the office without explanation the day before. But there was no time to worry about that. I left the store and drove straight to Lane's. I could barely keep the car on the road, I was so excited. Once again, I imagined myself as Dustin Hoffman barreling to Santa Barbara to stop the wedding. I couldn't get that damn movie out of my head. It was my proof that maybe, just maybe, this idea would work.

Lane wasn't home. I stayed in my car and smoked, cigarette after cigarette. I don't think I'd smoked that many since the last time I did Ecstasy. As soon as I finished one, I lit the next with its cherry. I knew it was a terrible idea. Lane didn't smoke, and I certainly wasn't putting my best foot forward by showing up reeking like an ashtray to ask her to marry me. But I couldn't stop.

As I waited, I couldn't shake the creepy feeling of being a stalker, sitting outside a place where I didn't belong. I hadn't called Lane. She wasn't expecting me. For all I knew, she didn't even want me there. But I couldn't stop. No matter how wrong it felt, I had to go through with it. If it worked, I'd be a genius. If she was repulsed, then I was crazy. Obviously, I was willing to roll the dice.

Finally, Lane pulled up.

"Hey, Crazy! What are you doing here?"

She stepped out of her car looking ravishing, burgundy lipstick pressed against her voluptuous lips, a royal-blue blouse paired with white slacks that showed off her lean figure. Yes. This was it. This woman would be mine.

"I thought I'd come see you," I said. It wasn't the right line to deliver with an engagement ring in my pocket, but there was no script for this.

"I only have a few minutes," she said. "I've got another class in half an hour."

"That's all right. I won't be long."

I followed her into the dim apartment. She still wouldn't meet my eyes, not shy, but wary. Damn. I felt creepy, but it was too late. If I didn't ask her now, I'd be standing here tomorrow with the ring in my hand. I had to do it. No matter what.

"Did you drive all the way from Atlanta?" she called from the kitchen.

"I had to see you," I said.

I touched her arm to stop her from moving around. At that point, I just wanted to get it over with. It was obvious she would say no. She could barely look at me, much less consider marrying me. I should have had a speech prepared or at least gotten down on one knee, but I didn't. I reached into my pocket and pulled out the case.

"Lane Johnson, will you marry me?"

She placed her hand on her heart and snatched the ring before I could slip it on her finger. Her eyes sparkled with glee. I had never seen such unbridled enthusiasm from her, and for a moment I thought the scheme might actually work. That was the strange part: this didn't feel like love. Not even lust. It was about probability, simple cause and effect. If I asked Lane to marry me, she would have to say yes. Who had ever heard of a woman turning down a marriage proposal?

"It's the most beautiful ring I've ever seen," Lane said.

I looked at it again. Suddenly, it seemed small. One carat wasn't much, and the extra money I had spent on color and clarity hardly made a difference to the naked eye.

"Let's just go and never look back," I said. "Everything will work out. I promise."

"Where would we go?"

"I say we get married in Gatlinburg."

"Gatlinburg?" She smiled, holding her hand in the air to admire the ring. "It even fits. How did you know my size?"

"You told me."

"That's right. I did."

Was it possible she didn't remember? That one detail—her ring size—had been enough to convince me to go through with this.

"What would we do for money? Where would we live?" she asked, still unable to take her eyes off the diamond.

"I've got money, and I don't care where we live."

"What would people say? Have you told anyone about this?"

"Why should I? It doesn't concern them."

Lane's brown eyes softened with sorrow. Before she spoke again, I knew she was turning me down. I wanted to argue, but I didn't want to beg. I was already humiliated for having pushed this far with such a reckless proposal.

"You know I love you, but I can't get married. Not now. Maybe someday. But not now."

"Why not now?"

"I have school, for one thing."

"You can finish school."

"I know, but… but—"

"If you don't want to, that's okay. I just had to ask. I had to know for sure. You can't blame a man for trying."

I was letting her off too easily, and I knew it. I wasn't pleading my case with the conviction I should have. But this wasn't like haggling with a used-car salesman. Either you're in, or you're out.

"I'm glad you asked me. I'm flattered," Lane said.

"Then why won't you marry me?"

"I'm just too selfish right now. I wouldn't be any good to you as a wife. Not now, at least."

I thought about hugging her but didn't. It would have been meaningless. Instead, I turned to leave. Lane ran to the door to open it for me.

"I love you," she said.

"I guess that isn't enough this time."

There were so many things I wanted to say, but I knew they would be pointless and only make an awkward situation worse. My proposal may have been pathetic, but at least I hadn't begged. Nothing was going to change her mind.

All I wanted now was to get that six-thousand-dollar check back from the jeweler, return to Atlanta, and try to piece my life back together.

It was a quarter till seven when I arrived at the jewelry store. I walked in and handed the case to the jeweler without preamble.

"She said no. How much do I get back?" I asked.

"I'm sorry to hear that."

"What do I owe you?" I had no interest in small talk. I wanted this finished, forgotten, erased.

"You must pay for the setting. That's three hundred dollars. You'll have to call and cancel your other check for six thousand and write me another for three hundred," the jeweler said.

"Why can't I just have the other check back?"

"I've already deposited it."

Back in Atlanta, I was surprised at how upbeat I felt over the next few days. I buried myself in work at my real estate company and pushed forward with night classes for my master's program at Georgia State. I tried to forget Lane, but it wasn't easy. Deep down, I still felt the case wasn't closed. That kind of thinking, stinking thinking, would prove to be my downfall.

The first real sign of paranoia came with a call from Justin Roberts, a friend in Charlotte. We had lived together in Aspen right after college. Now he was in law school at UNC and applying for an internship in Washington, D.C. He had listed me as a reference and wanted to make sure I understood not to mention our history of drugs and alcohol.

I was flattered. Here I was with my first real job, and someone thought highly enough of me to use me as a reference. It felt like proof that I was growing up.

When I hung up, I felt good. It was nice catching up, and I was glad he was doing well. But as I sat staring at my computer screen, the conversation began replaying in my mind. The more I thought about it, the stranger it seemed. Why would Justin put me down as a reference?

Then I remembered: when Lane and I were dating, I had shown her photos from my time in Aspen. She'd once commented that Justin looked like Patrick Swayze. My mind spun. Could Justin's call have been a coded message? Could Lane somehow be checking up on me, using old friends to probe into my past?

My thoughts spiraled. Was it possible Lane had used sex as a tool to coax my friends into revealing stories about me?

Over the next couple of days, my mind descended to depths I had never conceived. Suddenly, every call I received, every person I spoke to, every voice I heard, whether a friend or a stranger, filled me with suspicion. I didn't want to go to work. I didn't want to go to the grocery store. I didn't want to talk on the phone, not to friends, and especially not to family members. If Lane had slept with a friend, I could simply exile that person from my life. But if it were a family member, I would have to face them for the rest of my life.

Calls from my past kept coming in. If someone laughed about something ridiculous I had done, I imagined they had told Lane about it. If they mentioned other friends, I imagined those friends had double-teamed her. If they mentioned multiple friends, I imagined there had been a gangbang. Conversations as breezy as commenting on the weather took on completely different meanings when I was untreated. I assumed everything people said to me was a lie, so I would simply do the opposite. A friend might say that I should work more, which I took to mean that my boss was also sleeping with Lane. Or someone might suggest I give Matt a call to let him know how I was doing. To me, that meant Matt hadn't slept with Lane yet, and since he was supposedly a loyal friend, I should call him. Just the sound of my voice would put him in the position of having sex with her.

But why was this happening? Why was everyone lying to me? I never once thought Lane was doing anything out of the ordinary. I thought this was simply the way the game was played. I remembered her telling me she was selfish. Was she sleeping with my friends to show me that I needed to be more selfish too? Was she showing me that these people weren't really my friends, that they were just using me? And most importantly, how could I make it stop?

I bought caller ID so I could screen my calls. I didn't want to talk to anyone unless I had to. I thought about how women are attracted to powerful men. Then I thought about myself. Lane was showing me that I wasn't all I believed myself to be. After all, I was a struggling real estate agent, which is basically the same as a glorified telemarketer. Did I really think being a telemarketer was up to Lane's standards? Where did I get the gall to ask her to marry me?

Of course, I kept this information to myself. I hoped my suspicions were unfounded, but I doubted it. I was almost certain my friends were sleeping with Lane, and I believed it was my job to stop them, to prove I was man enough to fight for her. The whole scenario seemed logical. I thought all brides-to-be slept with the groom's friends before marriage, a way of sowing wild oats. The more attractive the woman, the more oats she wanted to sow. And Lane Johnson, with all her other attributes, was the most beautiful woman I had ever seen.

In my mind, the man I caught with Lane would be the best man, while those who had already been with her would serve as groomsmen. I even envisioned the wedding. By my rough estimate, it would involve at least fifty men. Could I stand beside my bride with pride?

Calls came in from all over the Southeast. I had no idea where many of these friends even lived. Once, I drove halfway to Charleston, South Carolina, before regaining a sliver of sanity and turning back. Another time, I drove all the way to Virginia Beach, only to ring the doorbell of a friend's empty house before driving eleven hours back to Atlanta. After one of those all-night trips, I convinced myself that my roommate had been with Lane just before I walked in. I imagined him shoving her out the door so she could hurry off to another of my so-called friends.

"What were you doing all night?" my roommate Phil asked. "I haven't seen you in days, and then you show up in the middle of the night?"

"Nothing for you to worry about," I replied, determined not to lose my cool. He knew exactly what was going on, he was just being coy.

We had a neighbor in our apartment complex named Jerry, a repulsive middle-aged man with about forty yellow teeth, the worst breath I had ever smelled, and an obese wife he berated nightly after drinking. He claimed to be a commodities broker, though he never left his apartment. He blasted Van Morrison on his stereo twenty-four hours a day while drinking alone. Phil and I often joked about what a loser he was. But at this point, no one was above suspicion.

Too exhausted one day to work after one of my all-night driving stints, I stayed home, chain-smoking cigarettes and thinking only of Lane. How was I going to prove to her that I loved her? How much longer could I stand it? That damn Jerry was blasting Van Morrison at full volume all day long. I used to like Van Morrison, at least I thought I did, but by then I hated every note.

I finally convinced myself that Lane was canoodling next door with that disgusting creature. What could be more humiliating than her having sex with Jerry while I sat on the couch, too proud to act, too scared to stop him, too stupid to understand what I had to do? Could this be happening? Could this be possible? Of course it could. Anything was possible.

At last I got up from the couch and marched next door. Without knocking I shoved open Jerry's front door and walked inside. My anger, which had been smoldering, burst into full blaze. Jerry jumped off the couch.

"Where is she?" I demanded.

"Where's who?"

He stood inches from my face, exhaling his foul, dragon breath. God, he was disgusting. I pushed him aside and headed toward the kitchen. He followed.

"What are you doing?" Jerry cried.

"Where's my girlfriend? Where is she?" My eyes scoured the apartment. If I could have laid this man in the middle of a deserted road and left him to die of exposure, I would have done it without hesitation. Instead, I bolted upstairs, taking two, maybe three steps at a time. I checked the master bedroom, the second bedroom, and then the bathroom. I yanked open the shower curtain. Nothing. Where was she?

"What are you doing? I'm a married man! How dare you accuse me of being with another woman?"

I shoved Jerry out of the way, stormed down the stairs, and walked out the door. He was in hot pursuit. Just then Phil came home from work. Judging by the look on his face, he was aghast.

"Tell him to stay out of my apartment!" Jerry shouted. "His girlfriend is not in my apartment!"

Jesus Christ, this was bad. I didn't want to explain to Phil what I was thinking. I didn't want to talk with anyone but Lane. What was happening to me? I hustled up the stairs, locked the door, and lay down on my bed. I didn't want to answer questions. I was completely out of touch with reality. How could I think that Lane would sleep with this pathetic piece of human flesh? The big problem was, despite overwhelming evidence to the contrary, I still wasn't convinced. I wasn't close to being convinced. I knew I was right. All of these men had slept with Lane. They were men. They wouldn't waste time with a woman just to talk with her. They were going to fuck her.

Phil knocked on my door. "Are you all right? What happened?" he called out.

"I'm fine. It was just a misunderstanding. Everything is fine."

"Come out here. I need to talk to you. I need to make sure everything is fine."

"In a minute," I said.

Under no circumstances did I want to have this conversation. I couldn't trust Phil. After all, he had slept with Lane. In fact, I couldn't trust anyone. I thought Lane was testing how I would deal under pressure. In that regard, I knew I was failing, but it wasn't from a lack of trying. This was a competition. And in the immortal words of legendary jockey Willie Shoemaker, "It doesn't matter where you are in the middle of the race. It's where you are at the end that counts."

I took solace from these words, and I was not going to back down. I was going to do my best. I was going to look the enemy in the eye and face him. Finally, I left my room and went downstairs. Phil was on the couch smoking pot.

"Can I have some?" I asked.

"Are you sure?"

"Yeah. I just need something to calm me down."

Phil packed the bowl and passed it to me. I took a big hit.

"What happened back there?" asked Phil.

"No big deal. It was my fault. I was out of line."

"You need to get hold of yourself."

"I know."

"Are you sure that you should be smoking pot?" Phil asked.

"Can't get any worse."

Phil set the bowl down on the coffee table and looked straight at me. "Things can always get worse."

CHAPTER 2

I was making a complete ass of myself, but what hurt most was that I was painfully aware I could not stop, and I had been headed full steam ahead in this direction for the past six months. But Phil was right. It could get worse, and it did. My friends and I joked about the "trap door." When you think you've hit your lowest point, the trap door opens, and you fall that much lower. That's what was happening to me, and I was almost striving to hit that low point, believing that only then would my place in the world be secure and the pain would melt away.

Over the next twenty-four hours I did my best to keep the demons at bay, but all I could imagine were my so-called friends having sex with Lane. Two at a time. Three at a time. Yelling and jeering about how a loser like me could possibly have the ego to think I deserved a girl like her. Men whose wives they weren't satisfied with. Men who were much more successful than I and regretted their choice of spouse. Men who didn't like me for whatever reason. Men who pretended to be my friend but loathed my existence.

Then I had a thought. Maybe there was a silver lining. Maybe something good could come of this. Maybe this was how married couples showed their friendship. Maybe sharing spouses was normal behavior. I thought of some of my friends' attractive wives. That wouldn't be too bad, but I never considered it a fair swap. I didn't want to share. I didn't want anyone besides Lane. Maybe I was different from other men. Maybe other men would relish the opportunity to have multiple partners. Come to think of it, that wouldn't be all bad. But more importantly, was that what Lane wanted? She could have had almost any man. *Why would she want to settle down with me? I was an ogre next to her. Where did I get the ego to think she would ever want to settle down with me?* Maybe having a beautiful wife had its faults. I felt guilty for wanting to take away Lane's freedom of choice, her freedom to spend time with other men, her freedom to pursue whatever in life she desired.

But how could I go on? Could I live with myself knowing that Lane had sex with multiple partners at the same time? Could I look these men in the eye with pride knowing what they had done with my wife? What would people say? Would they respect me? Would they respect my wife? It was too much. I didn't care if everyone fucked each other's wives. That wasn't the way I wanted to live my life. I wanted Lane all for myself.

It was beyond jealousy. This was a full-blown obsession, and I was losing credibility with my friends at an alarming rate. To this day, ten years later, I still feel embarrassed when I see them. I avoid people in malls or at football games. I rarely go to reunions. Okay, so everyone does that, but trust me, it's different. When I see an old friend, I wonder if I should say something about my mental illness so we can have a light moment and hopefully move beyond my checkered past, or if that would make the situation even more uncomfortable.

The memories are still there and have shaped my personality as much as my experiences in college or boarding school did. I don't trust myself the way I should. I have made so many horrific mistakes that I constantly second-guess myself. I didn't used to be like that. I used to run through brick walls, and that tough spirit was evident in those awful days back in 1998. I simply could not believe that I was wrong.

My best friend in Atlanta, Charles Laughlin, called. He was practically the last person left who would have anything to do with me. Just like Justin Roberts, we had lived together out in Aspen. There was nothing I wouldn't do for this guy. We skied together. Mountain biked together. Vacationed together. If there was anyone in the world I could have an honest discussion with about Lane, it was Charles.

But then I had another thought. Was Lane having sex with Charles as well?

I couldn't stand this. We would have to live on a deserted island, subsisting on berries she picked and fish I caught, before I allowed my best friend to have sex with Lane. In fact, I decided that was what I wanted most. If I could live out my dream, it would be *The Blue Lagoon* to live on a deserted island with Lane and raise a colony of little shitheads. Lane even kind of looked like Brooke Shields in the movie, and I had curly blond hair like the strapping young lad who defiled her.

By the time I hung up the phone with Charles, I was furious. I immediately looked up his address in the phone book. I had never been to his home but knew that he lived with his parents in the Virginia Highlands area of Atlanta. Just like the other times, I was going to stop Charles from having sex with Lane. Charles was going to be the best man.

I ran to my car and drove, fast. Too fast. I ran a stoplight, and the police pulled me over. I couldn't believe my bad luck. Charles was having sex with Lane at that very moment while I dealt with the cops. *Could the police be in on* it *as well?* Were they *slowing me* down *from stopping Charles?* The whole world was against me. No one wanted me to marry Lane, but I didn't give a damn. I was going to do my best. I might fail, but no one could say it was from a lack of trying.

After fifteen agonizing minutes with the police, I headed toward Charles's house. I drove through the streets, scanning house numbers until I found the right one. I may have failed so far, but, by God, I was going to finish well. Willie Shoemaker would be proud.

I'd be damned if I was going to ring the doorbell. I'd been polite long enough. Facing the house, I ran to the front door. I felt close—like the end was near—and I wondered how this would play out. Maybe my friends would have a party. Maybe Lane and I would get married on the spot. Maybe we would disappear for a couple of years until the dust settled. None of it mattered. I was ready for anything. Without hesitation, I took a running start and karate-kicked the front door. The wood splintered but didn't give. I kicked it again. Same result. Suddenly Charles opened the door.

"What the hell are you doing?"

I grabbed him by the collar. "Where's Lane? Where is she?"

Charles pushed back. "Take your damn hands off me and calm down!"

"Where is she?" I cried.

"Get a hold of yourself. I'm sure Lane's in Nashville. What's gotten into you?"

"Lane's sleeping with all of my friends."

"Stop! You're talking crazy. Now calm down and tell me what's going on."

Charles placed his hand on my shoulder. He's not a touchy-feely kind of guy, to say the least. We had always communicated with insults, but he was obviously concerned. I had never seen that look on his face, and I immediately understood that Charles wasn't playing games. Lane wasn't in the house.

I dropped my eyes. I couldn't even look at him. I wanted to, but I couldn't. I was so embarrassed. I turned away and walked toward my car. There was no way I could explain what I thought was happening. It was ludicrous. Not even Charles, one of my best friends, could possibly understand what I was going through, the shame I felt, the fear I could no longer endure. Before I made it to my car, Charles ran in front of me.

"I'm not letting you go until you tell me what's going on." Once again, he placed his hand on my shoulder. This time he squeezed. "It's going to be okay," he said in a soothing voice.

"I don't know about that."

"It will. I promise. Let's get something to eat and talk about it. You look like you haven't eaten in days. Eating will make you feel better."

"I'm not hungry."

"You need to eat something. It will calm you down."

"Let's get a beer," I said.

"Now you're talking. A beer sounds good. Then you tell me exactly what's going on. I promise, it's not as bad as it seems."

That comment didn't help matters. In my warped understanding of the English language, Charles was saying that my life was bad to some degree, just not awful enough to justify kicking down doors. I was back to not trusting anyone. Even Charles had turned his back on me.

But still he stayed by my side, trying to settle me down. Finally, after his pleading, I calmed enough to leave, and a beer sounded like the perfect remedy.

We stopped at an English pub called the Fox and Hound, just blocks from my apartment complex in Buckhead. It was nice to be in my neighborhood, and it was nice to have a draft beer in front of me. Unlike other bipolar people I've met through my "travels," I don't crave alcohol in a manic state. When I'm manic, I want to be perfect, and the lengths I will go to prove it are mind-boggling. However, at this point I wanted to reassure Charles that I was okay. Most of the time he is not a very serious person, but in this moment he was gravely concerned. Basically, I had scared the shit out of him, and he was trying to be a good friend and talk me down as if I were on a bad acid trip, which is probably the best way to describe my mental health at that moment.

"Sorry about trying to kick down your door," I said.

"That's all right. But what were you thinking? Why did you do it?"

"I told you. I thought you were inside with Lane."

"But I don't even know Lane," said Charles. "Why would she be in my house?"

To a sane man, that explanation would have sufficed. After all, none of the men I suspected even knew Lane. Most likely I hadn't even mentioned her in casual conversation. My behavior was beyond anything they could understand. People always said I was a little different, but this was past their comprehension. I tried to be rational. Let's get from point A to point B. Maybe Charles could help me, but it wasn't going to be easy. I didn't want to reveal too much.

"Do you think you'll ever get married?" I finally asked.

"Why do you want to get married all of a sudden? I've never even heard you discuss it until about a month ago."

"I'm twenty-five years old. I'm not going to live forever. What am I waiting for? I'm ready."

"You've got plenty of time to get married. Trust me." Charles looked at me out of the corner of his eye as he sipped his beer.

"But do you ever think about it?" I asked.

"I don't know. I guess so. That is, if anyone will have me." Charles laughed. "I need to get a job first."

"You don't seem like you're trying very hard."

"To find a job or a wife?" asked Charles.

"A wife."

"My stepdad once told me that the best way to get girls is not to think about them. It happens when you least expect it."

After a couple more beers, I relaxed enough that Charles felt he could leave me alone. With my spirited thoughts, I'm sure I was exhausting. I wasn't even listening to his voice of reason as he tried to explain the facts of life, not to mention the facts of friendship, but he had been surprisingly calm about the day's events. He didn't call me a dumbass or anything like that, and I appreciated the gesture. I'm sure he was afraid to say anything that might trigger another outburst. Instead, he just told me to think about what I was doing and not to drink too much of the hooch.

Since Phil wasn't home, I went upstairs to my room and opened my textbook, but I couldn't concentrate long enough to comprehend anything. Instead, I surfed the internet, looking for real estate companies that might be hiring. I found five companies that developed Publix grocery stores and wrote letters of inquiry. I placed stamps on the envelopes and dropped them in the mailbox.

All of this seemed like the right thing to do. I wasn't going to let a little breaking and entering get in my way. I was sending my résumé to some of the most prestigious real estate companies in Atlanta. Hell, maybe with my penchant for knocking down doors, I could land a job in demolition.

The beers had done their work. No one out of the ordinary called, and I slept well that night. The next morning I went to work feeling strong. I worked hard all morning and felt at peace with the world. Finally, I had a plan. I was going to be a real estate mogul. I was going to be a big man.

My stockbroker called that afternoon. We spoke about once a week. He was a fraternity brother and friend. It was 1998, and like everyone else, we were weaving gold in the dot-com boom. We spoke about my investments. Then he made a comment that disturbed me. Out of the blue, he said, "You know, Steve Marks and Nat Moore live in my neighborhood."

It was a strange comment. Both of these guys were at least three years older than me, and though they were fraternity brothers, I barely knew them, and I doubted they remembered me. My mind shifted into high gear. *Could the three of them be having sex with Lane? Is that what he was telling me?*

I reflected on the day before, when I had tried to kick down Charles's door. I couldn't do that again. That was obviously not the right thing to do. Not only were those guys big, but they were not nice. They would beat the hell out of me and make me watch them have sex with Lane.

I brooded the rest of the day at work with the same awful thoughts. I wanted to go over there and whip some ass, but I was trying to be rational. I tried to believe there was no way Lane could be sleeping with all those guys. But still, I wasn't sure.

When I got home at the end of the day, Phil was sitting at the dining room table, looking over some paperwork. His eyes lifted wearily when I opened the door. There wasn't anything to say at this point. Then the phone rang. By then I had become pathological about checking the caller ID before answering any call. If no one heard my voice, then no one could have sex with Lane.

The caller ID read "David Marks," but in my frenzy I thought it said "Steve Marks," the fraternity brother who lived in the same neighborhood as my stockbroker and Nat Moore. There was no doubt about what they were doing.

I let out a loud "AHHHH!" and ran for the phone book. Weeks would pass before I realized that it had actually been David Marks calling, David Marks, the older brother of one of my friends, an executive in real estate I had been trying to contact about a possible job. But my mind was moving so fast that coincidences collided daily. I thought they were signs from God. Karma from Buddha. Hell, I don't know what I thought. But I sure as hell didn't think they were nothing. And I couldn't take a chance. I couldn't do nothing. A loser does nothing.

I looked up Steve Marks in the phone book and wrote down his address. Breathing hard, sweating under my arms, barely able to control the car, I imagined a big fight was about to ensue. But I took strength in believing I was finally going to see Lane. This wasn't going to be easy. Trolling the dark streets, I searched for the right mailbox number. I didn't want to do this, but like everything else, I felt I had to. And I was scared out of my mind. I truly believed I was about to get the shit kicked out of me.

Finally, I found the house. All the lights were out, and there were no cars in the driveway. I sprinted around to the back. It was just as dark, which struck me as ominous. French doors led inside. Without stopping, I ran toward them and punched the glass with my right hand. I should have gone with the karate kick, the window didn't shatter, but my hand did. I had never broken a bone in my life, but I knew instantly that I had. A lump was already forming on the outer edge, throbbing in rhythm with my racing heartbeat.

I still wanted to go inside. It never crossed my mind that if someone had been home, they would have already rushed to the sound of breaking glass. But I wasn't about to punch that window again. Once bitten, twice shy.

I looked around for something to smash it with. Patio furniture circled a table. Too big. Flowerpots sat on the tables, too small. Then I spotted exactly what I needed: a stone bunny, about a foot tall, perched on the back porch. Without hesitation, I grabbed the bunny and hurled it through the French doors. The glass exploded. I reached through the jagged opening and unlocked the door.

I stormed through the house, checking every room, upstairs, downstairs. Empty. No one was home. Holy shit. This was serious. I had to get the hell out.

I bolted back to my car and drove off, steering with my left hand while my right throbbed in agony.

When I pushed open the apartment door, Phil was on the couch, probably smoking pot, that's what he usually did. But when he saw me, he jumped up.

"What the hell are you doing?" Phil asked.

"Nothing."

"You take out of here like a bat out of hell and then. . ." Phil saw my hand. By this time it was bleeding as well as being broken. "What the hell happened to your hand?"

"I broke it."

"Doing what? Did you get in a fight?"

"Kind of."

"With who?"

"You don't know him," I said

"We've got to get you to a hospital. We've got to get your hand looked at, and then you've got to talk with someone."

"What do you mean talk with someone?"

"A psychiatrist or something."

Under no circumstances did I want to do this, mainly because if I talked to someone, then Lane would probably have to have sex with them as well. But my hand was mangled, and I knew a doctor needed to look at it. I wasn't too worried about the psychiatrist. I could talk my way out of trouble. Phil was only telling me to see a doctor so that Lane could philander with my friends. I pictured Phil calling her and saying that he had finally gotten me tied up for a little while. The coast was now clear.

At the same time, it was confusing. Phil obviously did not want to be doing this. He wasn't rushing me out the door, and he was hunched over in despair, not the mannerisms I expected from him after his ploy to disarm me had worked. The real reason he was pissed was because he had concert tickets. I don't remember who he was going to see, but I do remember that he wasn't planning on missing out just because his roommate had broken his hand. He stuck around the hospital long enough to make sure I told the emergency room staff about my hand and that I wanted to speak with a psychiatrist, but he was ready to leave.

"Are you going to be okay?" Phil asked.

"Of course. Go on out. I'll see you tonight. Have fun."

As I waited to be seen by a doctor, I paced the waiting room, occasionally sneaking outside for a cigarette. I couldn't believe I had broken my hand, but at the same time I didn't feel like there was anything wrong with me. I didn't need to see a psychiatrist, but I knew what they were about. It was the dirty secret of my past, something I never spoke about with anyone.

My parents took me to a child psychologist when I was about eight years old. They thought I was too sensitive. Even then I was trying to be perfect, which is a wonderful attribute when it comes to sports or school, but in the more important aspects of life, like relationships, it can be a burden. The last straw with my parents came when they punished me for something I had done wrong. I replied, "I'm sorry. I guess I'm just a bad person."

Believing that an eight-year-old should not be questioning whether he was a bad person, my parents became concerned. But that's the way I was. I was wound tight, always trying to prove myself in school or on the ball field—both of which I excelled in. I was a good student and an even better athlete. But if I failed, as I said earlier, I was an extremely sore loser.

And that was where the emergency room psychologist came in. I have to take my hat off to Phil for making me seek help, but at this point I was mad as hell at him. He was not my friend; he was the leader of the guys who were having sex with Lane. I imagined him calling everyone and telling them what I had done, while Lane waited for her next fling, eager as a beaver to show me I wasn't worth a damn. All these other guys had slept with her, and none of them had stooped so low as to make a marriage proposal. I was the stooge.

After the orthopedist set the bone and wrapped it so it wouldn't move out of place, I met with a bearded man wearing glasses. To be honest, I don't know if he was a social worker, an M.D., a Ph.D., or an astrologer, for that matter. At the moment he was just some guy to whom I was going to explain, logically, what was happening to me. He would understand, after all, he was a professional. He looked at me with a grim face and pushed his wire-rimmed glasses up his nose.

"What seems to be the problem?" he asked.

"There's no problem."

"Then why are you here?"

"My roommate wanted me to talk to someone because I broke my hand."

"How did you break your hand?"

I was very careful not to lie. I was being judged, and above all else, lying was not acceptable. At the same time, I realized this interview was not progressing the way I had envisioned. I was already being pushed into a corner.

"I punched a window."

"Does that sound like normal behavior?"

"No. I don't know."

"Then why did you do it?"

"I thought my girlfriend was in there with him."

I'm going to stop right there for a minute. Lane was not my girlfriend at that moment, nor was she ever. We went out several times, but I never considered her my girlfriend. But at that moment, my story didn't make sense unless I said she was. Just like when I busted into Jerry's apartment and said, "Where is my girlfriend?" I was doing the same thing here.

"Do you still think that this man was with your girlfriend?"

"I don't know."

"Then why did you do this?"

"I asked this girl to marry me so I'm dealing with all of that stuff."

"What stuff are you talking about?"

"You know what a girl does when someone asks her to marry him." I couldn't bring myself to say what I thought. That a woman sleeps with everyone until the man stops it.

"No. I don't. Please tell me. What do women do?"

"You know what."

"No. I don't. Please tell me what she is doing."

I didn't say anything. I thought he was a damn good actor. I couldn't read anything into him. He seemed genuinely bewildered, but then again, he was a shrink. He could probably read my mind. He was probably in on the scam.

"Was she in the house?" he asked.

"No."

"Then why did you hit the window?"

"I thought that she was in there."

"Is this man a friend of yours?"

"Sort of."

"Did you want to hurt this man?"

"I don't know."

"Do you want to hurt anyone right now?"

"No. It was a mistake."

"How do you feel right now?"

"I feel a little jittery."

"I bet you do." The man looked me dead in the eye and said, "I think we need to transfer you to a mental hospital."

I was beyond shocked. I had heard of people going to rehab clinics for drugs or alcohol. I had even been to jail a few times, and I thought that was bad. But a mental hospital was beyond my comprehension. At this point in my life, I don't think I had even seen *One Flew Over the Cuckoo's Nest*.

"Don't you understand that I am in love? I'm just madly in love."

"Yes. I understand your situation, and you need to go to the mental hospital to be evaluated."

"What if I don't want to go?" I asked.

"Then I will be forced to call the police."

"But I'm not sick. Don't you understand that?"

The man looked at me sternly, and there was no changing his opinion.

"Stay in the waiting room until I can get an ambulance to take you over to the hospital. It will be a while, but like I said, if you leave, I will call the police."

I was stuck. These bastards had my address. My car was at my apartment. There was nowhere to run, nowhere to hide. I went out to the waiting room and watched people check in with broken limbs and whatnot. I felt like everyone was watching me, and this was just some elaborate scheme. These people trickling into the emergency room weren't sick. They were just actors. I thought this was another part of the elaborate test that Lane was putting me through to see if I was worthy. I felt I was doing excellently on this test, but they were trying to completely break my spirit—to see what it would take for me to give up. *Well, boys,* I thought, *you're going to see just how much of a badass I can be.*

A couple of hours passed while I rotated between the outside, where I smoked cigarettes, and the inside, where I kept warm. I remember it being chilly for a March night, and it was approaching nine o'clock. I was outside leaning against a pole, replaying conversations in my head about how I was going to talk myself out of this mess, when two men in uniform approached me.

"Are you Benton Savage?"

"Yes."

"Come with us."

Before I could even spout my rebuttal, the men took me by the arms so I couldn't run. There was nothing I could do. They didn't give a damn what I had to say. They were just doing their job, which was transporting me to the nuthouse. Without asking, they ducked my head and placed me in the back of an ambulance. There were rails on both sides and a couple of seats for the paramedics. I sat on a stretcher, and the two men sat in the back with me. They closed the door, while a third man drove.

We drove toward my neighborhood. I couldn't believe it. They were taking me back to my apartment. When they turned right onto Defoors, where I lived, I was certain. That was the way the game was played. They were going to take me back to the apartment, where I would be reunited with Lane. I leaned back, convinced I had aced the test. I knew all along they weren't taking me to a mental hospital. They were just testing me, checking to see if I was crazy. I almost wanted to hug those ambulance guys for making me so happy. All the pain had been worth it for this very moment.

But when we reached the gate to my apartment complex, they kept driving. There was no reason to pass my apartment. They could have taken another route. They were taunting me, rubbing it in my face. Screw that. I lunged for the door and tried to escape. But they were ready. I hoped this was part of the act and that they would let me go, but their viselike grip convinced me otherwise.

"Pull over! Pull over!" one of the men called out.

I struggled to free myself, but these bastards were strong.

"Hold him down! Hold him down!"

Both men pinned me to the stretcher, held me fast, and strapped me in until I was completely immobile except for my extremities. Only then did they release me.

"You weren't going anywhere, were you?" one of them said with a smile. They seemed to enjoy their job.

I averted my eyes in disgust. I had no choice but to accept my fate. I was going to the mental hospital.

Fifteen minutes later they parked the ambulance in a lot. I waited patiently as they powwowed outside about how to handle me. They opened the back door and lowered the stretcher to the ground. The three men surrounded me with grave expressions.

"Can we trust you to be good?" one of them asked.

I didn't say anything.

"If you promise to be good, we'll unstrap you."

"I'll be good."

They removed the straps but kept their hands on me. They still weren't sure about me, and they shouldn't have been. If it hadn't been for the threat of those damn straps, I would have fought them tooth and nail. Instead, I remained calm as they escorted me through the dark parking lot to an open door, where a Black man greeted us. He was wiry, with a thin mustache and veins visible in his arms.

"He's all yours, Otis," said one of the EMTs. "Keep an eye on him. He's already tried to run once."

"He'll be all right."

Otis led me through the door into a large but quiet room. Dining tables and chairs were lined up in rows, and it reminded me of a miniature school cafeteria. Across the room, huge windows looked out onto the vast hospital grounds. To the left and right stretched long hallways with closed doors on either side. Otis pulled out a chair for me in front of a charcoal-skinned Black woman. Another Black man walked through the room whistling. I don't consider myself racist, but I was wondering where the hell all the white people were.

"What's your name?" asked the woman.

I didn't speak. Speaking was what had landed me here in the first place.

"Here's his paperwork," said Otis.

The woman looked at it, then at me, flashing the whitest teeth I had ever seen. "What is the problem, Mr. Benton? You do not like me? I am only trying to help." She spoke in staccato with an accent that sounded African to me. With her calling me Mr. Benton, she sounded condescending, and I wasn't going to respond under those conditions, hoping she would grow frustrated and just go away.

"If you do not speak, I cannot help you. Please speak, Mr. Benton."

Once again, I was losing touch with reality. With the woman talking to me like I was a kindergartner, I wondered if it was a joke. Was I being punked? Was Lane here? Was this the way the game was played?

The woman looked down on me with her dark eyes and smiled. She didn't seem threatening. In fact, she seemed nice, so nice that I immediately didn't trust her. I turned my head so I wasn't facing her. When she stood up from behind her desk and walked away, I thought my ploy had worked. But a couple of minutes later she returned.

"Here is some medicine," she said. "It will make you feel better."

I knew about the medicine. Along with seeing a child psychiatrist in my youth, at my mom's insistence I had seen a psychiatrist in college as well. He prescribed me Prozac, which I took for a couple of months before giving it up because every time I mixed it with alcohol I blacked out. Being a good drunk in college was far more important than having a stable mind and making good grades. My transcript proves that.

"Please take the medicine, Mr. Benton."

The woman held out four different pills in a Dixie cup in one hand and a Dixie cup filled with water in the other.

"I will leave you alone if you take the medicine, but you must take it."

I looked up at her again. I didn't like her staccato way of speaking, but I took the cup of medicine and washed it down with water without even asking what I was taking. I didn't care. It was late, and all I wanted was to be left alone.

"Thank you, Mr. Benton. Now we must take your property, and then Otis will take you to your room. You will sleep better. You'll see."

I looked at Otis.

"Give me your shoelaces and your belt."

This did not surprise me. I had been to jail for underage drinking and DUI. I knew they took these things to prevent me from hanging myself.

"Do you have a wallet or keys?" Otis asked.

I handed them over as well.

"Anything else?"

I pulled out my cigarettes and lighter.

"Give me the lighter. You can keep the cigarettes."

"What good are cigarettes without a lighter?" I asked.

"We'll light your cigarettes when the time comes."

Otis led me across the room to an area with three rows of green lockers. He opened one of the metal doors and placed my property inside.

"You'll get your property back when you leave. Now I'll take you to your room."

A couple of other patients emerged from the shadows. They walked stoically, their arms behind their backs and their eyes on the floor. It was quiet except for the Black man who continued to whistle, but there was unspoken tension from everyone, including Otis, who I'm sure had seen his fair share of sneak attacks born of the kind of anger only a madman can possess. But I wasn't going after Otis. I kind of liked his silent way. He was the only one who hadn't hassled me.

"Here's your room."

Otis opened the door and flicked on the lights. There were two empty beds with white sheets, "Brawner Hospital" printed on the fabric, which was the first time I knew where I was. The hospital hadn't exactly brought out the welcome wagon when they admitted me. No introductions. No tour of the facility. No food. All they did was fill me with meds and take my property away. Not exactly what I look for in accommodations.

"Take your pick of which bed you want. We'll wake you in the morning."

I sat down on the bed and turned on the bedside lamp. I looked around the room and tried to take in my surroundings. The room was symmetrical: one bed, one desk beside each bed, the same stenciling on the sheets in a nonconfrontational light blue. The only difference was that one side of the room had a toilet and the other side had a shower. There was no artistic design whatsoever. They probably used three or four standard layouts in mental hospitals across the country.

Quickly bored with my analysis, I looked down at my broken right hand wrapped in a brown Ace bandage. No one had even asked about it. It was a boxer's fracture, the bone just below my pinky was broken. The wrapping felt tight. With nothing else to do, I fiddled with the bandage. Then I had the brilliant idea of loosening it a little and rewrapping it. What I didn't realize was how hard it would be to rewrap with one hand. I could barely manage it. After several grueling minutes, the bandage was so loose it did nothing but cover the fracture. My hand throbbed, and I couldn't believe no one was helping me.

Now that I had managed to make my life more miserable than it had been fifteen minutes earlier, I thought of the trap door. Yes, I had sunk lower once again. There was truly no way it could get worse. Amazing that I could still believe something so foolish after the last six months, but I am an optimist. Everyone who knows me says that. It is probably one of my best and worst attributes.

So it should come as no surprise that my thoughts returned to Lane. Could she be here too? Or was this another test? I couldn't be sure. I decided to do a little snooping around, to see what was happening in the old nuthouse at the midnight hour.

I walked back out to the main room, expecting to see the same black woman behind the desk, but she had been replaced by a red-haired man with an equally red goatee. Instantly I disliked him.

"Can I help you?" he asked.

"Just walking around."

"It's past lights-out," he said.

"I can't sleep."

The man looked at me with sinister eyes. Could he be sleeping with Lane as well?

"If you're quiet, you can stay up," he said. "Just don't disturb anyone."

I paced the hallways, looking for Lane. She could be anywhere. I walked every inch of the main room and started down the halls. There were at least ten rooms on each side. A couple of snorers were so loud I could hear them through the cinderblock walls. I thought about checking the rooms, but where would I start? Besides, Lane wouldn't bother with one of these flunkies.

After exhausting my search, I studied the red-haired man again. With his goatee and sinister eyes, he looked like the devil himself. Could Lane be under the desk? I had to know, though fear gnawed at me. Still, I wondered. I paced the room, edging closer to the desk. Every so often, the red-haired man stopped writing to glare at me. He knew I was up to something.

At last, I was only a few feet away. Summoning my courage, I lunged at him, shoving him out of his chair and landing on top of him. He seized me by the throat. I jammed my hand under his chin and forced it upward until he cried out, "You want to fight, do you?"

He flipped me, pinning me beneath him. "You picked the wrong guy! Otis! Come quick! We've got a live one!"

We rolled across the floor, locked in a desperate struggle, until Otis stormed in and wrenched me backward by the waist. Together, they shoved me out of the room and into another—bare, with only four walls. Otis yanked my pants down halfway. The red-haired man plunged a needle into my butt cheek.

Almost instantly, calm washed over me. The fight drained from my body. Within ten seconds, I went limp and sank into sleep.

CHAPTER 3

I don't know how long I slept, but I don't remember the next two days at all. I later heard from other patients that I roamed the hallways like a zombie, speaking to no one and scarcely picking at my meals, which, in the grand scheme of things, was probably a good thing. Memories of the mental hospital aren't good for the soul. When I did finally come through, I was much calmer. Lethargic might be a better word. Still, I was furious about my incarceration. That had not changed. Despite the evidence to the contrary, I simply couldn't accept that I needed to be in a mental hospital. Even then, I believed that everything I had done, I had done for a good reason.

Eventually, I met with a psychiatrist. He looked like a middle-aged former frat boy with short black hair, not a strand out of place. I suppose he looked normal compared to other psychiatrists, but it didn't matter. From day one, I had never liked psychiatrists. When I was eight years old, I saw one who was always wanting to give big hugs and play these odd games where we constantly congratulated each other for trivial things like coloring between the lines. I suppose he was trying to boost my self-esteem or help me get in touch with my inner self. Even at eight, I knew that was a crock of nonsense.

When I was in college, I saw another psychiatrist. He thought my priorities were out of order because all I wanted to talk about was the fact that I didn't have enough beer money. He may have been on to something, but he was a nerdy-looking guy who probably didn't drink his first beer until he was twenty-one, and he certainly didn't do a good job persuading me to his way of thinking. What I'm saying is, this shrink didn't stand a chance. His predecessors had already shaped my judgment. "Do you know why you're here?" he asked.

"No."

"Do you remember attacking one of the staff members upon your admittance?"

"Yes."

"Why did you do that?"

"Because I wanted to."

"Do you think that was proper behavior?"

"I want out of here."

"Do you understand that you have to take medication?"

"No."

"Would you like me to tell you what medicine you are taking?"

"I don't need it."

"I think you do. You are very depressed. It is an illness. You have an acute chemical imbalance."

"When can I get out of here?"

"We'll see how you improve and then talk about it."

"Is that it?"

"That's it."

I left his office and joined the other patients, men and women, young and old, Black, white, and Hispanic. Some talked. Some talked to themselves. And some didn't talk at all, which didn't bother me. The nuthouse isn't the kind of place where you network.

Usually, I hung around the TV room, where a group of young men watched astute programming such as professional wrestling, which, along with Jerry Springer, I've noticed is extremely popular with the mentally ill. We gathered around the television, hooting and hollering for the bad guy to win.

Most of the patients wore blue hospital clothes a couple of sizes too big and walked around in terry-cloth socks. I refused to change out of my street clothes. Getting into that horrible hospital wear would have been admitting defeat, and I was a long way from that point.

By this time, I had found the smoking room. At all times there were at least three or four patients inside, smoke hovering around their heads. They even had chairs for us to sit in, and a staff member lit our cigarettes. I can't imagine how much money this person made for simply flicking her thumb, but there are several jobs in mental hospitals you cannot attach a description to. Still, I was eternally grateful for this luxury. This was the only mental hospital where I was ever able to smoke. Of course, this was 1998, and not even California prohibited smoking in bars at the time, but still, it was a lifesaver.

"It's good to see that you are socializing with the other patients," the staff member said when she lit my cigarette.

I didn't reply but instead looked around the room. The black man who was whistling was there. He almost seemed like a friend, or at the least a familiar face.

"Why are you in here?" I asked.

"I'm crazy just like you," he said.

"I'm not crazy."

He smiled. "I saw you when they brought you in."

"I saw you, too."

"I'm surprised that you remember. You were pretty messed up."

"Who brought you here?" I asked.

"I brought myself here," he said.

"Why in the hell would you do that?"

"I was hearing voices."

"What were they saying?"

"They were telling me to kill myself."

"I guess that's a pretty good reason."

Clearly, I wasn't in the same category as this man. I had no desire to kill myself—the thought hadn't even entered my mind. My focus was singular: I wanted to get out of the hospital with as few people from the outside knowing as possible, and all my energy was aimed toward that goal. While gaining strength each day, I relentlessly hounded the staff, nurses, and doctor, who kept asking if I had family I wanted to call. They weren't permitted to call my family on their own; I had to call my mom myself, which was the absolute last thing I wanted to do. I didn't want visitors. I didn't want anyone to know about this. I just wanted to put this chapter of my life behind me and go home.

Although I was overmedicated to the point that I could barely keep my eyes open, the upside was that it slowed down my drive to find Lane. I no longer thought she was in the hospital, but I still didn't feel good about it. She was out there, and as long as I was in here, I wasn't going to be able to stop her. When I was coherent enough to have thoughts or ambition, they were still about her. Otherwise, I slept most of the time.

By the third day, it became clear I wasn't going home anytime soon, and I grew ornery. I stomped around the ward, yelling about how they had no right to keep me there. I would not shut the hell up. What bugged me the most was that the staff basically ignored me. There were no empty promises that I would be leaving soon. They didn't even tell me to quiet down. They had seen my kind before, and I knew that if I became too disrespectful, they would shoot Thorazine into my ass again. I didn't want that, but I pushed as hard as I could without crossing that fine line. Finally, at wit's end, I demanded my release.

"You can sign a seventy-two-hour letter asking for your release," said a staff member.

"What does that mean?"

"You go in front of a judge, and if he sides with you, then you're released," she said.

"And if he doesn't?"

"We can hold you another ten days."

"Ten days! I can't stay here for ten days. I have a job. I have a final exam to take. I have responsibilities."

"It would help if you called your family."

I fought the notion as long as I could. I did not want to have this conversation with my mom, but I feared they might never let me out if I didn't. There was a pay phone in the recreation room. I must have picked it up half a dozen times before I finally completed the call. When I did, I wasn't sure how to explain it to my mom, but I did the best I could while withholding the most incriminating details, like how I broke my hand or the marriage proposal to Lane.

My mom was surprised but not shocked. For years she had said she thought I should be on medication. She knew I was unstable. For that matter, everyone knew I was unstable. Everyone but me.

The next day my mom drove two hours down to Atlanta to see me. Visiting hours were in the afternoon. She greeted me with a big hug, which was unusual. We weren't a touchy-feely family. She handed me a homemade blueberry pie, my favorite. My apprehension relented somewhat. A nurse led us to the visiting room, where we could speak privately. Even in front of my mom, I was intensely embarrassed. Yet she never indicated disappointment in me.

"Are you doing okay?" she asked.

"No."

"Why not?"

"Because I'm in the nuthouse."

"Not forever."

"Long enough."

"Do you know what medications you are on?"

"No."

"Don't you think you should know what medications you are taking?"

"I don't know. I want out of here," I said.

"What drove you to this point?"

I didn't want to lie to my mom, but I wasn't sure she would understand. I also feared that if I told her, her boyfriend might sleep with Lane. My mind was still fixated on Lane, yet I hadn't mentioned the marriage proposal to any of the staff. At the same time, I was convinced my mom already knew. In fact, I thought everyone knew. I searched for a signal to confirm it, but when none came, I finally told my mom about the proposal. I felt I had no choice, I needed to unburden myself. I had carried that secret for four days, and I hoped admitting it would ease the turmoil in my head. To my relief, it did feel good to get it off my chest.

"Do you love her?" Mom asked.

"Of course I do. I wouldn't have asked her to marry me if I didn't."

"Do you have much in common with her? You couldn't have seen her much in the last couple of years. She is very young. Isn't she still in college?"

"Yes."

"What did she say?"

"She said no."

"Are you ready for marriage? I never knew you were that serious about her."

"You don't like her?" I asked.

"I don't know her that well, but what I do know, I like a lot."

I couldn't tell my mom the truth about what I was thinking. It was too grotesque. Besides, my mom had been married once. She knew what was going on. As much as I didn't want to think about it, I knew that at one time she had sewed her wild oats. All women did.

"I think it might be a little premature to ask her to marry you," my mom said.

"I know."

"But you were serious, weren't you? She means that much to you."

"She's different from any girl I've ever met."

"Sounds like she is handling it well. There are lots of girls who would marry the first guy who asked her."

"Yeah. She's been nice about it."

"Do you have much in common with her?"

"I don't know, but I don't necessarily believe that's important."

"Trust me. It's important."

"I disagree. I don't want a clone of me. I want someone who makes me look at the world in a different way. Someone to challenge me."

"That could work, but it'll be harder, and marriage is hard enough as it is."

"I never thought you and Dad had that much in common," I said.

"Probably more than you think."

I tried to imagine what my mom and dad had in common, though it had been several years since I had last seen my dad. He died of cancer when I was a senior in high school. Needless to say, it was a damaging blow to my already insecure world. Dad and I had a close but volatile relationship. He pushed me to the extreme in academics and even more so in athletics. On the surface it seemed to work. I became a very good high school athlete, earning all-state honors in both cross-country and track, but it warped me in other ways. I don't want to say my father was abusive, but he was explosive, and I have no doubt that his combative nature rubbed off on me. He was never abusive toward my mom, but they certainly had disagreements that often erupted into shouting. Still, there was never any physical abuse. They were simply both strong-willed.

"How did you end up here?" asked my mom. "And how did you break your hand?"

Despite the doctor's instruction to keep the wrap dry, I soaked it in the shower to the point that it was beginning to stink. I momentarily considered telling my mom the truth, but decided against it and told her that I couldn't remember. No doubt for the best. My mom was worried enough without telling her the whole sordid story.

"We'll have to get that looked at when you get out," she said.

"I need to have it looked at right now. It hurts."

"I have a six o'clock appointment with the psychiatrist. I'll talk to him about your broken hand."

"What are you going to talk with the psychiatrist about?"

"About you. And how we can get you better."

"Am I going to be at this meeting?" I asked.

"I want to talk to him alone, if you don't mind," said my mom.

"Okay."

"Is there anything you want or need?"

Even though my mom hated that I smoked, I did not hesitate. I needed cigarettes.

"Don't you think it's time to quit that nasty habit?"

"Mom. Please. I need something here. You don't know how it is. It's awful, and I've been bumming off the other patients."

"Anything else? Books or anything? Or are you able to read?"

"I don't know."

"It looks like they have you on a lot of medication. You seem kind of out of it."

That was an understatement. They had me on enough drugs to slow down an elephant. I could barely get out of bed in the morning. I could barely walk across the room. I showered when they made me. I ate when they told me. I took medicine three times a day when they told me. I didn't think about what they were giving me. I didn't care what they were giving me.

In the evenings I met with the psychiatrist. He spoke in a smooth, never faltering voice. He diagnosed me with Type I bipolar disorder. We spoke about what medication I was taking, and how it affected the neurotransmitters in my brain.

"I think I'm on too much medication," I told the doctor.

"Most of the medicines we are giving you are just to stabilize you. When you get out, we'll keep you on just lithium to start off. That's why we keep taking your blood. We need to find your optimum lithium levels."

"Then can I leave?"

"You are going to have to make some lifestyle changes. No more alcohol. No more drugs."

"I know. I know."

I agreed with him, but that didn't mean I liked him. After all, I thought that he was sleeping with Lane as well.

After enduring nine long days I was the only remaining patient from the original group. Everyone else had left, and now there was a fresh batch of loonies. Everyone else had been allowed to go home. I was irate. I wasn't even allowed to go outside for a walk like most of the other patients. I hadn't felt direct sunlight since I had arrived and was beginning to feel claustrophobic, not to mention bitter. I regressed back to raving.

"I'm the craziest of the crazies!" I announced in the recreation room. "Everyone else gets to go home, but I'm the craziest of the crazies, and I have to stay."

A couple of the patients looked over at me.

"Behavior like that is what keeps you here," said one of the staff members.

"Like it makes a difference. You're never letting me leave."

"You'll get out of here eventually. Trust me. We don't want you here anymore than you do."

CHAPTER 4

On the tenth day, the doctor released me from the hospital. Despite my persistent demands, I was not ready. There was no question about it, I was still clinging to my delusions. I was no longer speaking about Lane, but I still believed she was sleeping with my friends, and as soon as I got out, I planned to put a stop to it.

Despite the setback, I still wanted to marry her. I didn't care that she had been with other men. That was in the past. My eyes were fixed on the future, even as I replayed the past in my mind and devised what I thought was a solution.

After returning to my hometown of Cleveland, Tennessee, I went to the doctor and scheduled surgery to have a couple of screws placed in my hand. Finally, I decided to call Lane. Since leaving the hospital, she had been the only thing on my troubled mind, but I still didn't know what I wanted to say. Rather than apologize, I felt she owed me an explanation, or at least a sign that she appreciated my so-called chivalrous nature.

When I called, we spoke for a long time. The conversation was not what I had hoped for; it focused more on my illness than on our imagined future together. Still, the talk went well enough that Lane agreed to visit me the next day at my mom's house. She looked great, though thinner than I had ever seen her. I couldn't help but think the stress I had caused contributed to her weight loss. My mom spoke to Lane briefly before retreating to the bedroom so we could talk privately.

"I brought a book that I thought you might enjoy," Lane said and handed me *An Unquiet Mind* by Kay Redfield Jamison. "It tells the story of a bipolar doctor coming to terms with the illness."

I grabbed the book and then offered Lane a seat on the couch in my mom's living room. I wanted to sit as close to her as possible. I wanted to touch her. I wanted to kiss her.

"The reason I brought you this book is that you have always written me great letters, and I thought you might find it therapeutic to write about the thoughts you are having. It might help you come to terms with the disease. You are not alone. There are many people like you."

"You liked my letters?"

"Of course. I've saved all of them and have been rereading them recently."

"Really?"

"I've been thinking of you a lot," said Lane.

"Hopefully good."

"I'm worried about you. Everybody is."

"Have you told anyone that I asked you to marry me?"

"Just my family, and of course my roommate knows. It came as quite a shock. I had no idea that you felt as strongly about me as that."

The conversation awkwardly dropped. Lane looked like she had something important to say, but she wasn't ready to blurt it out. Realizing that she was probably doing this to spare my feelings, I didn't push her. I let the moment pass without saying anything else.

"How are you doing today?" Lane finally asked. Her mouth was rigid, and her eyes were concerned. It was painfully obvious that she'd come here only in support. Nothing romantic, and I was too weak to do anything about it.

"Okay. I guess."

"Was the hospital hard on you?" she asked.

"Harder than you can imagine."

"At least you got out of there. Hopefully you won't have to go back."

"It's just hard for me to understand. Why am I different?"

"It's just the way we're wired," said Lane.

"We?"

"I suffer from depression as well. I take medicine and have for the past few years," she said.

"I had no idea."

"I don't tell many people."

"I guess everyone knows about me. I made a complete fool of myself."

"I wouldn't worry about it too much. People understand that you were sick. There's no reason to live in the past."

I looked down at my shattered hand. "Some things are easier to forget than others."

"How did you break your hand?" asked Lane.

"I tried to punch through a window."

"But why?"

I didn't know what to say. I didn't know if I should say, but finally I summoned the courage to be honest. "I thought you were in the house."

"With who?"

"Steve Marks."

"Who's he?"

"A fraternity brother."

"Does he know that you broke his window?" asked Lane.

"I don't think so."

"Don't you think you should pay Steve for it?"

I watched the expression on Lane's face to better judge her reaction. I didn't expect her to tell me that she had slept with Steve Marks or anyone else, but when she referred to Steve by his first name, immediately I suspected the worst.

I reached out to touch her. I gently stroked her shoulder. Her eyes were cold. I had put her through a lot. Despite my good intentions, and Lane understood that they were, I had placed her in a tough position.

"I'm glad you came by," I whispered. I didn't want my mom to hear my sweet talk, but Lane was annoyed.

"Why are you whispering?" she asked.

I removed my hand from her shoulder. "I don't know."

"Do you still want to marry me?"

"I don't know. Everything is so weird for me right now, but that doesn't mean I don't want to see you again."

"So you don't want to marry me?" Lane leaned back on the couch. For the first time she seemed to relax.

"I didn't say that I don't want to marry you. I'm just in a very bad place right now."

"You know I can't marry you right now."

"I know."

We hemmed and hawed for a few more minutes. Shortly thereafter, she left. I knew that I had lost her. I didn't know if was forever, but I recognized that I wasn't going to be with her anytime soon. This chapter was closed.

CHAPTER 5

I never returned to work at my real estate company in Atlanta. I simply couldn't manage it. After several months of manic energy, the bottom dropped out, and I sank into a deep depression. I left my Atlanta apartment and moved into a furnished place in Cleveland, Tennessee. I wanted to live at home with my mom, but she somehow decided that wasn't a good idea. As supportive as she has been throughout my battle with bipolar disorder, I believe this was a mistake on her part. I needed to be around people, and living alone was not what I needed. I retreated into my self-absorbed thoughts and was downright miserable. To my credit, I didn't drink during this time, but I was still miserable.

I continued seeing a psychiatrist weekly and took the lithium he prescribed. Although it helped somewhat, I hated it. The side effects wore on me, short-term memory loss, constant thirst from the salt in the medication, weight gain from drinking so many fluids, and trembling hands that made even the simplest tasks, like tying my shoes or pouring a glass of water, difficult. I often held my hand out just to see how badly it was shaking.

Through my reading about the illness, I learned that many writers and artists were bipolar. I decided to make the most of it, to try to turn my madness into an advantage. When Lane suggested I write, she probably meant keeping a journal to better understand my condition, but I took it further. If writing a book was the fastest way to her heart, then I would write the great American novel.

I studied many of the 20th century American classics, Hemingway, Fitzgerald, Salinger, but the reading didn't go well. The lithium dulled my concentration, and I often had to read passages over and over just to understand them, if I had the energy to read at all. It was a hard time. I thought about Lane constantly, replaying our conversations and searching for any sliver of hope that we might someday be together. I knew I needed to let go. Obsessing over her was unhealthy, but it wasn't easy. Many days I simply lay on the couch and wallowed in self-pity.

I accepted that I was never going to be the Benton of old, the carefree and spontaneous Benton who took life as it came. I blamed lithium for that, and more than once I stopped taking my medication just to feel that rush of energy again, only to retreat when the pain returned. And when I say pain, I mean both mental and physical. As my psyche spiraled downward, I would become physically exhausted from battling delusional thoughts until I slipped into a full-blown psychotic state. Although the decline was slow, I found that the true bottom came suddenly, when I was no longer strong enough to resist the psychosis. Almost before I realized it, I was deep in an episode.

After three months, I needed something to bring joy back into my life. I needed a drastic change. I still believed Lane was sleeping with my friends, and as irrational as it sounds, I could not shake the thought. I knew the only way to ease that fear was to move away. I couldn't return to Atlanta—that was where everything had unraveled in the first place. Nor could I stay in my hometown. The thought of seeing old friends, who no doubt would look at me differently, was unbearable. I wanted to go somewhere no one knew me, or Lane. Somewhere far away. I decided on Northern California.

I am not a man who believes in indecision. After a couple of weeks of frantic preparation and no real send-off, I drove across the country. At first, I felt relief in cleansing myself of the people and places that had haunted me for months. I was going where no one knew my failures, but also where no one knew my successes. What I was unprepared for was the skepticism I encountered from strangers. Soon after my arrival in Palo Alto, I found myself bored and lonely.

The people in California were different from those in the South, more serious, less friendly. On more than one occasion, after I launched into a diatribe about the virtues of conservative government or why the Atlanta Falcons were better than the San Francisco 49ers, people simply turned their heads, or in some cases walked away. I had never felt discrimination until I moved to Palo Alto. Just as some judge others by skin color, I was dismissed as a simpleton for being a Southerner. With nothing better to occupy my time, I began drinking again, making up for lost time by drinking more than I had before. The results weren't pretty. A couple of times I got into fights defending my homeland and ended up banned from two of the more popular bars.

Even with my newfound friendships at the bar, I was still lonely. During the winter months I became so desperate for conversation that I began talking with homeless men on the streets. They certainly didn't mind a stranger's company. Eventually, I grew comfortable enough to invite three of them into my apartment. They slept on the floor and showered in the morning when they woke up. One man even pushed a shopping cart. I will never forget the time he rolled his cart into the building and took the elevator up to my floor, nor will I forget the look on my neighbor's face when he cracked open his door in the middle of the night to see what was making the racket.

I don't consider myself a saint. I used them as much as they used me. By then I was writing every day, becoming aware of how little I knew about people. Just as I was learning about the habits of liberal-minded Californians, I wanted to understand the underbelly of society as well. I wasn't judging them. If my last three months in Tennessee and Georgia had taught me anything, it was not to judge others.

When I took the time to speak with these men, I enjoyed the conversation. They kept up with current events through discarded newspapers they read cover to cover while sitting on park benches. In their own way, they were highly moral. They despised Bill Clinton—not because of his policies, though they had opinions on those too, but because he had cheated on his wife and then lied to the public. They were girl crazy, and though they knew they had little chance with women, they swore that if they did, they would never cheat on them.

As for my role, I bought them beer and listened. They appreciated it, and I listened to their life stories. Just as much as money, if not more, these men wanted to be heard. If a woman, any woman, gave a homeless man two minutes of her time, it would mean far more to him than a quarter dropped into his cup. No one wanted to hear his thoughts or feelings on any subject, and loneliness set in. Sure, many of these men were mentally ill and believed they deserved no better, but I found their conversation fascinating. Though their experiences were much different from mine, I listened with sincerity.

The three homeless men I befriended, William, Carl, and Lee, took no money from the public. They were proud that they weren't beggars, instead receiving a government check each month for about $775, which, according to their own peculiar moral code, they didn't consider a handout. They drew a distinction between taking money from the government and accepting handouts from citizens on the street. They needed some money, going through life with none at all would have been nearly impossible. Still, William made an attempt. He regularly rummaged through dumpsters, eating anything from discarded pasta to unopened canned goods.

William, however, was unlike anyone I had ever met. He lived like an animal. Even when I invited him up to my apartment, he had no desire to take a shower; he preferred to stay dirty. What mattered most to him was using my phone to call his sister. He even reimbursed me for the twenty-eight cents a minute the call cost.

William was also a natural entertainer. He roamed the downtown streets of Palo Alto singing at the top of his lungs, not for money, not because he thought he was talented, but because he was free. Because he could. He told me that he had been arrested several times for disturbing the peace, but he didn't care. To him it was just another experience. In a way, jail was a step up; at least he slept indoors for a couple of nights. He never paid the fines. Eventually, they just let him go.

William was also one of the most resourceful men I have ever met, and he found amusement in things I never would have noticed. Once, while in my apartment, he picked up a Popsicle stick from the counter.

"Can I have this?" he asked.

"Why?"

"I collect them."

"Really?"

"I collect pencils too."

"Why?"

"I'm a tree hugger. I hate to see people needlessly cutting down trees."

Somehow William acquired a Volkswagen bus for $300 and was always talking about taking a trip with me to San Francisco for a night on the town. Once, he opened the back of his bus to show me what was inside. I had never seen such a menagerie of worthless items. He must have had twenty broken umbrellas, clothes stacked to the ceiling, and multiple recycling bags filled with cans and bottles that he claimed he was saving to cash in on a rainy day. He kept everything, even picking cigarette butts off the ground and smoking them rather than buying a pack of his own. Since he spent almost no money, I suppose he saved his $775 government check. There's no telling how much money he was worth, but he didn't care. In his mind he had full use of the outdoors, and that was all he needed. Instead of my feeling sorry for him, he almost pitied me for giving in to society's norms. He was the winner. I was the loser.

CHAPTER 6

Even today, when most people claim that mental illness is no longer as taboo as it was twenty years ago, little understanding remains of the severity of untreated disease. When I told some people I was bipolar, several casually replied that they were bipolar too, as if it were no worse than catching a cold. Then they would add that they refused to take medication. That always floored me. The worst thing you can say to someone with bipolar disorder is that he does not need medication to live a normal life. Yet I have heard it countless times. If you are truly bipolar, you do not have a choice, you must be on medication. Without it, I would either commit suicide or spend the rest of my life in a state hospital.

At the time, however, I was still in the early stages of the illness and had not come to terms with it. The people who said I was weak for taking medication, or that I was using it as a crutch, eventually got to me. No matter how strong you are, or how much you know those statements are false, a patient always wonders in the back of his mind whether he might be fine without pharmaceuticals. Maybe he is being weak. Maybe the demons from the past have been vanquished.

That kind of doubt can get the better of a fragile mind. Without consulting anyone, I canceled my appointments with my psychiatrist and quit taking lithium and Paxil. At first I felt sharper. My thoughts seemed clearer. The sluggishness that had weighed me down for nine months lifted. Slowly, almost imperceptibly, the irrational thoughts crept back in. I did not wake up one day suddenly insane. The descent was gradual. My concentration dissolved. I could no longer absorb what I read, losing focus after a paragraph or two as my mind drifted toward the abstract and the illogical.

To dull the chaos, I turned to alcohol. It slowed me down and, in the absence of prescription drugs, temporarily blunted both the manic highs and the depressive lows. But there was a price to pay. The swings grew sharper, the crashes harder, and in the end the devastation was worse than before.

Sadly, Lane Johnson entered my mind again. It began with a conversation I had at a bar with someone I knew. The man made an unusual statement about an albatross, a strange word, to be sure, and one that I had used in the book I was writing. When he said this, I immediately thought that Lane had been entering my apartment and reading what I had written. Of course, she must have relayed this information to people I knew, many of whom were the very subjects of my writing.

With this revelation, my mind was off to the races. I had no doubt that Lane was in Palo Alto. Fortunately, I did not think she was sleeping with all of these men, but I did believe she was consorting with them. I retreated to my apartment. My writing about life in Palo Alto had not been kind, and I dreaded the thought of these people knowing what I truly thought of them. I stopped going to the familiar bars and withdrew to my apartment with my computer.

Even with mounting evidence, I've always struggled to determine whether I was in a manic stage, a depressed stage, or, worst of all, a mixture of both. In a mixed state, I experience the dark thoughts and hopeless ideas of depression, yet, because I am also manic, I have the energy to act on them. When I'm only depressed, life is miserable, but at least I lack the willpower to do anything drastic or cause much trouble. I just sit on the couch or lie in bed, and by the next day I don't feel the guilt of having made a fool of myself.

During my manic phases, I tend to anger people, or at least offend them, with my outlandish ideas and unchecked thoughts. My ego runs wild, and I come across as self-centered and conceited. I truly believe I am the center of the world. I don't imagine myself to be God or the resurrection of Jesus Christ, as some people with bipolar disorder do when off their medication, but I do get religious. I began reading the Bible with fervor, especially Revelation, and I saw parallels between my life and the words on the page.

For example, Revelations 2:8-10 reads:

> To the angel of the church in <u>Smyrna</u> write:
>
> These are the words of him who is First and Last, who died and came to life again. I know your afflictions and your poverty—yet you are rich! I know the slander of those who say they are Jews and are not, but are a synagogue of Satan. Do not be afraid of what you are about to suffer. I tell you the devil will put some of you in prison to test you, and you will suffer persecution for <u>ten days</u>. Be faithful, even to the point of death, and I will give you the crown of life.

Now I have never been an especially religious person, but in my convoluted mind the coincidence seemed too much to overlook. The mental hospital I stayed in was actually in <u>Smyrna</u>, Georgia, a small suburb of Atlanta, and they held me there for <u>ten</u> days, and I certainly did feel like I was suffering almost to the point of death. Maybe death would be even better. I thought at least the pain would finally go away.

I read further. Revelations 2:18-23 reads:

> These are the words of the Son of God, whose eyes are like blazing fire and whose feet are like burnished bronze. I Know your deeds, your love and faith, your service and perseverance, and that you are now doing

more than you did at first. Nevertheless, I have this against you: You tolerate that woman <u>Jezebel</u>, who calls herself a prophetess. By her teaching she misleads my servants into <u>sexual immorality</u> and the eating of food sacrificed to idols. I have given her time to repent of her immorality, but she is unwilling. So I will cast her on a bed of suffering, and I will make those who commit adultery with her suffer intensely, unless they repent of her ways. I will strike her children dead. Then all the churches will know that I am he who searches heart and mind, and I will repay each of you according to your deeds.

I could only think of Lane as Jezebel, which further confirmed in my mind that she was consorting with unrepentant men.

The cracking of hidden codes soon spread into other areas of my life as my thoughts grew increasingly erratic. I compulsively added, multiplied, or otherwise manipulated any numbers I encountered. For example, my address was 392 University Avenue. I would calculate $3 + 9 + 2 = 14$, or $3 \times 9 \times 2 = 54$, or $39 - 2 = 37$, or $3^2 = 9$. Most likely I did this just to keep my troubled mind occupied. Everything became mathematical, governed by cause and effect. Nothing seemed random, nothing left to chance. It was as if I were solving a riddle—or better yet, on a scavenger hunt.

Street addresses especially captured my attention. My psychiatrist's office was at 214 University Avenue, which I interpreted in several ways. At one point I believed it meant I would live to be 214 years old. At another time I thought it was the date I would marry Lane—February 14, not coincidentally Valentine's Day. Even license plates, whether mine or a stranger's, took on significance. They could represent anything from the day I would die to the number of children I would have.

At the same time I developed a case of temporary dyslexia. My thoughts were turning wrong side out. In my head I spelled words backwards and forwards, and I could not stop. For example, 'racecar' spelled backwards is 'racecar' and the drinking water 'Evian' spelled backwards is appropriately 'naïve.' Another good one is 'lived' spelled backwards is 'devil.' Walking down the street, I would see a sign to 'Park' and would immediately think of 'krap' or a 'Stop' sign would be 'pots.' These were the fun ones, since they at least spelled something reasonable, but most words don't do this. 'Siht od t'nod sdrow tsom tub.'

Coupled with these compulsive number games, I habitually formed acronyms within my head. For example, Best Of All Time is B.O.A.T. and Sack Of Shit is S.O.S. As In The Earlier Cases These Were The Fun Ones. AITECTWTFO is not so much fun and can be downright maddening when it occurs every minute of the day for weeks at a time.

Over the next 24 hours, I smoked cigarettes and replayed in my mind every conversation that Lane and I had. I thought about how, when I asked her to marry me, I told her that we should just go and not look back. If I truly meant what I said, I reasoned that I should dispose of my possessions. That was the only way I could prove to Lane that I was serious about marrying her.

Without hesitation, I gathered my belongings and carried them down to the dumpster in the basement. I took my clothes, desk, mattress, two cherry end tables, wallet with all of my credit cards and cash, radio, food, books, and computer, including all of the pages from the book I was working on, so I no longer had any record of what I had written. I didn't care. Lane would respect the spontaneity of my decision.

Around midnight the superintendent found me in the basement just as I was taping a piece of paper to my pile of belongings that read 'Free.'

"What are you doing?" asked the superintendent.

"Throwing my things away," I replied. I was sitting with my legs crossed on the cold, concrete floor looking up at him.

"Can I ask why?"

"I'm leaving."

"That's all fine and dandy, but you are supposed to give me thirty days' notice. I won't be able to give you your deposit back."

Of course I didn't care about that. I didn't want any money anyway. All I wanted was Lane.

"What are you going to do for money?" he asked.

"Things have a way of working their way out."

"How do you plan on leaving? By plane?"

"I'm not sure yet."

"What about your car?"

I had forgotten about my car.

"I don't have a driver's license."

"Don't do anything crazy with your car. I promise that you'll regret it if you do," said the super.

"I won't have any regrets."

"Does this have anything to do with that motley crew you've been hanging around with?"

"No. It doesn't have anything to do with them."

'Well. You're a grown man. I guess you can do what you want with your life."

I went up to my room. The couch was the only thing left in my apartment, too heavy for me to carry on my own. I lay down on it and waited for Lane to come. I waited for two days, but she never appeared. I didn't sleep. I didn't eat. I began to wonder whether people really needed sleep or food. I thought it might all be a scam, that only children slept, like believing in Santa Claus. Adults, I imagined, simply lay in bed at night pretending to sleep so their children wouldn't know any better. Since I was still a child emotionally, I slept, and I felt embarrassed by this. I tried my best to keep my eyes open.

But I grew hungry. *What was I going to do?* Lane still hadn't shown up. *What if she never did? What would I do then?* I had no money, no way of getting money, no way of getting food. Though I didn't want to, I had no choice but to call my mom. Since I had thrown away my phone, I walked across the street to a phone booth and dialed her 800 number, which she kept for emergencies.

"Hello."

"It's me. I've screwed up, Mom. I've screwed up real bad."

"What have you done?"

"I threw all of my things in the trash."

"Why in the world would you do something like that?"

"I don't know. I thought it was the right thing to do at the time."

"Do you think that was the right thing to do now?"

"No."

"Have you quit taking your medicine?"

"Yes."

"Did you throw it away too?"

"Yes."

"Are you going to start taking your medicine?"

"Yes."

"Then you need to go see your doctor and get him to write you a new prescription."

"You don't understand. I don't have any money."

"You threw away your wallet?"

"Yes."

"Oh Benton! What were you thinking?"

"I guess I wasn't."

"If I come all the way out to California to get you, are you going to take your medicine?"

"Yes, Mom."

"Promise?"

"Yes, Mom. C'mon, I need your help."

"I know you do. You need to think about these things before you do something crazy like this."

"I know."

"I'll have to book a flight. I'll try to get out there tomorrow. Will you be okay until tomorrow?"

"Yes."

"I'll call your sister to come up from San Diego to get your car."

"Thanks, Mom."

"I love you, Benton."

"I love you too, Mom."

CHAPTER 7

The next day my buzzer rang, and I let my mom, sister, and stepfather into the building. I heard the elevator stop on my floor and watched as my family came around the corner. They looked like people attending a funeral. My sister spoke first.

"Oh, Benton. Are you okay?"

While my mom often grew frustrated with my lack of responsibility in managing the disease, my sister was more patient. I was two years older than Emily, and Lord knows she dealt with a lot growing up as the crash-test dummy for the behavior I imitated from watching *The Three Stooges,* professional wrestling, or *The Incredible Hulk*—all shows my parents eventually forbade me to watch out of fear that I might seriously injure her.

As we grew older, I was never the overprotective brother when it came to Emily's boyfriends. I'm not saying I did nothing, I voiced my likes and dislikes from time to time, but by the time she started seriously dating, I respected her as a grown woman who could make her own choices.

Since I never babied my sister, acting more like a wise friend than a big brother, Emily treated me differently from my mother. She was more supportive than combative. In the months after my initial hospital visit, she took a week off from work in San Diego to spend time with me in Tennessee. Unlike my relationship with my mom, where I always felt defensive, I was more at ease with my sister, who really just wanted me to know she was there if I needed her.

That week, Emily and I went to movies, ate at restaurants, and shopped at the mall, basically anything she could think of to ease my mind from the troubles lurking just below the surface. I don't remember exactly how much I opened up about what was going on in my head, but I do remember that whatever little I did share, my sister told me straight whether I was being paranoid or whether it was a legitimate concern. Often, it wasn't a legitimate concern. Though I was embarrassed to share these revelations with my younger sister, I felt more comfortable with her than I did with a psychiatrist. Besides, I was certain my sister wasn't sleeping with Lane.

"You don't look too bad," my mom said as way of greeting.

"Yeah. Just a little shaken up," I said.

"How are you doing, Benton?" My stepfather held out his hand. He was the only one who was smiling.

"I've been better."

I held the door so they could enter my apartment.

"You really did throw everything away," Mom said.

"You didn't think I made it up, did you?"

"I guess I didn't realize that you threw *everything* away. I thought maybe you kept your bed and desk. How did you get all of your stuff to the trash?" asked my mom.

"It wasn't easy."

"Do you not even have a change of clothes?"

"I don't have anything."

"Is that why you still have the couch? It was too heavy?"

"Yes."

"Well. It is a good-looking couch," said my mom with the first sign of humor since they had arrived.

"Take a seat," I said.

"We really don't have time. We have a flight scheduled for tomorrow. I want to speak with your doctor and get your medication. You are going to take your medicine, aren't you?"

Something in the way my mom asked that question made me suspicious. Suddenly, I didn't trust her anymore.

"Well. Are you?"

"No," I replied.

"Now Benton," my mom said sternly. "You promised that if I came all the way out here to get you that you would take your medicine."

"I've changed my mind."

"Do you think you would have thrown all of your things away if you were taking your medicine?"

"Yes."

"Why would you do that?"

I looked over at Emily. Her eyes were glossy like she was about to cry, but she didn't say anything.

"Just think about it," said my mom.

"I have. And I'm not going to take my medicine."

"Will you at least tell me the name of your doctor so if you change your mind, you'll have it so you can take it?"

"Dr. Campbell."

"Where's his office?" My mom was trying to be patient. She's as strong as a bull, and it takes a lot to rattle her, but I was pushing her limits. I conceded that I should at least tell her where the doctor's office was.

"Three blocks down University Avenue," I said.

"Thank you," said my mom, and she looked me in the eye. I stared back at her in what I'm sure looked like hate-filled eyes. "We'll be back in a while, depending on how long it takes us to see the doctor. Would you like us to bring you some food?"

"No."

"I thought you said that you hadn't eaten in days."

"I'm not hungry."

"We'll bring you something anyway."

I didn't say anything.

"Will you be okay by yourself for a little while?" asked my mom.

"Yes."

My sister walked over and tried to hug me; I kept my arms at my sides. I wanted them to leave. If I went with them, I wouldn't see Lane, I would be giving up. Since I'd come this far, I decided to go the final mile and hold out as long as possible. I was doing this for Lane. I wouldn't compromise; I would do the best I could.

"And take a shower, you don't smell very good," my mom said.

"I don't have any soap or shampoo."

"If I buy you soap or shampoo, will you take a shower?"

"Yes."

"And will you at least consider taking your medicine? I hate seeing you like this."

I said nothing, and they left without another word. I relaxed on the couch. With nothing to do, I wanted to read, anything to pass the time, but instead I closed my eyes and fell asleep.

A couple of hours later my family returned. They had seen the doctor and filled my prescriptions. My mom wasted no time: she opened the bottles and poured the pills into her hand.

"Take these," she said.

My sister stood beside her and tried to hand me a soda to wash down the pills. I stayed on the couch. I no longer trusted them; I thought they were trying to trick me and wanted them to leave. I decided not to speak, surely that would send them away. Instead I glared at them with the most awful look I could muster; inside, I wept. I was so sad to be acting this way, but I had to. I had to do it for Lane.

"So now you're not going to talk?" my mom asked.

I lowered my eyes.

My mom looked at my sister and stepfather. "I guess that's a no."

"If I give you paper, will you write down your answers?" my sister asked.

I nodded. My sister retrieved a pen and paper from her purse and handed them to me.

"Why won't you talk?" my mom asked.

"I don't want to," I wrote.

"That's not a good answer," she continued. "What do you want to do?"

"Nothing," I wrote.

"Is there anything you want?"

"I want the book *To Kill a Mockingbird*," I wrote.

It had been a long time since I had read the book, but for some reason the title struck a chord with me. I felt like people were mocking me. I didn't want to kill anyone, but I did want them to stop. Then I made another unusual connection: my preschool teacher's name was Mrs. Harper and my first-grade teacher's name was Mrs. Lee. The author of *To Kill a Mockingbird* is Harper Lee; I thought the two of them had somehow written the book together under a pen name.

"Did Mrs. Harper and Mrs. Lee write *To Kill a Mockingbird*?" I wrote.

They all looked at each other funny.

"Why would you say that?" asked my sister.

"They have the same name."

My mom smiled. "No. That is only a coincidence."

I didn't write anything.

"If I get you this book, will you take your medicine?"

I didn't say anything. I really wanted this book.

"We'll buy you some more clothes as well."

They left again. They returned a couple of hours later.

"We bought you some clothes," said my sister.

My mother was carrying a red plastic bag with the words "Stanford University Bookstore" on it. My stepfather had a couple of black plastic bags in his hands.

"We brought you some food as well."

My stepfather pulled out a box of cereal, a carton of milk, a jar of peanut butter, a jar of jelly, a loaf of bread, and a carton of orange juice.

"All your favorites."

My sister emptied the contents of the red bag and pulled out a Stanford University sweatshirt, T-shirt, and sweatpants. "I thought you might like a change of clothes."

They were being so nice to me it was practically breaking my heart not to speak.

"Here's your book, too," said my sister with a grin as she handed me To Kill a Mockingbird.

"Thank you," I wrote. It was hard to be mean to my sister. My mom and I had many arguments through the years, and I knew her skin was as thick as an alligator's, but my sister was different.

"Are you going to eat?" asked my mom.

I didn't write anything. I didn't even acknowledge their presence. I turned my head, hoping they would leave.

"We're not going to stand here and be ignored. You broke the deal. You said if I came out here that you would take your medicine. And now you're not going to do it?"

I didn't move.

"All right. I guess we'll go to the restaurant where you used to work then. Can you at least tell us where it is?"

I wrote down the address.

"We'll be back tomorrow."

As soon as they left, I tore into the food. I ate two peanut butter and jelly sandwiches and two bowls of cereal. That night I tried to read *To Kill a Mockingbird* but couldn't concentrate. I slept on the couch and waited for my family to come back the next day. They showed up around ten in the morning.

"I spoke to your landlord," said my mom. "He has agreed to give your deposit back if there's no damage to the apartment."

I didn't say anything. I didn't write anything.

"Are you not coming home with us?"

I shook my head.

"What do you plan on doing?"

"Staying here," I wrote.

"Do you mind if your sister takes your car? You can't drive it, and she needs a new car," said my mom.

"Why did you lock yourself in the trunk?" my sister asked.

"Because I wanted to," I wrote.

My mom looked at me. She was losing her patience. "You're acting like a five-year-old."

"Younger," I wrote.

My mom smiled, but it was forced. She was not amused. "I don't know what you plan on doing, but you're not going to last long with no money and a loaf of bread."

My mom attempted to be calm. She knew me well enough to know that asking for my obedience would fall on deaf ears, and most likely I would retreat further into my shell. But her restraint was unprecedented. My mom is not afraid to let me know exactly what she is thinking. However, in this case she didn't press. I was surprised at the time, but I understand now. If something drastic happened, like a suicide, my mom didn't want her last words to be something horrible. I spoke to her later about it, and she admitted that all three of them wondered if I would try.

"You need to leave," I finally said.

"What did you say?" my mom asked.

"I said. You need to leave."

"All right, Benton. If that's what you want, then that's what we'll do. But don't come calling me for help again when you finally realize that you are helpless."

"I won't," I wrote.

"You leave us no choice. We're going to leave you here all by yourself. We have a plane to catch."

My mom and a teary-eyed sister gave me a farewell hug, and my stepfather offered his hand to shake. I did not reciprocate. They left, and despite being a complete ass, I felt little remorse. My mind had reached a point where logical thinking was nonexistent, and there was no convincing me that I was, in fact, wrong and that I must take the medication.

Another day passed. It was Thursday by then. I had eaten all my food. That didn't matter. I didn't need to eat. I didn't need to sleep. I didn't need anything but Lane. However, I was concerned that she wasn't going to show up anytime soon. How long should I wait? How long could I wait? The night slowly crept by. I eventually went down to the laundry room to watch TV. It was miserable. I watched an infomercial about how to make millions by placing classified ads.

I went back to my room. As I lay on the couch, I began to hum "Dixie." I didn't know much of the song, so I just hummed the refrain over and over until a radical idea came to mind. Memorial Day was the upcoming weekend. All my friends from Tennessee celebrated by going to Ocoee Lake. It would be a huge party. Lane would probably be there as well. I didn't sleep a wink that night. At 9 o'clock sharp, I was in the superintendent's office to turn in my key.

"So you're hitting the road, are you?" the superintendent asked. "Yep."

"Do you have any money?"

"Nope."

"Would you like to borrow some? I suppose I could give you a loan from your deposit."

"I'm fine."

"Well. I guess it's bon voyage. You sure are a strange kid."

"That's what they tell me."

I embarked on my journey by walking out of the office and straight to University Avenue. I wore khaki pants, a Stanford sweatshirt, and running shoes without insoles, which I had taken out during my trashing to signify that I had no "soul" or something to that effect.

I headed east on University until it ran into Interstate 101. I expected a friend, any friend, to drive up in an 18-wheeler, pull the horn, wave me into the truck, slap me five, and then push play on an eight-track of the Smokey and the Bandit soundtrack as we roared down the open highway on our way across the country. I wondered what friend it would be, John, Jay, Matt, Michael. I didn't care. I smiled, thinking about it. This would be the greatest story ever told!

When no one showed up, I took off running. I had convinced myself that I could run across the country like Forrest Gump. At the time, this seemed entirely logical. I started slowly, trotting across the hot asphalt. This wasn't so bad, I thought. All I had to do was keep putting one foot in front of the other. I could run forever if I gutted out the pain. It was simply a case of mind over matter.

Cars whizzed by me at seventy miles an hour. Though the wind was at my back, I was in terrible shape from lack of exercise and a pack-a-day smoking habit. The California sun beat down on me, and my boxers crawled up my leg. Not only could I not run across the country, but I also couldn't run to another zip code. After a mile, I was completely winded. I placed my hands on my knees and tried to catch my breath.

What could I do now? I couldn't turn back; I no longer had the key to my apartment. I decided to continue heading south with my thumb out. I intended to catch a ride across the country with truckers.

I planned to make it back to Tennessee by Monday. I had hitchhiked in Georgia once when I ran out of gas and was picked up in a matter of minutes, but California proved different. No one stopped. After several miles, a state trooper pulled up behind me and turned on her lights. I kept walking until the car parked behind me.

A female voice commanded me to stop. I turned around. The state trooper, blonde hair pulled back and mirrored sunglasses in place, stepped out of the car.

"Sir, can I ask what you're doing?"

"I'm trying to get back to Tennessee."

"You're what?"

"I'm trying to get back to Tennessee."

"I'll be honest with you. I've never heard that one before. Are you serious?" she asked in a smoky voice.

I didn't answer but gave her a halfhearted smile.

"Do you have any identification on you?"

"No, ma'am."

"Do you realize that it's illegal to hitchhike on the interstate in the state of California?"

"No, ma'am."

"You do now. Consider yourself warned. If I catch you out here again, I'll be forced to write you a citation."

"If I can't hitchhike on the interstate, then where can I hitch?"

She paused, wiping the sweat from her brow before answering. "You can do it on state highways only. I can take you to a place where panhandlers frequent, if you want."

"I'm not panhandling."

"Look. Do you want a ride or not?"

"Sure."

I hopped in the back seat of her car. She drove me to the next exit, where she dropped me off with another warning not to get back on the interstate.

I had been hiking for four hours and was exhausted. I stood at the exit with my thumb out for close to an hour, but no one stopped.

Screw the state trooper. I had to keep moving. Tennessee was waiting, and I needed to be there by the end of the week. I walked the two blocks back to the interstate and pushed on for another couple of hours.

Another patrol car pulled up behind me. I kept walking, steady, as if I didn't hear him. I was obeying rules six and seven: Do not look. Do not listen.

This one wasn't so patient. He ran up from behind and threw me to the ground. My cheek hit the hot asphalt. He twisted my right arm behind me, hard, like he was ready to cuff me.

"What's your problem? Are you deaf?" he growled.

"No, sir."

He let go, pulled me up. His eyes studied me, suspicion fading into curiosity.

"What are you doing out here?"

"I'm trying to get back to Tennessee."

"Got any identification?"

"No, sir."

He smiled then, shoulders easing. "So you're saying you want to get back to Tennessee. Wouldn't it be easier to take an airplane?"

"I don't have any money."

"You don't have money, and you plan to hitchhike across the country?"

I said nothing. Rule number eight: Do not say a word.

"Do you have any family you can call?"

Silence.

"If you're not going to speak, then I can't help you." He scratched at his mustache, spat. "Do you hear me?"

"Yes."

"What's your name?"

Still I hesitated.

"You better tell me, so I can run a check."

"Benton Savage."

"So you can speak after all."

I nodded.

A few minutes later he came back from his car. "Everything turned out okay. I'll follow you to the next exit, but I'd better not catch you on the interstate again. Do you understand?"

I kept my eyes down and nodded. I walked toward the exit, maybe a quarter mile ahead. Cars roared past, and each time I turned, his headlights were there, close behind. At the ramp he sped up and passed me.

This time I listened. I stayed off the interstate. I followed a state highway instead, its strip malls and gas stations glowing in the dark. Night closed in and I was exhausted.

I thought of Hank Williams, drifting through the night like a voice I couldn't shake. At the convenience stores, I lingered in front of the coolers, aching for a drink I couldn't buy. More than once, I thought about stealing one. But I didn't.

Sometimes I sat in the grass to rest my blistered feet, but I knew I couldn't stay. I had to keep moving. By morning I was on back roads, cherry orchards on both sides. I reached for fruit, hoping for something to keep me going, but the cherries weren't ripe.

After walking in the dark all night, I watched the sun rise above the horizon. I came to another community and found a bench, where I sat down to rest my legs. I now knew I was in trouble. I was too far from Palo Alto to turn back, and I had no idea how I could sustain myself. I desperately needed water. Food would help, but fluids were essential.

Around 11:00 a.m., I spotted a small Mexican restaurant. I walked in through the front door. I can't imagine what I looked like, but I hoped my appearance was pitiful enough to earn me a cup of water and perhaps a plate of food. I approached the counter and simply stared at the cashier. Apparently, she could read my mind.

"Would you like some water?"

"Please."

She filled a large paper cup with ice water and handed it to me. Without stepping away from the counter, I gulped it down, then looked back at her.

"Do you have any money?" she asked.

I shook my head.

"Would you like something to eat?"

I nodded.

"I'll get you something, but you need to wait outside. The owner would kill me if she caught me giving away food."

Fortunately, there were tables outside. Though there was no shade, I rejoiced at having a place to sit. A few minutes later, the woman came out with a burrito wrapped in tinfoil.

"Would you like some more water?"

"Thank you."

It wasn't the best bean burrito I had ever eaten, but in my history of great meals, this one stands out as one of the best. I could have eaten another, but pride kept me from asking. After finishing, I threw the trash away and continued down the road under the sweltering sun. I was about seventy-five miles south of San Francisco, and I couldn't help thinking of the inaccuracy of the line attributed to Mark Twain: "The coldest winter I ever spent was the summer I spent in San Francisco."

The comfort of the meal spoiled me a bit, and I began scheming about how I might get another one. In the meantime, I tucked myself under a highway overpass to escape the sun, which was becoming more and more of a factor in my frail existence. Walking again, I saw a telephone booth, and I knew I couldn't pass it up. My plan to hitchhike across the country was ridiculous. I needed help. There was no other way of looking at it.

"Got yourself a little problem there, don't you, Benton?" my mom said when she answered.

"Yes, ma'am."

"I suppose I can call the Morrises and see if they can pick you up and take you to the airport, but without identification I don't see how you'll board a plane." The Morrises were cousins who lived in San Francisco.

"How will they find me?"

"You don't know where you are?"

"Not really."

"I guess you can call the police. They can take you somewhere, and then you call me from there, and we'll arrange the pickup."

"Thank you."

"I guess it goes without saying that if I do all of this for you, you have to start taking your medicine again."

"Yes, ma'am."

"Okay, Benton. Call the police, and I'll see what I can do on this end."

I didn't relish calling the police and explaining my situation, but I was exhausted, dehydrated, and slightly disoriented. A half hour later, the local police picked me up.

"What are you doing out here so far from home?" the officer asked.

"I was trying to get back to Tennessee."

"Tennessee! And you were walking?"

"I was trying to hitch."

"You can't hitchhike in California. Wouldn't it be easier to take an airplane?"

I let it pass without a smart-aleck remark. "Where are you taking me?"

"We're taking you to a church where the homeless come every evening for dinner. I believe they also have beds, if you need to stay overnight."

CHAPTER 8

The church was cool and comfortable. I drank several cups of water and began to feel better, relaxing somewhat. A few minutes later, the receptionist brought me some cookies. I scarfed them down in about two minutes and then remained in the lobby for a couple of hours until the homeless people started showing up around five o'clock.

This was a large church with a gymnasium. Volunteers wearing red aprons and warm smiles served hot food. I watched the homeless men pile fried chicken, mashed potatoes, and baked beans on their plates. As much fun as I had clowning around with my homeless friends in Palo Alto, I did not belong, and I felt awful for taking advantage of the situation by accepting free food. While these men endured hardship out of personal plight, I had simply discarded my possessions and was now waiting to be transported back to my mother. I felt ashamed of my behavior and prayed no one asked questions. Fortunately, none of the men questioned me. We ate with minimal conversation. I finished two plates and then returned to the lobby, relieved to be away from their desperate eyes.

Though my cousins lived on the West Coast, they were as close as family could be, despite our living on opposite sides of the country. They had two daughters about the same age as my sister and me, and we all got along very well. When my dad was alive, I remembered a family adventure when we flew out to stay with them just outside San Francisco, and they visited us a couple of times in Tennessee. Now, as I waited for them in the safe confines of the church lobby, I hoped they wouldn't show up driving too nice a car. I felt like a fourteen-year-old kid being picked up by his parents at the mall right in front of his peers. It was a ridiculous desire under the circumstances, but among these homeless men, who were struggling just to stay alive, I couldn't bear for them to see me drive away in luxury.

Even though I knew I would never see these men again, it still seemed important not to flaunt my privileged upbringing. Of course, my cousins showed up in a Mercedes-Benz. But as I scampered out the door and into the car, I don't remember anyone noticing, and looking back, I doubt any of them cared. They had bigger worries.

Instead of concerning myself with the opinions of men I would never see again, I should have felt more self-conscious about the burden I was placing on my cousins. However, I was simply relieved to be around people who cared about me. They didn't make me feel guilty. They were kind. Rather than embarrassing me with pointed questions about how I had ended up in this situation, they asked about the book I was writing.

"I'm not writing anymore," I said.

"Why not?" asked Susan.

"Everything has been said. There's nothing new to say."

"There are certainly a lot of new books coming out for there to be nothing more to write," said Susan.

"That's true. But none of them are any good."

We arrived at the airport a couple of hours before my flight. They took me out for another meal. After being solitary for so long, I felt downright jubilant with the fresh conversation among people with whom I felt comfortable. My worries were temporarily behind me. I was meeting my goal. Though the means of transportation were different than I had hoped, I was making it back to Tennessee before the end of the weekend, and I would be seeing Lane again in a matter of hours. Feeling good and finally secure, I don't know what the hell I was thinking, but I ordered a beer with my dinner, maybe even a second one. I don't remember. But obviously I wasn't feeling too guilty about my poor judgment over the past few months.

At the ticket counter my cousins vouched for my identity, and I was escorted to the gate. I caught the red-eye out of San Francisco. Since there was no direct flight to Chattanooga, I transferred in Atlanta and arrived home midmorning on Saturday. My mom had medication in her hand when I hopped in the car. I refused it.

"But you swore that you would take it," said my mom.

"I don't need it. I'm fine."

"You are not fine. I just got you back from California because you were lost. You are not fine."

"It was just a bad spell. I'm fine."

"You're not staying in my house if you aren't going to take your medicine," she said.

"Where am I going to stay?"

"That's your problem. I'm washing my hands of you with a guilt-free conscience. I told you the deal, and now you're breaking it. Again."

Despite her claim that I couldn't stay at home, she took me there. I went downstairs to my room and lay on my bed. I hadn't slept much in recent days, and I fell into a deep slumber, not worrying about what the future had in store for me but instead almost proud of the ruse I had pulled. A few hours later my mom and stepfather entered. My mom had a piece of paper in her hand.

"Are you still not going to take your medicine?"

"No."

"And why not?"

"I don't need it."

"You don't think that you are bipolar?"

"No."

"Can you explain why you are acting the way that you are?"

"No."

"What are your plans?"

"I don't know."

"Why don't you have any plans?"

"How am I supposed to know what's going to happen next? I take life as it comes."

Of course I was lying. That's true for everyone, and certainly true for a person suffering from bipolar disorder. I was always dreaming of something, whether it was advancing my career, planning a vacation, or even getting people to go out on the weekends. When I was in Atlanta, working in commercial real estate, I was constantly looking for a better company to hold my real-estate license. When I was in California, working as a bartender, I always kept my eye out for a better and more lucrative establishment to serve drinks in. But now, as I lay on my bed in my mother's home, none of those things seemed important to me anymore. The only thing on my mind was being with Lane. The problem was, I had no idea how to go about it. So in that sense I was telling the truth: I had no real plans.

"Do you mind if I give you this test I found on the internet to determine whether you are bipolar?" my mom asked.

"What is it?"

"Twelve questions that you are supposed to answer with a number from one to five depending on how strongly you feel about your response."

"Sure. I'll take the test, but it won't make any difference. I know I'm not bipolar."

"At times I feel more talkative than others," was the first question.

"Very much."

"I get into moods where I feel very speeded up or irritable."

"Very much."

"My self-confidence ranges from great self-doubt to equally great self-confidence."

"Often."

This went on for twelve questions, most of which I rated four or five. I answered completely honestly. I was sure I had aced the test. I was sure the results would deem me sane.

"You scored forty-two," my mom said.

"And?" I said with a smile. This was one of those times when I felt great self-confidence.

"Any score over ten indicates that you are most likely bipolar," my mom said.

"Over ten?"

"Yes. Now do you believe that you are bipolar?"

"No."

My mom looked at me. "Benton! I know it's the illness that is making you act this way, but you need to believe me. You need to take medicine. You are bipolar. There is no other way of looking at it."

"No. I'm not."

My mom glared at me. "You're not staying in this house if you're not going to take your medicine. It's as simple as that."

"That's fine. I'll just go somewhere else."

"Like where?"

"I have friends. I'll stay with them."

"Believe me. They won't put up with this any more than I will," my mom said with a kind of fake laugh. She was clearly beside herself.

"We'll see."

"Yes. I guess we will."

I smiled at her just to be an asshole.

"You're not eating dinner with us. Don will bring your meal down to you."

After my mom and stepfather went upstairs to prepare dinner, I called my friend Everett, who I knew would be hosting a Memorial Day party up on Ocoee Lake. He was my oldest friend. Though I hadn't spoken with him much in the past year, mostly because I suspected him of having slept with Lane as well, I assumed he would be happy to see me. We talked for a long while, and I kind of invited myself up to his cabin for the day. Like I said, we were old friends, and of course he didn't mind. I neglected to mention the circumstances of my return home, instead glossing over most of the details by simply saying that I had grown weary of my life in California and was glad to be back in the South. We made plans for him to pick me up the next morning.

I went upstairs to rub it in my mom's face that I already had somewhere to go.

"Do you really think that's a good idea?" she asked.

"I don't see why not."

"I'm sure there are going to be a lot of people up there. Do you think that it is a good idea to be drinking beer in your condition?"

"I don't see why not."

"I'll tell you why. Because twenty-four hours ago you were wandering in the middle of nowhere with no money and no place to sleep."

"That was yesterday."

"Did you tell Everett what happened yesterday?"

"I didn't see any reason. That's in the past."

"History has a way of repeating itself."

I went back downstairs. A half hour later I received a call from Everett.

"Listen, Benton. I don't know if it is such a good idea that you come up to my cabin with me tomorrow. There's going to be a lot of people, and you know. I just don't know if it is a good idea."

"Did my mom tell you to say this?"

"That's not important."

"It is to me."

"I'm not trying to be a bad friend. I'm trying to be a good friend, and sometimes that means tough love."

"That's not cool," I said.

"Just the same. It's my decision."

We ended the conversation and went upstairs to speak with my mom.

"How dare you call Everett and tell him not to invite me up to his cabin tomorrow," I said.

"I didn't tell him not to invite you to his cabin. I just told him the circumstances that you came home. It was his decision. Not mine."

"But you influenced him," I said.

"Benton. I'm trying to help you. Don't you understand that?"

"No."

A few minutes later my stepfather brought dinner down to my room. I hadn't been invited to eat with them. I'm not exactly sure what it was, but it looked like a huge peach cut in half with an empty hole in the middle, shaped like a vagina. In the middle of the fruit—or vagina, were three tiny white seeds. I have never spoken to my mother about this, and I don't know how I could broach the subject, but I felt they were trying to get under my skin by illustrating the seeds inside Lane from all the men having sex with her.

I wasn't going to take this without a fight. I didn't take one bite of the meal; instead I snuck into the garage and laid the plate on the front-left tire of my stepfather's car so that when he drove, he would break it. I stayed outside and hid behind a tree. I wanted to see my action come to fruition.

I must have waited an hour. Since it was probably close to eight o'clock, I could have waited all night. Sure enough, my stepfather came out to his car. I heard him turn on the engine, then the shattering of the plate as he backed out of the garage. I watched through the shadows as he inspected the damage and then went inside to tell my mother. Just as I was about to sneak back into the house, my mother met me at the door.

"Benton! What the hell are you doing?"

I didn't say anything. I tried to walk past her, but she was blocking the door.

"You can't come in here! I don't want you in my house!"

I slid past her and walked toward my room with my mother yelling at me as I went. "This isn't going to last! I want you out of my house!"

Everything was calm until the next morning, when I woke and went back upstairs. My mother was reading the newspaper in the kitchen.

"Don has gone to exercise, and I'm about to leave, too. But before I go, we need to have a talk," she said.

My mind was already drifting. I did not believe my stepfather was exercising; I believed he was with Lane. I was sure of it. I was also sure my mother knew about it, and somehow, in my twisted mind, I had concluded that she had approved of him sleeping with Lane, that this was some kind of reward for stymieing my personal pursuit of Lane.

"Don's not exercising," I said.

"Then what is he doing if he's not exercising?" asked my mom.

"You know what he's doing."

"No. I don't. What is he doing? Please tell me."

"He's with Lane."

My mom laughed and shook her head. "Benton. You are crazy. Don isn't with Lane. He's at Bodynamics working out."

"Call him. You'll see."

"You want me to call him at Bodynamics?"

"He's not there," I said.

"I'll call him just to prove how ludicrous you really are."

My mom picked up the phone and dialed the number. She asked for Don. A minute later she was having a conversation with him.

"Here. Talk to Benton. He doesn't believe that you are at Bodynamics. He thinks you're with Lane doing God knows what."

My mom tried to hand the phone to me. I didn't take it. I walked out of the kitchen and down to my room. How could I have been so wrong once again about my stepfather being with Lane? Even then, I wasn't convinced I was completely wrong. Sure, I believed my stepfather was at the gym at that time, but that didn't erase my suspicions that he had been with Lane in the past. This was an ongoing conspiracy that was not going to stop until I cracked the code. The only problem was, I had no idea what needed to be done. But I was willing to try anything, no matter how ridiculous it sounded. No stone would be left unturned. I repeated a phrase in my head that I had learned in a high school history class: "All's fair in love and war."

Since I considered Lane the most amazing woman I had ever met, I knew it was going to be tough. Just as a great war is won by a brilliant, overwhelming tactic in battle, I scoured my brain for the atomic bomb. I needed to do that one thing that would bring this awful situation to an end. Nobody would stand in my way. I would never surrender.

I went outside for a long walk. I must have been gone for three or four hours when a storm blew in and I was a couple of miles from home. When I arrived back, I was drenched from head to toe. I tried to retrieve the key from its secret hiding place, but it was not there. The key had never before failed to be where it was supposed to be.

I rang the doorbell. No one answered. I rang it again. This time my stepfather came to the door.

"Benton, I can't let you in here," he said.

"What are you talking about? It's my house."

"It's your mother's house, and she doesn't want you in here. You broke the deal. You're not taking your medicine."

I pushed my stepfather aside and walked in. I went downstairs to my room. I stripped out of my clothes and dried myself with a towel. Still naked, I lay in bed and pulled the covers over my body. I was tired and wanted to sleep. I didn't give a damn what my stepfather said. I hadn't done anything wrong. All I wanted was a dry place to lay my head and a couple winks of shuteye.

Half an hour later I heard strange voices and then loud footsteps coming down the stairs to my basement room. I pulled the covers up to my chin. Two uniformed police officers entered. Without hesitation they rushed toward me and pulled me out of bed. I went limp as they dragged my naked body across the floor.

"What did I do?"

"This is not your house. You pushed your dad, and they want you to leave."

"Put some clothes on him," I heard my mom say.

A moment later, the officers jerked me around with brute strength as they slid my khaki pants up my legs. Then came the sweatshirt. I couldn't believe this was happening. After dressing me, one of the policemen grabbed my arms, while the other grabbed my legs. They carried me up the stairs, out the front door, and pushed me into the back of the patrol car.

By the time we arrived at the police station, I had straightened up enough to realize that my life would be a great deal easier if I walked by my own means. They brought me into a small room, processed me, and issued an orange uniform and a pair of plastic sandals. I was scheduled to see the judge in the morning.

The officers led me through the station into my living quarters, a common area with four double-roomed cells surrounding it. All the other prisoners were young, like me. I walked into my cell, where another inmate lay on the bottom bunk. Without saying a word, I climbed to the top bunk.

"What are you in for?" he asked.

"Battery," I replied.

"On whom?"

"My stepfather. What about you?"

"Domestic violence," Johnny said.

"How long you in for?"

"Until they say I can leave, I reckon. What about you?" By this time, Johnny was standing at the toilet, going to the bathroom.

"As soon as I take my medicine, I think."

"What medicine?"

"My mom thinks I'm bipolar, but I'm not."

"You're telling me you don't have to be here if you take your medicine?"

"That's what I'm saying."

"Then why the hell won't you take it?"

"You've got to stand up for something."

Now Johnny was standing beside me, about eye level. This was the first time I got a good look at him. He had dark brown hair parted down the middle, a little acne on his face, and eyes set a bit too close together—an imbecilic look that I thought could possibly be the result of Appalachian inbreeding. He couldn't have been more than twenty-five years old.

"But you're just acting dumb," he said.

"At least I didn't beat my wife."

Silence filled the room for a few seconds. Then Johnny spat on the floor. His face was about three inches from mine, and those strange eyes were now filled with anger.

"Are you looking for trouble, partner?"

"Not any more than you are." I pushed myself up off my stomach, ready if he started feeling froggy.

"You just keep your mouth shut."

"Then don't ask me any more fool questions."

I lay back down on my bunk. He wasn't going to do anything, and we both knew it. I shut my eyes and acted like I was going to sleep. A moment later, I heard Johnny lie down as well.

As I lay there with my eyes closed, I thought about other ways I could possibly get in Johnny's head, or the other prisoners' heads, for that matter. Finally I came up with a plan: I wouldn't have a bowel movement or take a shower. With the toilet unguarded in the corner of the room, there would be no mistaking when nature called, and I thought it would be funny to hold it in just to freak these guys out. I had been in situations with these reptiles of society before, and the best way to gain their respect was to be unpredictable, keep them guessing.

The next day I was brought before the judge. Because I wore an orange jumpsuit, I felt like a hardened criminal. I looked into the seats and saw my mom and stepfather sitting there. They did not make eye contact with me.

"Sir, do you know why you are here?" asked the judge.

"Yes."

"Why don't you tell me, then?"

"I pushed my stepfather."

"Yes, that is true." The judge paused for a moment as he searched for the right words. "I understand that you are bipolar."

"That's not true."

"Regardless, from what I understand, if you agree to start taking your medicine the battery charge will be dropped and you will be allowed to go home."

"But I don't want to take the medicine," I said defiantly.

"Then I guess we'll keep you. In the meantime, I will order a psychological evaluation."

I remained standing in front of the judge.

"You're dismissed," he finally said.

The next day I was taken to Moccasin Bend, the mental-health institution in Chattanooga. The doctor asked me why I was there. Apparently my mom had faxed him a letter describing my situation.

"My mom is just getting in the way," I said. "She can't handle that I'm growing up. Sure, I have mood swings, but who doesn't? That's just the way I'm made. I don't need medicine."

"I'll be honest with you," the doctor said. "In my fifteen years as a psychiatrist, I have never had a mother write me a letter to convince me that her child is mentally ill."

"Maybe she belongs in the mental hospital," I said.

The doctor smiled. "I think you are an extremely intelligent young man, and I don't see any sign that you are mentally ill."

Finally, someone was on my side. This was exactly what I wanted to hear. I needed a professional opinion to solidify my beliefs. It gave me the strength to stand my ground because even then I was beginning to question whether it was all worth it. But I was afraid to give up. The next thing I did might be the secret code I needed to win Lane's heart. I had no doubt Lane was following the progress of my recovery. In my mind, to be with Lane I had to be drug-free. Why would someone as perfect as Lane agree to be with someone who wasn't nearly as perfect? I certainly couldn't hold a candle to her looks, but I could control my brain. Giving up would be an example of me being weak, and Lane would never settle for a man who was weak.

On Thursday, my cousin Mark White came to visit me at the jail. Not only was he my first cousin, he was also one of my best friends. He wore a coat and tie for work. At first I was happy to see him, he was the only visitor I'd had all week. Of course I was pretty sure he was sleeping with Lane as well, but at least he had the courtesy to take the time off and come see me.

"How are you doing?" he asked.

"Obviously I've been better."

"Tell me what happened. I've only heard your mom's side of the story. I want to hear yours."

"As far as I can tell, it seems like a joke. I barely even pushed Don, and now they've thrown me in jail. You've got to be kidding me."

"I can assure you it's not a joke," Mark said.

"Then why am I here?"

"I think you know that it's more than just pushing Don. From what I understand, there are other things that have happened."

With that comment I immediately stopped trusting Mark; he had sided with the enemy.

"Even the doctor said he doesn't think I'm bipolar," I said.

"That's beside the point. Why don't you just take your medicine so you can get out of jail?" Mark asked.

"I'm not going to lie about it," I said. "I'll stay in jail for as long as I need to. Hell, I'll go to a jury trial if need be."

"But why?" Mark asked.

"Why not? I've got nothing better to do."

"You understand the whole family is worried about you."

"Everyone knows?" I asked.

"Of course everyone knows. We're all concerned."

I laughed, more angry than amused. "There's no reason to be concerned. I'm fine. Make sure you tell everyone that as well. There's absolutely no reason to worry about me."

"Still, we are concerned."

"Am I acting like I'm crazy? Be honest. Am I?"

"You seem a little keyed up," Mark said.

"The doctor didn't think so."

"I'm just telling you what's happening. They're not going to let you leave until you take your medicine."

I'd heard enough. I stood up and looked at the guard who was overseeing the conversation.

"Ready?" asked the guard.

Mark stood as well and walked toward me. He offered his hand to shake. I turned my back without saying a word. Besides the doctor, no one was backing me up.

After four more degrading days of listening to prisoners' stories about the women they had bagged and the mouthwatering food they would eat when released, I went in front of the judge again on Friday. Once again, my mom and stepfather were present. The judge said the charges had been dropped—that I was free to leave. After being processed and after all the proper paperwork had been handled, I was released.

As I walked outside for the first time in a week, there was no banner hanging from the roof commemorating the event, nor a ticker-tape parade trumpeting my triumph over evil. My mom and stepfather weren't there. My cousin Mark didn't meet me either. I was free but had nowhere to go. I started walking. My family had a cabin on Ocoee Lake. Though it was about twenty miles away, without any money or credit cards, it was my best option.

Even though Cleveland, Tennessee, is a thumbnail in the anatomy of the United States, I wasn't familiar with the jailhouse neighborhood. Three hours later it was dark, and I was staggering along a desolate road. The only thing I knew was that this road was not Highway 64, which leads to Ocoee Lake, but I was certain I was walking in the right direction.

As night crept by, I began to tire. I had been walking close to seven hours and had no idea where I was. There were no streetlights and no signs of commercial development that might indicate I was headed the right way.

I grew desperate and thought about squatting for the night under a tree. Very few cars passed me. Another hour slipped by. Sweat gathered under my arms, and my lips were chapped from long exposure to the elements. I needed to sleep. I needed to find some place safe. Even though it was by no means a good road for hitchhiking, I held out my thumb to the occasional passing car. For at least two hours, no one stopped.

Close to 2:00 a.m., a car slowed down and pulled to the side of the road. I ran to it.

"Do you know where Chilhowee Campground is?" the passenger asked.

I leaned down to look through the window and saw there were only two guys inside. I couldn't believe my luck. The entrance to Chilhowee Campground was right across the road from my cabin.

Twenty minutes later they dropped me off at my cabin, and I pointed them toward the campground. Unfortunately, I didn't have a key, but there was a pontoon boat parked at the floating dock. It was as safe a place as any to stay for the night. No matter how uncomfortable my accommodations were, at least I could lay down my head without worrying about being woken up and arrested for vagrancy. Thoroughly exhausted, I stumbled down to the boat and found a boat cover I could use as a blanket. Minutes later, I was asleep.

CHAPTER 9

The sound of a motorboat speeding across the lake woke me the next day, and the sun beating down on my face kept me awake. I stood and stretched. Even in the mountain air I could smell my body odor from not showering the entire week I was in jail, and my teeth and gums felt like moss had grown on them. After walking into the woods and relieving myself of a week's worth of backed-up food, I went to the end of the dock and cupped my hands to splash water on my face and rid my eyes of sleep. My stomach growled. Unless I planned on catching fish with my bare hands, I had to head back into town.

My wallet was still at my mom's house. I started walking the twenty miles back into town again. The balls of my feet were already blistered from the jaunt the previous night, but with a hot meal like a pot of gold under the rainbow, I pushed forward. During that walk I decided that I had to go someplace else. Where? I was not sure, but obviously I wasn't welcome at my mom's house. She had already successfully alienated me from my friends and the rest of my family. Despite all of this, I really wasn't mad at her. I could not forget that she had rescued me from my certain demise in the farm country of northern California. That carried a lot of weight with me. Not to mention, she dropped the battery charges. After spending a week in jail, I felt like I had paid my debt to society and that the slate was wiped clean.

By this time I was not looking directly for Lane; rather, I was in search of clues about how I could win Lane's heart. I wasn't exactly sure why I had set my mind on Key West. It was probably because I'd spent the last Christmas with my dad before he died there, and I had been thinking of him a lot lately. More than once in my negotiations with my mother over the last year she had said how disappointed my father would be if he were still alive. My mom assumed that remark would cut deep, but I was numb to that kind of blatant manipulation by then. I recognized this was her way of taking the gloves off in her fight to make me seek counseling, and though it did make me reconsider, I was so far into the depths of mania that only a sign from God could make me change my ways.

Just before nightfall, I arrived back at Mom's house. I rang the front doorbell. A moment later, my mom answered, cracking the door only slightly.

"You can't come in here," she said immediately.

"That's fine. I just need my wallet and checkbook."

"Where are you going?"

"None of your business."

"I have a right to know where my son is going."

"And I have a right to my wallet and checkbook."

My mom stared at me coldly.

"I'll leave immediately, but you've got to let me have my wallet," I said.

"Where is it?"

"On my desk in my room."

She shut the door in my face. A moment later, she returned with my wallet.

"Where are you going?"

"To the bus station."

"And then where?"

"Key West."

"Key West? Why there?"

Since my last Christmas with my father had been in Key West, I thought maybe he had been trying to relay a message to me. I hoped that if I went back there, I could discover what it was. It was a long shot, but I had no better ideas. Like I said, I was willing to do anything to solve the riddle that held the key to Lane's heart. Not to mention, it sounded like a good time. I had lived in a big city, Atlanta, grown up in a small town, Cleveland, Tennessee, and lived in a mountain town, Aspen. But I had never lived on the ocean. Key West seemed like a cool spot, and hopefully I would find that indefinable link to bridge my way back into Lane's life.

"If you wait a second, I'll take you to the bus station," my mom finally said.

This was a welcome change. It was at least another three miles to the bus station, and I didn't relish the thought of trekking there on foot.

"I appreciate that. Can I please come in?"

"No, you stay out here. I'll drive around to the front of the house."

I hadn't thought of it until then, but I realized that I was about to take on the future without even a change of clothes, carrying with me a stench that even the grittiest of Greyhound passengers would probably find offensive. It had been so long since I had showered that my fingernails were black with dirt, and I had a perpetual itch all over my body.

A few minutes later, my mom drove around to the front of the house. I limped down the driveway and climbed into the car. Two bottles of medicine sat on the seat.

"Will you at least take the medicine with you?" my mom asked.

"Mom, I told you. I don't need it, and I'm not going to take it with me."

Until then, I had only seen my mom cry a few times, but there was no hiding the fact that she was holding back tears. Her lips trembled; her face was splotchy.

"I'll be fine," I said.

"Why don't you just take your medicine? Then you can come back in the house and get your life back in working order."

"My life is in working order."

Her eyes cleared; she was once again angry.

"What is it going to take?"

"Nothing."

My mom kept her eyes pointed straight ahead as she drove through the streets. I could tell she was scouring her mind for the perfect thing to say, that one home-run statement that would make me realize the error in my judgment. When she didn't say anything, I realized she had given up hope. She knew the only way I was going to learn was from the school of hard knocks.

"Call me when you get to Key West," she said. "I'll worry about you. You remember the 800 number, don't you?"

"Of course."

"Don't be afraid to use it."

By this time we were parked at the bus station. Mom stepped out of the car. I expected her to give me a hug, but instead she stuck out her hand to shake mine. It was an odd gesture, I wasn't exactly sure what it meant, but it triggered something in my mind that brought even greater horror than I'd already imagined.

I thought back to the time I drove up to Nashville to see Lane and proposed to her. As you may recall, after I told her how I felt we kissed briefly and then she bit my lip. I thought she was just being playful; at the time that explanation sufficed.

But, like many things during this period of my life, the passing of time warped what things meant. I changed the meanings to something outlandish and disturbing. For example, my first name is Benton. Phonetically it sounds like "bitten," or at least close to "bitten." Since Lane had "bitten" me the night we kissed after I proposed, I came to believe that, rather than sex being the true sign of love between Lane and me because of my name, biting was my threshold of physical intimacy. A man named Jack would have a handjob as his height of intimacy, while a man named Bob would be limited to blowjobs for the "bobbing" of one's head. Frank would be French kiss since both words start with "Fr." Jay would be naked as a jaybird. John would be a top-shelf man. Dick would only get fondled. I thought that one's name controlled a person's destiny. I thought that, as far as I could go sexually with a woman, it was the biting stage. That was what my name meant, and that was my destiny. I didn't like it, but at the same time there was nothing I could do about it.

It was crazy, and I can assure you that I didn't like nor understand it, but as quickly as my mind was connecting what were in reality mere coincidences, it seemed completely reasonable. I didn't know if these rules applied just during the courtship, or if after being boyfriend and girlfriend, or even married, they moved on to a sexual relationship, or if they stayed at the same level of physical intimacy. I had to rationalize human reproduction, but of course I came up with an explanation for that as well. Couples were allowed to have sex when they were trying to have a child. I never did come up with a decent excuse for the number of condoms being sold, nor could I explain my past sexual relationships. Youthful indiscretion was the best reason I could come up with.

The next bus to Florida did not leave until morning. I looked around the waiting room. This was not a big bus station with concession stands and a gift shop; it was only one large room with a soda and candy machine. I could not even buy cigarettes. I had no choice but to sleep on the floor. I lay down on my back and looked up at the ceiling. Why should I take my medicine? I did not feel depressed in the least. If anything, my mind was moving fast and furious. That was what made the disease so difficult for me to put my arms around. I understood depression when my thoughts were morbid and slow, but at this point I had not come to terms with the dangers of the manic phase, which is where I spent much of the time, slowing myself only by self-medicating with alcohol so I could sleep at night.

In my mind I defined manic depression as acute depression rather than a state of existence that consisted of large mood swings. Despite all the setbacks, I felt strong. I was right, and the rest of the world was wrong. Not for one second did I second-guess any of my decisions. Booming with energy, I did not sleep well that night.

By the time I boarded the bus the next morning, I was already planning my itinerary for Key West. The most important thing was getting a drink, and I had my heart set on going to Sloppy Joe's and ordering a mojito and a cheeseburger. Unfortunately, it was a twenty-four-hour ride to Key West, which gave me too much time to get confused in my thoughts.

This was my first Greyhound trip, and, believe me, the "dirty dog" attracts a different breed of passenger. During the various layovers on our journey south, I got off the bus to stretch my legs. Inevitably the cigarette poachers and town drunks would be eyeing their marks just outside the station, asking whoever came across their path for a cigarette or a quarter, depending on their poison of choice.

The bus filled with more passengers as we drove farther south. When I boarded, I had two seats to myself and felt comfortable. By the time we left Atlanta, the bus was full, and I became claustrophobic. I bought a magazine, but my mind was too restless to focus long enough to read.

On the bus there was nothing to do but dwell on my misgivings, and I began to get paranoid. What the hell was I going to do down there? Why did I think this time was going to be different? I understood why I had to leave home, but why come to Key West in the dead of summer, when even the dumbest tourists had the sense to stay away? And why Key West, when Lane was in Nashville—or California? Would she follow me down here as well? I decided to reverse course and head back to Nashville. That was where my heart lay. That was where Lane was.

I was in Central Florida. If I turned around for Nashville, I could expect another twenty-four-hour ride the other way. Even in my crazed condition, that was too much to ask. But I knew I should get off the bus before going any farther. In Miami we stopped at the airport. I got off only to be greeted by a stifling sun and a swarm of people that rattled me after the relative tranquility of the bus.

I still wanted a beer. Rather than finding the bus terminal so I could buy a ticket for Nashville, I wandered inside the airport in search of a bar. The empty faces of the travelers began to spook me. I saw the resemblance of someone I knew in everyone's appearance, whether it was the way they walked, the clothes they wore, or the way they smiled. Everyone looked familiar.

I found a bar and bellied up. I dug into my pocket and realized I had only a five-dollar bill, not enough even for a draft beer at the inflated airport prices. For some reason I didn't try to find an ATM but instead attempted to hustle up some money. I walked over to Baggage Claim and offered to carry people's bags like I was a porter. I didn't even ask, I would just walk up to someone and pick up his suitcase. By the third time, airport security was on to me.

"What are you doing?" asked an airport security officer.

"Helping people with their bags," I replied.

"Only airport employees can do that. You are breaking the law."

"I didn't know. I need the money for a cab."

"You'll have to find it someplace else."

By this time, the security officer had his hand on my elbow and was hustling me out of the airport. Back outside, I looked for the bus stop, but I had lost my bearings. Besides, there was no way I could hop back on a bus. I couldn't possibly remain seated long enough to make the trip back to Nashville. With no idea where I was going, I started to walk. It seemed like the only thing that could ease my mind. Just keep moving. Don't look back.

I thought I would find a hotel. There had to be one near the airport. I walked across the day parking lot and onto the main highway out of the airport. A few cars honked at me until I remembered that pedestrians were supposed to walk on the left side of the road. The sun set, and the early evening breeze cooled my sweat until I shivered. Physically and mentally exhausted, I began to get disoriented. I was in a Black neighborhood, and many people were loitering on the street or sitting on stumps in front of what I assumed were apartment buildings. Where was I going to sleep?

Obviously, I had walked the wrong way, because I didn't find a hotel. I looked for a park or an overhang where I could lie down for the night. Finally, I found a bus stop. A bearded Black man with a snaggle-toothed smile sat on the bench with a Styrofoam plate filled with fried chicken and rice. A place to sit, and maybe a bite to eat if I played my cards right. I sat down beside the man and pressed my beaten hands to my face. I started to cry, but as bad as I felt, as helpless as I had become, my plight seemed reasonable. Sure, I had never sunk this low before, but I was surrounded by other men in the same predicament. I wiped my face and decided to be strong. The world has no place for whiners.

I looked over at the bearded man and watched as he tried to chew his food with what few teeth he had. I guess he felt my pain, because without saying a word he held the plate up and nodded his head to signal that he was offering me a bite. I reached into my pocket and pulled out two cigarettes, offering them in trade. He shook his head but raised the plate again. I reached over, grabbed a piece of chicken, and began to chew. The man smiled as I ate, then resumed his own meal.

The world was not so bad, I thought. People helping people. I would be all right. Instead of looking down this time, I looked up at the heavens. The sky was a shade of purple, and I felt a drop of rain land on my cheek. I thought of the song "Purple Rain" by Prince.

"I only want to see you laughing in the purple rain."

As if the man could read my mind, he looked at me and laughed. Despite his earlier good nature, I didn't like this man anymore. I could see nothing to laugh about. This was serious. Maybe he was accustomed to hard times, but I wasn't. I stood up and looked at the bus schedule to see whether I could find a Greyhound bus station. I was so turned around by this point that I couldn't possibly have backtracked to the airport.

As I walked through the dingy streets under the purple rain, I couldn't quit singing the Prince song. What did the song mean? What could be the significance of laughing in the purple rain? I had always assumed it to be a happy song, but for the life of me I couldn't fathom that emotion now. I wrestled with the idea of going back to Nashville, or not "looking back" and remaining in Miami and attempting to start some semblance of a life. At this point I wasn't too impressed with my life skills. Clearly, I was no hustler who could make it on my own. I leaned my head against a telephone pole and tried to rest. A couple of Black men walked over to me.

"What are you doing here?" one of them asked.

"Taking a rest."

"Do you smoke crack?"

"No."

"Don't you know this is a crack neighborhood?"

"No."

"Get the hell out of here!"

Without looking up, I continued down the street. No one wanted anything to do with me. Not even crackheads. I walked a half-mile in the other direction. I considered going back and telling those guys that I did smoke crack. Maybe I should be a crackhead. More songs crept into my head. I started to sing The Clash.

> Darling you got to let me know
>
> Should I stay or should I go
>
> If you say that you are mine
>
> I'll be there till the end of time
>
> So you got to let me know
>
> Should I stay or should I go.

I needed some purpose in life. Something to fill my time. Something to make me proud. Something to make the world a better place. I was determined to make the most of my situation. No one would laugh at me. Not even some toothless man sitting by himself at a bus stop.

I saw an empty white trash bag on the ground. I considered it a sign. I should pick up trash. What could be more noble than cleaning up the planet? I would become an icon. A saint. People would offer me food because of my generosity. I would be like my homeless friend William from Palo Alto. I would live on the street and just pick up the trash. I would travel the country for my cause. I would be like Johnny Appleseed. It wasn't what I had planned to get out of life, but things had changed. Life was different than I thought only twelve months before, but everyone had to play his role in life, and I was determined not to be bitter about mine.

Though it was dark, I picked up the trash bag and filled it with bottles and cans that dotted the landscape. This wasn't so bad. I even laughed when my mind started acting like a jukebox as different songs popped into my head as I worked. I welcomed the interruption since they prevented me from morbid reflections on life that had been so pervasive recently. The songs carried special meaning, as if they had somehow been created with me in mind. I sang Arrested Development's "Tennessee."

> Take me to another place
>
> Take me to another land
>
> Make me forget all that hurts me
>
> Let me understand your plan.

I thought about what the song meant. Did they or didn't they like Tennessee? It was hard to determine. I decided that they were bittersweet. I could relate to that.

I then sat on a bench to rest my weary legs and take a break from my newfound occupation. I sang the first verse of Jethro Tull's "Aqualung" over and over in my head.

> Sitting on a park bench
>
> Eyeing little girls with bad intent
>
> Snot running down his nose
>
> Greasy fingers smearing shabby clothes.
>
> Drying in the cold sun
>
> Watching as the frilly panties run
>
> Feeling like a dead duck
>
> Spitting out pieces of his broken luck.

Another song whose words I had never seriously considered, but they had somehow ingrained themselves into my subconscious. This song was about a homeless man, but what did "Aqualung" mean? I did not know, but I would soon find out.

Cars raced by me. I sang Widespread Panic's "Airplane," which was how I wanted to get back to Nashville.

> Sitting around waiting for an airplane
>
> Don't know how to fly but that's okay.

I couldn't help but notice my choice of songs had been in reverse alphabetical order from Arrested Development to 'Aqualung' to 'Airplane.' What was next, AIDS? Then I worried that I somehow had contracted the AIDS virus, even though I hadn't been sexually active in a while. I remembered that I had given blood for a lithium test just a few months before, and there had been an article in the Palo Alto newspaper about a scandal in a medical center about contaminated needles. Hell, anything was possible these days. I took a deep breath and tried to collect my thoughts but couldn't. It had to be after midnight, which led me to singing Eric Clapton's 'After Midnight.'

> After midnight we're gonna let it all hang out
>
> After midnight we're gonna shake your tambourine
>
> After midnight it's gonna be all peaches and cream.

Next came The Meters' 'Africa.'

> Take me back to the Motherland
>
> Africa oh Africa.

I was dehydrated. I saw a half empty Mello Yello bottle lying on the side of the road. I couldn't stand the thirst any longer. I picked it up and finished the bottle. It was still cold, and the citrus tickled my parched throat as it went down.

I marched down the street before eventually stopping and once again plopping down in a patch of grass. I picked up a piece of grass and stuck it into my mouth. Hank Williams Jr.'s song 'A Country Boy Can Survive' played in my head. I lay flat on my back and relaxed. I fell asleep but only momentarily. There was too much noise for a long nap. I rose to my feet again and continued marching to my own beat.

Around this time the lyrics from one of Van Halen's songs came to mind: "Open up your mouth and say Aahh." I knew that I was in trouble. I had almost made it to the first of the alphabet. I yelled 'aahh' like I was at the doctor's office. A person in a car stopped at the light and let out a wicked cackle of a laugh. I gave him the finger, and he drove off.

Then something very unusual happened that scared me shitless. In my mind, like an old timey gas pump, the letters AAAAA changed to five O's very slowly.

Arrested Development

Aqualung

Airplane

AIDS

After Midnight

Africa

A Country Boy Can Survive

AAAHH

AAAAA

OAAAA

OOAAA

OOOAA

OOOOA

OOOOO (Flashing)

I immediately fell to my knees and lay on my back. Cars and trucks honked their horns all around me. I was sure that I was the devil. Revelations came into my head, and it was then that I thought I knew the secrets of the world. It was true that I didn't need to eat or go to the bathroom. It was also true that my father wasn't dead but was merely six feet under and sleeping soundly as was everyone else who was buried. But what did the five O's mean? I had to find out. I rose from my horizontal position and ran for some people. . .any people. There were no pedestrians on the street, so I ran towards a strip mall. I saw a sign for a pub and sprinted to it. I dashed inside and frantically grabbed the first employee I saw.

"I just hit five O. What does it mean?"

"Hawaii Five O?" he said. "I don't know. Let me get the manager."

Several people stared at me, which was not surprising, considering how filthy I was from wallowing in the grass. The manager came from the back.

"What's your question?"

"I hit five O," I yelled out. "What does it mean?"

"You hit five O?" he said quickly.

"Yeah."

"Get the hell out of here!" he yelled in my face.

Welcome to the jungle

We got fun and games

We got everything you want

Honey we know the names

We are the people that can find

Whatever you may need

If you got the money honey

We got your disease

'Welcome to the Jungle' signified that I had continued past the beginning of the alphabet and was regressing further in the opposite direction from Z down to W. The story of William Tell splitting an apple off a person's head with a bow and arrow entered my head. Symbolically, that was what I had done. I had gone off the beginning of the alphabet and started at the end. Instead of splitting an apple, I had split the alphabet. Just like 'Welcome to the Jungle,' William Tell started with W as well.

Though I attempted to believe that this made me a hero rather than a villain, I gained little solace. I somehow convinced myself that Judgment Day had come, but there was one problem. I was still alive. How could this be? There could be only one answer. My soul had expired but my body lived on. I had to do something about this. . .and fast.

I had to go back the other way in the alphabet. From W back up to A. That was the only way I had a chance. The first thing that crossed my mind was how do I get back to Z. Then a stroke of brilliance crossed my mind. ZZZZZs. I would just go to sleep. I lay down and closed my eyes. I felt an itch on my lower back. I jumped to my feet and saw an ant hill underneath where I lay. I quickly brushed the ants off my body and sprinted up the street to a highway overpass. My life was ending. I had to think of something quick. Time was of the essence. If I was going down, I sure as hell wasn't going to be caught. With my soul expired, if I got caught, they might bury me alive, and then there was no telling how long I would live underground. I was going down fighting. I sure as hell wasn't going to be buried alive. I finally made it to the bridge. I peered over the edge at the cars driving beneath. I was scared as hell.

"I don't want to die but sometimes wish I had never been born at all."

Quote from Queen's "Bohemian Rhapsody."

Q: Not the direction I wanted to be headed.

My mind raced to mortality, and once again I thought I was immortal, that merely jumping off a bridge might not kill me. I didn't know what to do. I vaguely remembered the Bible saying that suicide was a one-way ticket to Hell. I didn't want to go to Hell, nor did I feel I deserved it. But what were my options at that point? What could I do?

I thought back to my father's death from cancer, a noble way to go: painful, yet much more honorable than throwing oneself off a bridge. But I didn't have time to plan a suitable death. I snuck another peek at the cars below. I curled up in a ball and planned to roll off the bridge like an egg. The people in their cars honked and yelled at me.

"Go for it!" they shouted.

"You can fly!"

I closed my eyes and said the Lord's Prayer, then a silent prayer that I would somehow live through the fall. I felt my judgment would be determined by how I fell, I would be judged on originality. I had to die in a way no one had ever done before. I thought of different dismounts I could take. After briefly considering the backwards "Nestea Plunge" and the spread eagle, I returned to my original idea of rolling off the bridge like an egg.

I thought about writing a note, but there was no time, and what would I say if there were? The only thing that came to mind was an old Irish toast: "May the Devil find out thirty minutes after I die."

I had nobody to blame for my problems but myself. I didn't want to add to my family's grief by leaving a note. I curled up in a ball and counted to three, but I just couldn't do it, not because I'd had some revelation that everything was peachy keen and that I had every reason to live, but because of plain and simple cowardice. I was too chicken-shit to take the plunge, and it absolutely disgusted me. After all the screwing up I'd done over the past several months, I couldn't do the one thing that would make it right. I was even a failure at killing myself. I couldn't even come up with a way to end my life. I couldn't do anything on my own.

Tears ran down my face as I walked away from the overpass. Then an idea came to mind, an original one, I thought: another way of killing myself that would certainly not be noble, but a way to die.

I headed for the closest gas station. I hobbled into the convenience store and asked the clerk for the key to the bathroom. I marched to the bathroom and locked the door behind me. I got on my hands and knees and made a silent prayer for God to give me the strength to follow through on this suicide attempt. After a moment or so, I dunked my head into the toilet, blowing out bubbles to relax me. I imagined what people would think when they found me and realized that it would seem to be a suicide. I yanked my head out of the water and began banging my head against the sink, reasoning that a bump on the noggin would make it appear as a freak accident. There would be honor in that.

I hit my forehead against the porcelain sink several times as hard as I could muster, and then dropped my head in the cold water again. My entire face, except for my ears, was submerged. I heard the turning of the doorknob. I had to act quickly if I wanted to make this a successful death. I tried to relax and fall asleep in the water, but just as I approached blackout, I involuntarily lifted my head. I tried it once more with the same result.

I looked down at the toilet and saw the words American Standard stenciled into the porcelain. Damn! This wasn't an original way to kill myself. This had been done before. This was American Standard. I heard the twitching of the knob again. I decided to abort the mission.

I stood up and ran my hands through my hair to shake the water out. I glanced at the mirror and was halfway surprised I cast a reflection. There wasn't a trace of a smile on my face, and my pupils were fully dilated. I grabbed a paper towel and dried my hands and face. As I left the bathroom, a short, balding man was waiting, smoking a cigarette. After the door shut behind him, I wished I had asked him for a smoke. If there ever was a man who needed a cigarette, it was me. I was too disoriented to wait for him. I must continue forward. There was no looking back. I etched in my head "No looking back" as rule number twelve. I then got mad at myself for making another rule. I was almost dead already; there are no rules for the dead.

I wanted to go down in a blaze of glory. I considered sticking up the convenience store but had no gun. I thought about robbing the store with the old finger-under-the-shirt trick but quickly gave up on this as unfeasible. Besides, I couldn't fathom raising my voice at this point, but I had to do something.

I wanted redemption. I thought of Job from the Bible. He had been tested by God and was rewarded for his faith. My mind started making acronyms again. J-O-B: Jump Off Bridge. Yes, that was the ticket. If I jumped off a bridge, my sins would be expunged.

I wandered the streets of neighborhoods looking for a bridge and finally came across the Atlantic Ocean at the end of a street. There was a man fishing with a bamboo pole and a bucket sitting next to him. Should I jump in the ocean? I thought of Jonah being swallowed by the whale and spending three days in his tummy. Yes. That was it. I would jump in the water and stay underneath for a length of time and would be cleansed of my sins. I was thinking maybe something like twelve months. That should be long enough. I thought I would be able to breathe under water. Maybe I would swim all the way from Miami to Cuba. Though I didn't think of the song 'Aqualung' at the time, this state of mind was what inspired the song. A homeless man thinking he could breathe underwater instead of Sitting on a park bench Eyeing little girls with bad intent.

But I was nervous. And how did Jethro Tull know this? I didn't know what to do next. Should I leave a note? I saw a pack of matches on the ledge. Maybe I could make words with the matches explaining my final decree.

As I stood there trying to get up the courage to jump in, five neighborhood kids sprinted down the street. None of them could have been older than eight. One of the kids threw a wooden box into the ocean.

"We'll catch some squid with this bait," he called out.

I stood to the side admiring the enthusiasm of these youths but questioned their innocence. Could this youngster be making fun of me? Could I be acting so ridiculous that this half-pint looked down on me? Could I be squid bait? A mother of one of the children strolled down the street behind them.

"Do you have a girlfriend, Charlie?" she asked the boy standing closest to me.

"No."

"Are you afraid of girls?" she asked.

"I don't know."

I watched as the boy looked down at the ground with embarrassment. *Could this woman be making fun of me as well? Was that my problem? I was afraid of girls. Had I placed Lane on such a pedestal that I was afraid of her? Had I done this with all women?*

I watched as the boys danced in the street, laughing and pushing one another. I realized I was the one being childish. What kind of idiot jumps into the ocean? Without another look, I walked back the way I had come, relieved at my revelation and by the thought that I wouldn't have to submerge myself for redemption. A couple of hundred yards down the road I saw a man in his yard.

He called out angrily, "Turn around. You're scaring the women."

I thought maybe I had been right in the first place. Maybe I should jump into the ocean. Maybe that was what God had planned for me. Maybe it was my only chance at redemption. By the time I returned to the ledge the children were gone, but the matches were still there. I wasn't going to leave a message; I would just disappear. I didn't know how I would reenter society, but I supposed I had twelve months to figure it out. I took off my shoes and left them on the ledge beside my wallet, though I kept my debit card, thinking I would probably be hungry after twelve months of not eating unless I developed a penchant for seaweed.

It was about a five-foot drop into the ocean. I turned around one last time to see if anyone was watching, then jumped in. The current was swifter than I had expected. I moved through the water with only my head bobbing above the surface. I took a deep breath, exhaled, and sank until my feet touched the sandy bottom. I imagined myself standing on the ocean floor, very still, for the next twelve months as the rest of the world went about its business.

Thirty seconds later, I was back on the surface. I took another deep breath, and the same thing happened. I wasn't trying hard enough, I thought. I repeated the exercise again and again. My feet dropped to the ocean floor, where I tried to dig in; the current then pushed me with the tide until I ran out of breath and my head emerged from the water. This clearly wasn't going to work. Still, I wasn't disappointed. I had made the effort, and that was what mattered most. If I tried something that didn't work, I could cross it off the list and move on to the next thing.

Eventually I just swam in the ocean. I am a strong swimmer, so I never felt my life was in danger, but as a couple of barges drove by,

I began to feel foolish. However, when I looked along the shoreline I realized there were only cliffs, no beaches to swim toward. I was going to have to swim a long way to find a place to pull myself out. Maybe I'd have to swim all the way to Cuba.

I fluttered in the ocean for at least another hour. The waves made it difficult to maintain any kind of rhythm, so I had to mix it up. Sometimes I swam on my stomach, sometimes on my back, sometimes on my side, and sometimes I just tread water. All the while I was looking for a place to get out. I had begun to tire when I saw a bridge in the distance; surely I could get out there. But as I swam with hard, almost violent strokes, the current pushed me so fast that I was in jeopardy of being swept right past the bridge before I reached it. I sharpened my angle so I was practically swimming against the tide. Fifteen grueling minutes later, I was near land. Huge rocks lined the shoreline. When I finally reached them, I grabbed hold and tried to catch my breath.

"What are you doing down there?" a male voice called from above out.

"Just going for a little swim," I replied.

"Are you crazy? You'd better get out of there before you get in trouble."

"I don't give a shit. I've done dumber things."

I pulled myself out of the water and clambered up the cliff until I reached a guardrail along the road. After stopping to catch my breath once again, I threw one leg over the fence and followed it with the other.

I started up the sidewalk. I had no idea where I was going or what I would do when I got there, but I had a credit card in my pocket. I didn't have a driver's license, so I didn't know if it would suffice, but it was better than nothing. Surely someone would understand and let me use it.

With tiny pebbles scattered across the road, every barefoot step felt like walking on needles, and it wasn't long before it became agonizing.

I thought about walking on the grass, but the ground was covered with broken bottles and rusty cans. I was afraid I would take a wrong step and cut my foot. I stayed on the sidewalk and walked on my tiptoes to alleviate the pain. I was sure I looked ridiculous, but I had long since passed the point of caring what other people thought.

"Where are your shoes?" a driver of a van yelled out as he rode past me.

"Don't have any," I called back.

I was positive the driver hadn't heard me, but a moment later the van circled around the block, and this Good Samaritan hopped out of the car and handed me some loafers.

"Put these on," he said and walked back to his car barefooted not even waiting for a thank you.

Though the shoes were at least a size too large, I slipped them on my feet and felt better. As I continued up the road without having to worry about my tender tootsies, I began to get hungry. Suddenly, an ambulance pulled up beside me. Two E.M.T.s bolted out the back door and rushed toward me.

"Are you okay? We received a call that there was someone walking the streets without shoes. What's your name?"

"Benton Savage."

"Where did you get these shoes? We heard that you were barefoot."

"Someone gave them to me."

"Do we need to get the stretcher, or can you walk to the ambulance?"

"I can walk."

They drove me to the hospital. After more questions about the last time I had eaten or drunk fluids, they issued me a bed, hooked me up to an IV, and fed me a chicken salad sandwich. The relief I felt over finally being indoors where it was cool trumped any misgiving I may have had about being back in the hospital. I was almost giddy. This was as close to comfortable I had been in a long time. I was joking with the nurse, trying to get a discussion going about her favorite book.

My biggest concern was the enormous blisters I had developed on the balls of my feet from walking so much. A nurse treated my feet with a balm and bandaged them up. That night I was transferred to the mental health unit of the hospital.

The staff asked me who my emergency contact was. I answered that I didn't have anyone. I wasn't going to call my mom; I had run that course. But when they offered me medicine, I finally took it. I was too tired to fight it, and to be honest I was a little freaked out over the attempt to disappear in the ocean. They had given me a soft place to sleep and some decent meals. I was thankful for that, and if I had to take medicine for a short while in order to obtain these luxuries, I hoped Lane would understand.

Since I didn't have any insurance, the hospital released me seven days later and gave me three sets of clothes. I slipped on a tee shirt with the face of Curly from *The Three Stooges* on it. They packed my other clothes in a garbage bag and drove me to a homeless shelter with orders to take my medication.

CHAPTER 10

The homeless shelter was about twenty miles south of Miami in Homestead, Florida, situated on a former naval base destroyed by Hurricane Andrew in 1992. I had never been to a homeless shelter, but this facility had to be the Taj Mahal of homeless shelters. There were pool tables and ping-pong tables, kind staff members, and sixty-four beds in one large room for the males.

They processed me in a large, air-conditioned office where they questioned me about my special needs. Once again, I was evasive about my background, and they did not press much for details. Though they treated me as an equal to anyone else, I could not help but think I did not belong. After all, I was a college graduate and had attended an elite boarding school. I had a trust fund that supplied me with ample income and several thousand dollars in a personal bank account. Of course, I did not relay this information, and they immediately sent me to a social worker, who spoke to me about applying for SSI, a government program that gave $775 a month to the mentally ill. The social worker also implied that I might be eligible for an additional $800 if I could come up with a way to prove that I was disabled. Not bad money for doing nothing, but I politely declined when they said that if I obtained a job, then I could not accept this money. An interesting system, to say the least, but even though I had not worked in four months, I certainly planned on working someday in the future.

After the interview they issued me a bunk and gave me soap, shampoo, a towel, a toothbrush, toothpaste, a comb, a razor, and shaving cream. I walked through the lavish surroundings. With the neatly manicured landscape and open-air courtyard, it more resembled a resort than housing for the unfortunate. I placed my clothes and toiletries in my personal cubbyhole and then lay down on my bed. There was no one else in the sixty-four-bed room, and it was very quiet. Soon one of the staff members shook my arm to wake me up.

"You can't sleep in here now," the man said.

"Why not?"

"No one's allowed in the bunkhouse between eight and five."

"Where am I supposed to go?"

"Anywhere else but not in here."

I went into the recreation room where there was a group of old timers watching a movie about the history of The Temptations. In the back of the room men spoke softly so that they wouldn't interrupt the TV watchers. A young Black man walked into the room. The empty pockets of his jeans were turned wrong side out.

"What are you watching?" the young man asked.

"The Temptations," replied one of the men.

"Oh hell! Again? How many times have you watched this?"

"Not enough."

"Why don't you listen to some real music?"

"Like what?"

"Like Tupac."

"Rap isn't any good. That's the problem with you youngsters. All rappers sing about is fast cars and putting a cap in someone's ass."

"I like that."

"Why don't you sit down and get educated? This is real music."

"C'mon, Pops. Let's watch something else."

The old timer let the conversation die, and the young man left.

"Hey Curly!" called out a voice.

"Me?"

An older Black man with a kind face and a shaved skull was looking at me. His legs were crossed, and I noticed his Converse high top sneakers. I took that as a sign that he was someone I should 'converse' with. I liked him on sight.

"Aren't you Curly?"

I looked down at my tee shirt and saw my favorite Stooge. The nickname was appropriate. To go along with my shirt, I have naturally curly hair. "Yeah. I'm Curly," I said with a laugh, and that's how I met Jimmy.

"What are you doing here? You don't look like you belong," said Jimmy.

"Why not? I'm homeless just like you."

"How'd you get here?"

"I came from the mental hospital."

"Oh. You're one of those. What's wrong with you?"

"I'm bipolar."

"Hmm. Take medicine?"

"I'm supposed to, but I don't."

"Hardly blame you."

"How'd you get here?" I asked.

"Just released from prison," Jimmy said.

"And they brought you here?"

"Don't have anywhere else to go. My family doesn't want to see me."

"What were you in prison for?"

"Grand larceny."

"What did you steal?"

"I was a truck driver and sold everything in my truck to some gangsters."

"How much did you get?"

"Twenty-five thousand."

"No. I meant how many years did you get?"

"Five. Just released me three days ago."

I sat down in the chair beside him.

"Do you happen to have a cigarette, Curly?"

"Nah. I guess you don't either."

"I don't have any money," said Jimmy. "I just filled out the forms for S.S.I., but that takes at least four weeks."

"I have a beat-up debit card but no cash," I said. My card was washed and dried with my clothes at the mental hospital so it couldn't be used at a cash machine, but I hoped a clerk could manually enter the numbers.

"There's a convenience store about a half mile away," said Jimmy.

"Let's go."

The land around the homeless shelter was barren, dry, and treeless. It almost felt like the desert. Few cars were on the road, and due to Hurricane Andrew there was no other development in the area besides the standalone convenient store. The clerk accepted the card, and I bought Jimmy a pack of Newports and myself a pack of Winston Lights.

"I appreciate it, Curly. You'll see. I'll pay you back when my S.S.I. checks come thru."

"Do you mind if I smoke one of your menthols?" I asked.

"Of course, Curly. You bought them."

I lit the menthol cigarette with a match and blew out some smoke.

"Like a breath of fresh air," I said.

Jimmy laughed. "I like you, Curly."

It was five o'clock when we arrived back at the shelter. A long line of men and women were waiting for dinner to be served. Inside the cafeteria, there were 15 or 20 picnic size tables where we could sit. Jimmy and I sat at a table with four other men.

"You're new, aren't you?" one of the men asked me. He was probably in his mid-forties with salt and pepper hair parted down the middle and a woolly mustache. His name was Ralph.

"Just got here today," I replied.

"I wash dishes after the meals. Do you want to help?" asked Ralph.

I didn't, but I was too yellow to admit it, so I said, "Sure. Does it pay?"

"No. But you can have an extra plate of food if you want it," said Ralph.

"Sounds good to me."

"Good. I'll take you back to the dishwasher when we're finished eating," said Ralph.

"That's good, Curly. Some of these people just sponge off the system. You're giving something back," said Jimmy.

"Do you want to help, Jimmy?" I asked.

"Nah. I think I'll just stay a sponge. I've just about given up on life, but I'll tell you what you have. You have optimism. That's good, Curly."

"I've heard that before, but not about my work ethic," I said.

"What is it then?" asked Jimmy.

"I'm optimistic about women," I replied.

"Oh well. I gave them up a few years back too. About the same time I went on the lam for a year and realized it's everyone for himself in this world."

After dinner, I followed Ralph back to the dishwashing room. Trays stacked high and plates scraped clean were piled around the sink. I had washed dishes for free meals at my fraternity house in college, so I knew the routine.

I felt noble for helping and immediately began to imagine what life would be like if I stayed at the shelter, working as a dishwasher for an extended time. Ever since I had befriended the homeless men in Palo Alto, I had thought about how much I would enjoy working to improve the lives of homeless men, whether as a full-time employee or even as a volunteer. I believed I would find satisfaction in making a difference for people whom others would most likely cross the street to avoid.

"Here's an apron," Ralph said.

I draped it over my head and tried to tie the strings in the back, but my fingers shook from the Lithium being in my system again.

"First job requirement is that you have to be able to put on the apron correctly," said Ralph, but I could tell he was joking.

"It's the drugs. They mess with my fine motor skills," I said.

"What do you take?" asked Ralph.

"Lithium and Paxil."

"I take Zoloft," said Ralph.

We stared at each other for a moment, not saying anything else, but I suppose a bond was made from our similar circumstances. It took us an hour to wash the dishes. Due to the humidity both inside and out, my tee shirt was drenched by the time we finished.

"Do you want to help out tomorrow too?" asked Ralph.

"Sure. It wasn't too bad."

"Something to pass the time at least. What did you do for work before you came here?" asked Ralph.

"I'm a writer."

"Really? I write poetry," said Ralph.

"I'd love to read some of your stuff."

Ralph looked at me suspiciously. "I don't share my poetry with anyone."

I let it drop.

Lights out was at eleven o'clock. Breakfast started at seven. After a breakfast of eggs and bacon, Ralph and I washed the dishes again. When we finished, I ate another breakfast and went out to the corridor and sat in a chair beside Jimmy. It was sunny outside, but there was a slight breeze that kept the humidity down.

"Do you have a girlfriend, Curly?" Jimmy asked.

"No."

"Are you looking for one?"

"I'm always looking."

"How about that one?"

Jimmy pointed across the way to a morbidly obese woman. I knew that Jimmy wasn't serious, but at the same time I recognized that it was some sort of test. I didn't want to come off as someone judgmental.

"I don't see why not," I said.

"Really?"

"Sure."

"Have you ever been married, Curly?"

"No. How about you?"

"Still am."

"Then where is she?"

"Living with another man, I think."

"Why don't you go back to her?"

"She was an ugly old bitch."

"That's not very nice," I said.

"Just being honest."

"Why'd you marry her?"

Jimmy laughed. "Desperate, I guess. Just got back from Vietnam, and I was walking down the street in my neighborhood. She whistled and then asked me to come over. I did have a kid at least. That's the one good thing that came of it."

"Son or daughter?"

"Daughter. She went to Penn State on a basketball scholarship. Pretty girl, too. I was afraid she would turn out like her mother and be all dark and fat, but she's light-skinned like me."

"Did you go to any of her games?"

"No. I was in prison by then. She wrote me a letter once when I was in prison and said that half of the girls on the team were lesbians, and they all stared at her in the shower."

Jimmy laughed and pulled out a cigarette.

"What was Vietnam like?" I finally asked.

"Awful place." Jimmy blew out some smoke. "Fucked me up for a while when I got back. Still does, to be honest."

"I can imagine."

"Ate dog while I was down there, too. Not especially proud of that either," said Jimmy.

"Dog?"

"Oh yeah. Everyone ate dog. The best place was called 'Number One Chop Shop.'"

"Taste like chicken?"

"Quite a bit tougher than chicken, but it really wasn't bad."

Word had gotten out that I didn't mind working, which was an anomaly in the homeless shelter. A Black man named Inman approached me after lunch. He walked with an awful limp; at first I assumed it was from a leg injury, but I later learned it was caused by a severe hernia. He was trying to secure money from the government to have it repaired. The condition hardly slowed him down. He was constantly helping wherever he was needed, though I couldn't quite figure out his angle. Perhaps he simply wanted to stay occupied, something most of the others should have considered.

"Do you want to help me mop the kitchen after you wash the dishes?" asked Inman.

"Does it pay?"

"No."

"How can I get a job that pays?"

Jimmy told me that some of the residents were getting hired to perform janitorial duties and were getting paid eight dollars an hour.

"Talk to your social worker," said Inman.

"All right."

"And I'll take you to where you can get some more clothes."

I looked down. I was still wearing my Three Stooges tee shirt.

"I'll come find you after lunch."

Romances between the guests weren't uncommon, though I don't see how there could have been much physical intimacy with the complete lack of privacy. A couple of them were even married. They had to sleep with their own sex like the rest of us, no exceptions. The women slept in one building, while the men slept in another.

The main problem was that with all these horny guys hanging around with nothing to do, the men would hawk down on the women with no regard for etiquette. Wives were generally considered off-limits, even by the worst of these reptiles, but girlfriends were considered fair game.

I befriended a young man who had brought his girlfriend up from Key West. Besides not having two nickels to rub together, he was one of the ugliest sumbitches I had ever seen, with long, stringy hair, a touch of acne, and a raunchy set of teeth. His jagged teeth stuck out in all directions from his pink gums so that I could barely look at him when he smiled.

Steven had arrived before I did and had just lost his girlfriend to one of these poachers. I had seen her in the cafeteria being squired by another young man. Surprisingly, she was a cute girl, even if she couldn't have been five feet tall in a pair of four-inch stilettos.

Steven didn't receive much sympathy from the other male residents. The consensus was that a homeless shelter was no place to bring a girlfriend. In other words, he got what was coming to him. But Steven was depressed, and since I had nothing better to do than nose around in someone else's business, I became his confidant.

"It's not so much that she left me," Steven said. "It's that she left me for him. I just don't like that guy. He'll end up hurting her."

"Leave her," I said. "Even if she comes back, she'll do the same thing again. I guarantee that."

"We've been together for a month," said Steven. I could tell from the way he said it that he felt that was an eternity.

"Where did you sleep before you came here?" I asked.

"On rooftops."

"Must have gotten kind of hot with no overhang."

"Yeah. It was her idea to come here, not mine. I would rather drink beer every day then mope around this dump."

Alcohol and drug use were strictly prohibited. Though the rule didn't deter some of the wiliest veterans, most people abided by it, mainly because they didn't have enough money to even buy a forty and get good and proper. If you were caught with booze or drugs, it was grounds for dismissal, but generally people received second and third chances. No one wanted to be responsible for putting someone back on the streets.

In the afternoons, Inman and I mopped the kitchen and dining room. Sometimes I helped with food preparation, skinning potatoes or cutting vegetables. I didn't really enjoy it, but considering I was neither the cleanest person nor much of a cook, I rationalized that I was learning life skills. Not to mention, it eased some of the guilt I felt over the free stay.

I had not taken my medication since leaving the hospital, and about a week later I once again began to have creepy thoughts. Of course, Lane came to mind. Though I enjoyed the camaraderie of the homeless shelter, I couldn't help but think I was wasting time. I needed to get back to Nashville. Despite having played all my cards by asking Lane to marry me, I still felt there was more to say. I used Jimmy as a sounding board for my dilemma, asking him if I should return to Tennessee to claim her.

"Some men would," said Jimmy.

"Like whom?"

"None of these men here. I'll tell you that."

"But why not?"

"You need to understand. Some are bigger men than others."

"What does that mean?"

"It means you're not going to find real men in a homeless shelter," said Jimmy.

"But you're here."

"Listen. I'm a convicted felon. No one wants to hire a convicted felon. I couldn't get a decent job even if I tried. I will have a better lifestyle living off the government than I would bagging groceries. In a few months they'll set me up in Section Eight Housing, food stamps, and a monthly check. I'll be home free."

"You're giving up?" I asked.

"I consider myself retired. I've paid my dues. I served my country. I protected our so-called way of life."

"But there's more life to live. How old are you?"

"Fifty."

"And you're giving up?"

"Listen, Curly. I'm not a bad person. I no longer smoke crack. I don't do drugs anymore. I'm not going to hurt anyone. I just want to wind my life down."

"Am I a real man?" I asked.

"You're doing the best that you can, Curly. You're helping in the kitchen. You're not breaking any rules. That's more than most of us can claim."

It had been close to a month since I had spoken to my mom. I knew she was probably worried. I may not have been the best son, but I didn't want to burden her. Like most of my behavior those days, my intentions were good, but my thinking was wrong. As Jimmy had complimented me on my work ethic, I figured I was doing well. Never mind that I was living in a homeless shelter with no prospects for improving my situation, I felt good enough to call my mom.

"I'm living in a homeless shelter in Homestead, Florida," I said.

"I thought you were going to Key West. Where's Homestead?"

"I made a little pit stop. Homestead is just south of Miami."

"Is that where you want to be?"

"It will do for right now. It's not like I'm going to retire here."

"How did you end up there?"

"I was in the hospital for a week. They brought me here."

"Are you taking medication?" I could hear the hope in my mom's voice.

"No."

"Benton. What's it going to take?"

"Let's not get into that again. I just called to let you know that I'm okay."

"What are you doing with your time?"

"I wash dishes."

"At least it's a start."

"I'm meeting some interesting people."

"Well. I'm sure that there are some colorful characters there. How can I get in touch with you?"

"I'm calling from a payphone. You can call me here."

I gave her the phone number.

CHAPTER 11

When my father died, he left me a substantial sum of money along with a handwritten note saying he wanted me to become anything I wished in life and never have to worry about finances. He had worked as a teacher for his first couple of years out of college and believed it was the most rewarding profession, but he also recognized that he could not sustain the lifestyle he wanted on a teacher's salary. One of the reasons he worked so hard as a businessman was to give me the opportunity to choose any path I desired.

After I graduated from college, I wanted to be a businessman too. I was good with money. I wasn't a millionaire, or anywhere close, but I didn't buy an expensive car, and I invested my money wisely. My one vice was an obsession with the all-encompassing pursuit of new experiences. What I wanted most out of life was to have a good time, and for that I spared no expense. My mom once said, "Benton, if you can't drink it or smoke it, you won't pay for it."

She meant that all my money went into alcohol, which was a fairly accurate assessment. When I planned vacations, I often calculated the cost in six-packs. At the time, nothing gave me more joy than drinking beer with friends, the laughter, the self-deprecating conversations, the dreams we shared. Having new experiences mattered more to me than making money, and in that sense, I believe I was successful. That is part of the reason I wanted to become a writer.

But while I lived in the homeless shelter, even my writing ambitions were set aside. I went to my social worker, Robert Peterson, to ask about work. I knew I couldn't become a staff member yet, but I thought starting as a "sanitation engineer" would be a good way to prove my work ethic.

Robert was something of a misfit himself. Without going into detail, he told me he had recently had a finger amputated from his left hand. When I went to his office hoping to land a job, I knew he would give me the straight story.

He pushed his glasses up and snorted. "We don't have anything available for you right now."

"But other people are getting jobs. They just hired someone yesterday," I said.

"If you work, you won't be eligible for S.S.I."

"I told you. I don't want S.S.I. I want to work."

"Are you sure that you are capable of holding a job?" asked Robert.

"I'm a college graduate. I think I'm qualified to be a pooper scooper in a homeless shelter."

Robert leaned back in his chair and placed his hands behind his head, but he still wasn't smiling. He studied me for a minute. "I know that you are a college graduate. I spoke to your mom yesterday."

I was embarrassed. I hadn't expected my mom to call the shelter. After all, I was almost twenty-seven years old. I didn't need her looking after my affairs. I could take care of myself.

"What did she say?"

"She's very concerned about you."

"I know."

"She also said you haven't been taking your medication. Is this true?"

"Yeah."

"Why not?"

"I don't need it."

"I'm no doctor, but I have been around long enough to recognize that a person suffering from bipolar disorder needs to be on medication."

"I'm not bipolar."

"Didn't you come here from a mental hospital?"

"Yes."

"What did they say was wrong with you?"

"They said I was bipolar, but they're wrong."

"And that's why you're not taking your medication?"

"Pretty much."

Robert placed his deformed hand on the desk and tapped his remaining fingertips. He leaned forward, pulled some papers from a drawer, and handed them to me.

"At least fill out the S.S.I. paperwork. We'll take it one step at a time. It can't hurt to be prepared, just in case you change your mind."

"Have you been listening to me? I don't want to be on S.S.I."

"What are you going to do for money?"

"I'm a writer."

"Your mom mentioned that too."

"What did she say?"

Robert finally smiled. "She said you threw all your writing away when you were in California."

I didn't say anything. What could I say?

"Does that sound normal to you?" Robert asked.

"I didn't like what I had written." By this point I was steamed at my mom, and I wasn't exactly crazy about my nine-fingered friend either.

"Do you think you can make a living as a writer? I don't know much about the industry, but I'm sure it's difficult."

"I'm not doing it for my health, that's for sure."

"Funny you should mention that. Your mom also said she thought your writing might make your bipolar worse."

This was at least partly true. The introspection of writing was hard on me. My stories didn't usually have happy endings with a group hug because somebody's dog had puppies. They more accurately detailed the antihero's demise into hell on earth.

"I'm going to do more with my life than wash dishes for free. I'll tell you that much."

"We'll see," Robert said, though he didn't sound confident.

"Can I at least get a pen and some paper?" With his rebuff of my employment inquiry, I decided to change direction.

"Do you think that is a good idea?"

"I have to do something."

Robert walked over to the printer and removed a stack of blank paper. Then he reached inside his desk and pulled out a pen and handed both to me.

"Just consider filling out the S.S.I. paperwork. At best it will be some time before you get anything published. We are looking to place you in permanent housing, and you are going to need money."

I walked out of Robert's office and went to the cafeteria. Along with the privilege of an extra plate of food, I was allowed to cut to the front of the line so I could start washing the dishes as soon as possible before they piled up.

After lunch Ralph wasn't there to help me out, so I had to do the dishes by myself, and I wasn't pleased. The joy of pitching in out of the kindness of my heart was wearing thin. When I finally finished two hours later, I went looking for Ralph. I found him sitting in a chair in the corridor. His eyes were aimed at the ground, and he appeared very stiff. Obviously he was sad about something, but this didn't deter me from giving him a piece of my mind.

"Where the hell were you? I had to do the dishes alone."

"I can't do the dishes anymore," said Ralph. He looked up at me with bloodshot eyes. He had been crying.

"Why the hell not?"

"I stole a knife from the kitchen and got caught."

"Why'd you steal a knife?" I asked.

"I was planning to slit my throat."

"Oh." I didn't know what to say next, but the first thing that came to mind was that poets are likely candidates for suicide. Even more so than dentists, though I imagine their reasons are very different.

"I've quit taking my medicine," said Ralph.

"Why'd you do that?"

"It makes me feel funny. I don't like it."

"Better than slitting your throat."

"I know."

"What are you going to do now?"

"I guess I'll take my medicine."

"That seems to be the key element in recovery."

"Hopefully you'll continue to take your own advice."

Though Ralph was at least twenty years older than me, I felt like I was talking to a child. Funny thing was, I had thought about slitting my throat with a kitchen knife as well. Ever since I almost jumped off a bridge, I continued to think of different ways to kill myself. There were pills, which was the most obvious, but I also considered weighing myself down with cinder blocks and jumping into the ocean, and when I saw a lengthy extension cord, I always imagined tying a hangman's noose and kicking the chair out from under me.

My writing is what ultimately gave me solace. It was a long-term goal that at least gave me a way of looking into the future. I dreamed big. I wanted to be an icon with my writing, displaying the toughness of Hemingway, the crudeness of Bukowski, and the vulnerability of Salinger.

When I wasn't working in the kitchen or having discussions with Jimmy, I wrote on the printer paper Robert gave me. Visions of grandeur kept me going. I basically rewrote what I had thrown away in California. It was a fictional story about my experiences with bipolar. I was too embarrassed about some of my antics to write a memoir, feeling I'd bring discredit upon myself, so I fictionalized my story.

The biggest problem was that unlike many books, where a good work of fiction can tell the truth better than reality, the opposite is true for a book about mental illness. My thoughts were so jumbled that I couldn't imagine how to explain them. They don't even make sense to me now. Even now, when I desire to give full disclosure, some of my thoughts and ideas were so awful and hateful to people that I cared for that I can't possibly retell them.

It was also confusing. The more I wrote, the more detached I became. It was proving difficult and almost impossible to fictionalize my life in the homeless shelter while I struggled with the realities of my life within it. The temptation to act differently in order to invoke a story was too strong. Often in conversation, when I heard someone say something interesting, I immediately thought that would be something beneficial to my book.

This proved to be especially contentious when I began to suspect that people were reading my writing when I wasn't around. I wasn't being paranoid. This was almost certainly true. Since there was no privacy in the shelter besides the stall in the bathroom, I wrote in the open and right in front of people. This set off red flags. No other resident was hunched over writing. Given the free time all of us had, I hardly blame them for nosing around in my book.

I can't remember exactly what triggered this revelation of their snooping, but I got the feeling that people were mistrustful of me. Not Jimmy nor Ralph. I had told them what I was doing, and they seemed secure enough in our friendship to realize I wasn't going to slander them to write a good book. But there were others who stared at me when we crossed paths.

Then again, maybe it was paranoia. It doesn't matter. It was paranoia that got me again this time. Not to mention, it had been over a month since I had taken my medicine. I was beginning to learn that a month was about my breaking point.

Fortunately, Lane didn't come into the picture this time. Don't get me wrong. I was thinking of Lane. But the lack of privacy worked well in this situation. Not even I could construe how it would be possible for Lane to be sleeping with the other residents. There was nowhere to hide.

This time my thoughts were much grander. Once again, I believed I had a higher purpose in this world. Just as I had drawn parallels between my life in California and the Bible, I now read messages in what was happening in Florida. For instance, the hurricane that destroyed the town of Homestead was named Hurricane Andrew. My middle name is Andrew. I thought I was somehow responsible for this hurricane. I believed God had placed me in this shelter so I could witness the destruction I had caused. My mind strayed to the innocent people I imagined I had killed, the families I had destroyed, and the lives forever changed. The guilt I experienced was so strong that I had fits of crying.

"What's wrong, Curly?" Jimmy asked.

"Just thinking," I mumbled.

"Don't do that. It will just give you trouble. Smoke a cigarette and relax. You've got your whole life in front of you."

"That's the problem. I can't stop thinking about the future, and I can't stop thinking that I don't have choices."

"What are you talking about? We always have choices."

"You don't think things happen for a reason?"

"Not really. People want to believe in something so it makes them feel better," Jimmy replied.

"That's the problem. I feel worse."

"Don't worry about those kinds of things, Curly. Just sit right here with me. We can grow old together, sitting in rocking chairs and talking about the good ol' days."

"It's hard for me to think about the good ol' days right now."

Jimmy didn't say anything for a minute. Then he stood up. "It's time for lunch, Curly. Let's go eat some food. That will make you feel better."

"I'm not hungry."

"You've got to eat, Curly."

"I don't feel like it."

"Who's gonna do the dishes?"

"Let someone else do them for once."

"Suit yourself."

Jimmy walked away. Other residents soon followed, and a line formed in front of the cafeteria as people waited for the doors to open.

I lit a cigarette. I had been smoking at least a pack a day. Jimmy wasn't far behind. I bought him a pack of cigarettes every day. He owed me over a hundred dollars, but I wasn't worried. His S.S.I. check was due any day, as he reminded me every time I handed him another pack.

Enrique, a Colombian, walked up with his hands stuffed in his pockets and a sneaky smile on his face. He was among the many who had gone bottoms up due to their crack habit. He was a worthless fellow all the way around, always complaining how the system was out to get him. How the white man had held him back. I think he believed that when he came to this country he was going to be like Tony Montana in *Scarface*.

"Hey dude. What's up?" asked Enrique.

"I'm starting to feel as blue as you," I said.

"Fuck 'em. Don't take any of their shit."

"I try not to, but I feel like I'm already in a world of shit."

Enrique looked up at me. He was a skinny little fellow and talked out of the side of his mouth like he was always telling a secret, or at least saying something that he didn't want eavesdroppers to hear.

"I've decided something," said Enrique.

"What's that?"

"When I come into some money, I'm going to buy a gun and light some asses up. I'm tired of taking shit. When I came to this country for freedom, I thought that I was smart enough to become rich. Now I just don't know."

"No reason to kill innocent people over it."

Steven walked up behind me. He wasn't much better than Enrique. A conversation didn't go by without him bitching about his girlfriend dumping him. He wanted to go back to Key West and sleep on rooftops.

"I'm the same way," said Steven. "I would love to open fire in a mall or something."

"What the hell are you two talking about?" I asked.

"What do I have to lose?" said Steven. "I'm in a homeless shelter. Prison can't be much worse. Might even get a private room."

"That's what I'm saying," agreed Enrique.

"But then you've given up hope. There's still a chance to work our way out of the homeless shelter," I said.

"Only change that would mean is that I'd have to work all day for minimum wage. Been there. Done that. It's no way to live," said Enrique.

"At least you could have a girlfriend," I said.

"Until she dumps you for someone else," said Steven.

"If I came into money, I would just blow it on crack," said Enrique. "I'll be in better shape living off welfare. Then I won't have enough money to smoke crack."

"Is crack really that good?" I asked.

"No. It's really that bad. I've seen nothing worse," said Enrique.

"You guys are crazy," I said. "You're making me feel worse than I already do."

"Can I borrow a quarter?" asked Enrique.

"What for? Are you putting money toward your crack endowment?"

"I need another quarter to buy a cup of coffee."

I had come into a little money selling cigarettes for a quarter each. I only sold two or three a day, but these vultures smelled their opening and were always hitting me up for some change so they could buy coffee or candy. I'd never met so many candy freaks until I moved into the homeless shelter. I didn't have enough money for beer, so they looked for a sugar high.

At this point my mind was once again connecting things at a torrid pace. For instance, my cousin, Mark White, had once given me a painting of the Greek goddess Nike as a gift because I was a groomsman at his wedding. The painting showed a woman's body with wings attached to her back but with the head chopped off. I had stared at and studied this painting many times, trying to determine its exact meaning. After Ralph revealed that he wanted to slit his throat, I thought my cousin was somehow telling me that I needed to cut my head off, just like Nike. I didn't think my cousin had given me the painting out of malice but out of love, it was his way of telling me what I had to do: that a painless way to commit suicide and ensure instant death was simply to decapitate myself.

My thoughts quickly vaulted to The Legend of Sleepy *Hollow*, the Headless Horseman, then to Ichabod Crane, who may or may not have been part of the same story. That was the way my brain was working. In my version of the story, Ichabod Crane had tried to dig up a grave, and I found myself thinking about digging up my dad's grave to see if he was dead or merely resting. Maybe he was alive, even waiting for his son to dig him up and free him from his incarceration.

As I considered my options, my mind flipped to my father's mother, who lived in Columbia, Tennessee. Could Enrique from Colombia be trying to tell me something about my relationship with my grandmother? I had not written or spoken to her in a while, sometimes not even sending thank-you notes when she had sent me a check for my birthday. Was meeting Enrique part of a larger plan? I had done cocaine several times, and I knew that a lot of cocaine came from Colombia. Was this important? How was I to know these things would come back to haunt me? How could I right these wrongs?

I had come into a little money selling cigarettes for a quarter each. I only sold two or three a day, but these vultures smelled their opening and were always hitting me up for some change so they could buy coffee or candy. I'd never met so many candy freaks until I moved into the homeless shelter. I didn't have enough money for beer, so they looked for a sugar high.

At this point my mind was once again connecting things at a torrid pace. For instance, my cousin, Mark White, had once given me a painting of the Greek goddess Nike as a gift because I was a groomsman at his wedding. The painting showed a woman's body with wings attached to her back but with the head chopped off. I had stared at and studied this painting many times, trying to determine its exact meaning. After Ralph revealed that he wanted to slit his throat, I thought my cousin was somehow telling me that I needed to cut my head off, just like Nike. I didn't think my cousin had given me the painting out of malice but out of love, it was his way of telling me what I had to do: that a painless way to commit suicide and ensure instant death was simply to decapitate myself.

My thoughts quickly vaulted to *The Legend of Sleepy Hollow*, the Headless Horseman, then to Ichabod Crane, who may or may not have been part of the same story. That was the way my brain was working. In my version of the story, Ichabod Crane had tried to dig up a grave, and I found myself thinking about digging up my dad's grave to see if he was dead or merely resting. Maybe he was alive, even waiting for his son to dig him up and free him from his incarceration.

As I considered my options, my mind flipped to my father's mother, who lived in Columbia, Tennessee. Could Enrique from Colombia be trying to tell me something about my relationship with my grandmother? I had not written or spoken to her in a while, sometimes not even sending thank-you notes when she had sent me a check for my birthday.

Was meeting Enrique part of a larger plan? I had done cocaine several times, and I knew that a lot of cocaine came from Colombia. Was this important? How was I to know these things would come back to haunt me? How could I right these wrongs?

"I heard there was someone who was going to help me. I'm Larry," said the man with a moronic look on his face.

"I'm Benton."

"Lot of dishes. Glad you're here," Larry answered.

There was something odd about Larry. He seemed to be taking too much pleasure out of this menial job. Ralph and I had just kind of labored through the work with a general understanding that it had to be done, and we might as well be the people that did it.

"You take the sink," said Larry.

The sink was full of water. I grabbed a tray and dipped it into the hot water. Immediately my hand began to burn. When I yanked my hand out of the water, it was pink, and a couple blisters on the knuckles. Could this be in retaliation for masturbating in the bathroom? How did they know? And what did Larry put into the water to make my skin react and not his?

I put my hand back into the water, and it burned worse. By the time I yanked my hand out a second time, the blisters had popped and instead my hand was bright red and growing.

I quickly walked out of the kitchen and went to the main office to see the on-site nurse. I gave my name to the receptionist and sat down in a chair. There were several other people waiting to be seen. I felt that they were looking at me. I kept my hand covered and waited patiently. My skin felt like it was burning away. Periodically I would bring my hand to my face and look at it. After another half hour of excruciating pain, I was called.

"What seems to be the problem?"

"I wash the dishes, and the skin on my hand had a reaction to the bleach or something."

The nurse grasped my hand and ran her fingers over the sores. "This is strange. Does it burn?"

"Like fire."

"I think we need to take you to the emergency room. Take a seat, and I'll call someone to drive you to the hospital."

By this time I was angry. Who cared if I masturbated? It was a natural thing to do, not the most pleasant of behaviors, but it wasn't like I had done it out in the open. That was no reason to try to burn my hand. Or was this an act of God for my killing all those people in the hurricane? What could happen next? Was the world going to end this time?

My eyes darted around the room. I saw fear in everyone's faces. I had to do something. I didn't want to hurt anyone else. I had to save the world.

Finally the driver of the van came. He drove me to the hospital.

"What's wrong with you?" he asked.

"I held up my hand," I said."Good God! What happened?""I was washing the dishes.""It looks like you've been exposed to plutonium."

Could this be true? Could a nuclear holocaust be in the works? How could I stop this? I didn't want the world to end. I stopped speaking for the rest of the ride. The driver dropped me off and told me to call him when I was done.

In the emergency room I felt everyone was staring at me. After giving my name to the receptionist, I paced the room. The floor and walls were white and shiny, and the chairs were blue. I tried to sit on one of those chairs but couldn't stay still. I felt the walls closing in. I felt that the world was going to end if I didn't do something. But what?

I had to show that I loved the world. I would do anything to save it from destruction.

Then I came up with an idea of how I could save the world. I had to kiss a woman. My sole drive to win Lane had been selfish; I had to show that I could love someone else. But which woman? There were many to choose from in the emergency room. Also, there were many children. Obviously I wasn't going to kiss any of them, but they gave new meaning to my plight. These innocent children would die if I didn't do something. It was one thing for adults to die, we had lived a life, but children dying before they had experienced life was different.

By this time I was angry. Who cared if I masturbated? It was a natural thing to do, not the most pleasant of behaviors, but it wasn't like I had done it out in the open. That was no reason to try to burn my hand. Or was this an act of God for my killing all those people in the hurricane? What could happen next? Was the world going to end this time?

My eyes darted around the room. I saw fear in everyone's faces. I had to do something. I didn't want to hurt anyone else. I had to save the world.

Finally the driver of the van came. He drove me to the hospital.

"What's wrong with you?" he asked.

"I held up my hand," I said. "Good God! What happened?" "I was washing the dishes." "It looks like you've been exposed to plutonium."

Could this be true? Could a nuclear holocaust be in the works? How could I stop this? I didn't want the world to end. I stopped speaking for the rest of the ride. The driver dropped me off and told me to call him when I was done.

In the emergency room I felt everyone was staring at me. After giving my name to the receptionist, I paced the room. The floor and walls were white and shiny, and the chairs were blue. I tried to sit on one of those chairs but couldn't stay still. I felt the walls closing in. I felt that the world was going to end if I didn't do something. But what? I had to show that I loved the world. I would do anything to save it from destruction.

Then I came up with an idea of how I could save the world. I had to kiss a woman. My sole drive to win Lane had been selfish; I had to show that I could love someone else. But which woman? There were many to choose from in the emergency room. Also, there were many children. Obviously I wasn't going to kiss any of them, but they gave new meaning to my plight. These innocent children would die if I didn't do something. It was one thing for adults to die, we had lived a life, but children dying before they had experienced life was different.

CHAPTER 12

Isprinted for the door, dodging people as I went. Loud, angry voices called behind me. I knew I had screwed up. Outside, it was bright and sunny. I continued running through the parking lot. I looked for a bridge or an overpass. Anywhere I could jump off. That was the only thing that could give me redemption. But I saw nothing but rows and rows of parked cars. I stopped running. Should I turn around and apologize? Yes. That's what I should do. Everything would be okay if I apologized. I turned around and saw two police officers in pursuit. Instead of running away, I sat down on the curb and placed my face in my hands. How could I have been so wrong? I was only trying to save the world.

"Why did you kiss that woman?" asked one of the officers as he grabbed me by the arm and pulled me to my feet. I didn't struggle. I didn't say anything.

"Not going to talk to us?" sneered the officer.

I shook my head.

"Choosing to remain silent. Probably a good idea, pervert."

A police car drove up. By this time a band of rubbernecks had gathered. With everyone watching, the policeman pulled me across the parking lot and shoved me into the back of the police car. He slammed the door shut. I sat in the backseat and looked out the window. The police officers were clearly discussing what they should do with me.

An angry man with a goatee and a shaved head ran up to the police officers. I knew that he must have been the boyfriend or husband of the woman I had kissed by the way he kept glaring at me in the back of the squad car. A moment later he bolted toward the car and beat on the window.

"Motherfucker!" he called out, his face contorted in a grotesque expression.

I dropped my head in disgust and began to cry. I couldn't help myself. A few minutes later the police officers drove me to the station. I thought of ways that I could kill myself, but there was going to be no way now that I was in police custody. As always, they took my shoelaces and belt. They put me in a cell by myself.

"We're putting you in here by yourself for your own safety, weirdo."

I sat on the cold floor of the jail cell and looked at my throbbing hand. Maybe I was going to fall apart limb by limb, a very painful death, I imagined. Then I came up with an idea. Maybe I could kill myself by holding my breath. Without delay I lay on the floor and closed my eyes. I held my breath for as long as I could and then breathed again. I did this repeatedly, and each time I held my breath longer than before. I hoped I would be dead by the time the guard came back. Soon he returned. I remained motionless on the ground with my eyes closed and held my breath once again.

"What the hell are you doing?" the guard asked.

I remained motionless, trying to hold my breath. He reached down and tugged on my arm. When I didn't move, he laughed.

"I know you're not sleeping." He tugged on my arm again.

My breath was running out, and I tried to take a short breath so that the police officer wouldn't notice. I thought I would fake my death. I thought a person could decide when he wanted to die. I imagined lying very still as they lowered me into the coffin.

"I know you're not dead either. I can see your chest moving up and down."

I didn't move. The guard pulled me up to my feet. I gave up and opened my eyes. Faking one's death is not an easy chore to do.

"What the hell is wrong with you?" asked the guard.

I didn't say anything.

"We're taking you somewhere so that you can be with other people just like you." The officer reached down to grab my hand. "What the hell is wrong with your hand?"

"I think I've been poisoned."

"You're so dirty it's probably infected. Go to the bathroom and wash your hands."

They led me to a bathroom, and though I didn't want soap to further hurt my hand I rinsed water across it and squirted a tiny bit of soap out of the dispenser. Instantly my hand improved. The scabs washed away, and now they were just small wounds. A miracle, I thought, but I had no time for reflection.

Two officers walked me through hallways and up elevators. Other police officers passed us with criminals in their custody. I wondered where they were taking me. Five minutes later we stopped in front of a door.

"You'll like it in here," said the officer, laughing again.

He opened the door and shoved me through. Inside were what must have been two hundred other prisoners, most of them Black. There were no chairs, no benches, and no windows. In the corner, a man sat on the toilet with his pants around his ankles, while a couple of others waited beside him. I decided I could hold it. There was no way in hell I was going to the bathroom with two hundred people watching.

Everyone else sat on the floor, packed in like rats. I joined them. I had never been surrounded by mostly Black people before, and I was scared to death. I guessed that was how Black people must feel when they were in the minority and surrounded by mostly white people. The sound of the voices was unlike any I had ever heard, it sounded like gibberish, almost as if they weren't speaking English.

I pulled my knees to my chest and tried to go unnoticed. I must have succeeded, because no one spoke to me. After a while, I began to panic a little. How long were they going to keep me in here?

A couple of hours later, an officer opened the door and led all two hundred of us into the hallway. Rounding us up like cattle, they marched us outside to buses. We boarded two to a seat. I still hadn't spoken to anyone. Half an hour later, the buses stopped, and we filed out. I looked around. It seemed like some kind of farm in the middle of nowhere. It certainly wasn't like any jail I had ever been to. One of the officers held a sheet of paper and began calling roll. When he called "Benton Savage," I didn't say anything.

"Benton Savage," he repeated.

I still didn't say anything. I hoped that if I didn't answer than I could change my identity. I no longer wanted to be Benton Savage.

"Benton Savage!"

Everyone turned his head to see where Benton Savage was. Finally, I said, "Here."

"Don't you know your name?"

The other prisoners laughed. I still didn't say anything.

"Well. Do you?"

"Yes sir."

"Then answer us next time."

There were several small houses on the property. Inside mine were fifteen bunk beds. The lighting was dim. On one of the walls hung two payphones. Of course, none of us had any money, but that didn't stop people from calling collect. The bathroom was disgusting. Above the urinal someone had taped a sign that read 'Piss' with an arrow pointing down. Above the regular toilet was the word 'Shit' with an arrow pointing down as well.

I lay on the top bunk and tried to blend into my surroundings. Everyone seemed to be enjoying themselves. They laughed loudly, told stories, and in general ran around the room playing grab ass.

Meals consisted of cheese sandwiches and apple juice. In no shape or form did this jail remind of the Cleveland, Tennessee Jail. I didn't make any wisecracks or attempt any of my mind games. I feared they would strangle me with their bare hands if I did. I remained on my bunk with my single sheet pulled up to my chin.

After two days I wondered when I was getting out. It seemed like they were planning to hold us for eternity. I withdrew from my shell somewhat and learned that this was the Dade County holding area for criminals who have no way of posting bail. These people literally had no money whatsoever. They weren't even worth two dollars. I had been grouped there because I told the arresting officers that my address was the homeless shelter, and they assumed that I had no money as well.

Once a day a minister dropped by our shack and read from the Bible. I always attended in hopes that my salvation would come sooner in the name of freedom. Of course I was paranoid as well. Instead of thinking that I had come to save the world, I now thought that I was the devil, and that I was surrounded by vampires. That was why the lighting was so dim. That was why they slept during the day rather than at night.

After breakfast on the third day, a barber came with clippers and offered free haircuts. It had been at least three months since I had a haircut. There was a long line. Everyone wanted a free haircut, everyone except me. My childhood barber used to remark on a mole on my scalp when she cut my hair. An observation I didn't think much of at the time. Now I feared they would shave my head and that the numbers 666 would show on my scalp like they did on Damian in *The Omen*. So which was I, 666 or Five-O?

I listened in on conversations to see if I could decipher what I should do next. I thought that everyone was talking about me and that they knew I was "Five-O." When they laughed, I assumed they were laughing at me. When they spoke, I assumed they were speaking of me. I couldn't stand it.

I decided I was going to have to kick some ass if I wanted to earn their respect. Though I had barely even spoken to him, my bunkmate was the obvious target, but I was scared. I didn't know if I could get up the nerve. I wondered what he would do if I started beating him. I wondered what the other prisoners would do. Finally, I decided it didn't matter. Once again, I thought people didn't really die. This jail was for people who couldn't afford a proper burial. We simply disappeared from society without a trace. We would stay here in these death houses forever, eating cheese sandwiches and washing them down with apple juice. I'd be damned if I was going to be forgotten without a fight.

I jumped down from my bunk like a madman, rushed my bunkmate, and pushed him onto the bed. I used my left hand to hold his head while I punched him over and over. He raised his hands to protect his face but didn't fight back. He squirmed to turn over onto his stomach, but I wouldn't let him. I wailed on him some more.

"What did I do? What did I do?" called out the man.

"I'm Five-O!" My punches landed on his face and neck.

Finally, people pulled me off him. Someone ran to the door. "You'd better bring someone in here before we kill this guy!" a voice called out.

A moment later two guards ran into the room. "What happened?"

"He's trying to fight me," said my bunkmate.

"Why?"

I didn't say anything.

"I think I know where you belong," said one of the guards.

By this time the prisoners had huddled around me. The guard hooked my arms and escorted me towards the door. The prisoners moved and made a pathway. No one said a word.

"Where are you taking me?" I asked when we were outside.

"The eleventh floor of the police station. You'll like it up there."

The eleventh floor turned out to be the mental-health unit. Lunatics yelled and screamed at all hours of the day and night. They rotated us from cell to cell throughout the week so that we wouldn't spend too much time with one person. I had five different roommates the week I was in there.

The nurses tried to get me to take medication, but once again I refused. They offered me the use of a phone so I could call my loved ones; I refused that as well. They fed me three times a day, but I basically refused that too, only eating a banana or an apple at mealtime. One of my roommates called me a 'fruit' because that's all I would eat.

At the end of the week a social worker came by to see me. Word had trickled down to her that I wasn't participating in their 'rehabilitation' efforts. We talked just outside my cell. She was an attractive woman with a soothing smile.

"I'm trying to get you out of here," she said.

"That's good. I'm ready to leave."

"You'll have to go to a shelter."

"That's fine. That's where I was staying before I came here."

"Problem is, we can't take you back to Homestead. It's too far. We'll have to take you to a shelter in Miami."

"That's fine."

The next day I was released. A police officer drove me over to a shelter about five minutes away.

"But I don't want to go to a shelter," I said.

"Believe me, they don't want you there either."

Unlike the shelter in Homestead, this one was tiny, only a couple of rooms and not many beds. Residents without beds slept on mats. I sat at a table. I stayed there through dinner. I didn't speak to anyone. No one spoke to me. The entire time I was plotting my escape. I kept my eyes on the door, waiting for a time I could skirt out. I was nervous, but I knew I had to do it.

After dinner I tried to sneak out the front door.

"Hey, you! Come back here," yelled the social worker.

I turned around to face him.

"You don't want to leave here. You have no place to go."

"I don't belong here. They don't want me here," I said, echoing what the police officer had told me.

Suddenly all the other guests filed out of the shelter and began lying on the sidewalk around me. I was so disillusioned that I didn't know what the hell was going on. Maybe they were trying to help me, trying to show that if I didn't sleep in the shelter I would have to sleep on the sidewalk. But the shock of it all was too much for my system. Without saying a word, I turned around and walked down the road by myself. I didn't look back.

"Come back here," I heard the social worker call out again.

But it was too late. I had already made up my mind that I was going to tackle the world on my own terms. For the next two days I wandered the streets of Miami. I nourished my body with water from fountains I found on my journey. Once, when I saw a McDonald's, I went to the dumpster and scoured until I found a half-eaten chicken sandwich someone had discarded. I took a bite.

I thought about my homeless friends in Palo Alto. Had they been introduced to me so I would learn survival skills? Was living on the street and eating out of trash cans how I was to spend the rest of my days? Once again, not what I had planned for my life, but there was plenty of company for me, so who was I to say.

Another homeless man crept out from behind a tree and offered me a banana, but when he patted me on the head, I feared he was making a homosexual pass at me. I walked away. I wasn't playing that game.

I thought of my family. I thought of everyone. I must have replayed every conversation I could remember and undoubtedly created many conversations that never occurred, fabrications construed in my twisted mind. I was trying to determine who in my life had tried to help with good advice and who had tried to hurt me with their lies. Then I realized everyone was against me. Everyone was trying to tell me that I wasn't worthy of being a spoke in the wheel of society.

Everywhere I walked I tried to find something to jump off. I walked for miles through seedy neighborhoods. The balls of my feet were blistered again, and I could barely keep my eyes open. My mind moved at such a fast clip that everything I saw I felt I knew what was coming. Everything was happening for a reason. Everything was a sign. My mind was so fragmented at the time that I had visions of both misery and elation, sometimes stemming from the exact same sign.

For instance, I remember seeing the word 'Haley' carved into the sidewalk. I knew a girl named Haley. In fact, I had been thinking of her earlier in the day. Nothing specific, but she had just crossed my mind.

Then I thought of Haley's Comet, or did it mean Haley's 'Comment.' Could this be a sign that someone like me comes every 88 years? Did I meet Haley for a reason? Was this a bad thing or a good thing? On the surface everything seemed bad, but I was suffering so much that maybe I would be rewarded for my faith. Much like Job. Which brought me back to <u>J</u>umping <u>Off</u> <u>B</u>ridge again. How else could I show such faith in God than by hurling my body over the edge with the understanding that God would save me from death or even injury?

Finally, I found a bridge crossing a dirty stream. There was a van parked at the edge of the stream. I thought of the *Saturday Night Live* sketch when Chris Farley talks about living in a 'Van down by the River.' Was this skit about me? Was it part of a sick joke the world had played on me? Was this van left there for me? Was this my way out? Instead of suicide I could just live in a van down by the river. Fine. I would live down by the river, but I would do it with pride.

I took the steps down. My shoes got muddy as I trudged through the marsh. I didn't know if there would be anyone in the van, or if someone left the keys for me, or what the hell I should do. I looked around to see if anyone was watching. I certainly didn't want to go back to jail for breaking and entering. I pulled on the handle. The door was locked. I tried the passenger door. It was locked too. Okay. I'm not supposed to live in a 'van down by the river.'

I looked at the river. The Grateful Dead came to mind.

I will walk alone by the black muddy river.

Sing me a song for my soul.

Swaying trees hung across the narrow river. I walked closer and then decided that I didn't give a damn what the song said, I didn't want to 'walk alone by the black, muddy river,' but I couldn't decide what I wanted to do. One minute, I wanted to go back to Tennessee and see Lane; the next moment, I thought the idea ridiculous, and turned around and walked in the other direction. My mind was so caught in a circular loop that I walked fifty feet in one direction toward Tennessee before turning around and walking the other way. Every time I switched directions the length of my walk became less and less until I was down to 20 feet, then 10 feet. Then I just stopped, too confused to take another step. The Clash song once again played in my head with the never-ending debate.

Darling you've got to let me know

Should I stay or should I go.

Finally, I sat down on the curb. The summer sun beat down on my neck. I tucked my chin on my chest. A young woman walked by. She looked worse than me, with rotted teeth, stringy hair, and shabby clothes.

"Are you doing this for a woman?" she asked.

How could she know that? It fueled the fire in my mind that everyone knew what I was doing, and that it was some sort of sick joke the world had played on me like in the movie *The Truman Show*. But what did I do to deserve this kind of treatment? I wasn't a bad person. I wasn't perfect, but I couldn't think of many instances when I purposely hurt someone. Still, I couldn't look at it any other way. Every sign seemed to show that I had a special place in this world.

I began to play the "What is my biggest nightmare" game. I remembered reading somewhere that "a man's worst nightmares will become a reality." What was my worst nightmare? First, I came up with no more sex for the rest of my life. Pretty bad, I supposed, but plenty of people lived through this fate. Then I thought of being buried alive. That was awful, but before long I came up with what I thought was probably the worst affliction. I was going to live forever. I would be a million years old and still living on the street. No one even talking to me. No one showing me any kindness whatsoever. How would the world remember me? Surely, I would be respected for the enormous sacrifice I made for humankind. Like Jesus giving eternal life to those who believed in him, my job was to live forever so that other people could die. Up was down, and down was up. I didn't want that. I wanted to be like everyone else. I wanted a normal life with a beginning and ending.

I rambled through the streets. When I saw a bench, I took a rest. Once, a woman walked by me and tried to hand me a dollar. I refused it. I wasn't going to be a beggar, but then I thought of the Mexican restaurant where I accepted the handout. Suddenly, I realized I had already begged for food once. Did it mean that I was grouped into the homeless category forever? I couldn't change the past. Once a beggar always a beggar.

Finally, I found a hospital. It was the middle of the night. I had recently read a book by Cormac McCarthy called *Child of God*, where an escaped mental patient kills many people and at the end of the book, before he is captured by the police, he just checks back into the mental hospital, where he spends the rest of his life in solitary confinement and dies when he is ninety years old or something. Was I similar to this character from the book? Should I check back into the mental hospital? Was that the only place I would be accepted? After all, I had killed all those people in Hurricane Andrew.

Despite the fear that I might be sentenced to solitary confinement in the mental hospital for eternity, I decided life in a mental hospital was better than one on the streets. I walked past the security guards and into the emergency room.

"I want to check into the mental health unit," I said to the receptionist.

"We can't do that until eight o'clock," said the woman.

I looked at the clock behind her. It was four in the morning.

"What am I supposed to do until eight o'clock?"

"You can sit in the waiting room."

Frustrated, I walked outside. I thought I was so worthless and beyond redemption that they wouldn't even give me a bed and a hot meal in a mental hospital. I saw a parking deck just outside the hospital. It must have been ten stories high. I thought this hospital and this parking deck had been constructed so I would jump from the top and kill myself. That was the plan that God had for me. This was where the Benton Savage story would end.

At the top, I walked to the ledge and looked down. In a normal state of mind I have few phobias, but a fear of heights is probably the worst one I have. As I looked down, I couldn't get out of my mind that I might be immortal and that I might not die if I plummeted. I would be a quadriplegic at best. At worst I would lie on the ground in agony with no one helping me, exposed to the elements for eternity with no food or water, yet still unable to die. I imagined I would be some kind of freak show, where people would come to see the ruins of the man who saved the world. The man who lived forever so that the rest of the people could die.

I looked at the clouds. There was a breeze, and the clouds moved through the night sky. In one cloud formation I swore I saw the faces of my mother and sister drifting by. They were smiling. They wanted me to jump. I had embarrassed my family and myself long enough. It was now time to do the right thing. It was now time to jump.

I took off my clothes and threw them to the side. I was going to die the same way I had been brought into the world. I would be found naked. When I looked over the ledge again, I saw someone looking up at me. He sat on the curb. The sick bastard was waiting to see if I was going to jump. He wasn't going to try to stop me. I imagined him smiling at the thought of seeing my ultimate demise.

I stood on the platform with only a three-foot concrete wall standing between myself and death. I knew it would only take me a split second of courage to make this happen and end my life. I knew this was the thing to do, the thing that would make myself proud for doing the right thing. But there were so many other things I wanted to do with my life, and what if I was wrong? What if I didn't have to die? What if Lane and I might one day be reunited? At least that was the excuse I was using at the time. Truth is, I couldn't muster up the courage, and it disgusted me. This is one of the few occasions in life when it is good to be chicken shit.

Still, I couldn't bring myself to walk away. I knew that I had to stay there until I finally summoned the strength to jump. I put my clothes back on and stood there at the ledge. The sun began to rise. Even the man who had been watching from the bottom had grown bored and walked away. Two police cars drove to the top level of the parking garage. Four men hopped out.

"Don't jump, son. She isn't worth it," said the officer.

How did they know what I was thinking?

I made one last pathetic lunge for the wall, but I was never going to jump. Truth is, I didn't have the courage. I just wanted it to go on the record that I had at least tried. Two officers grabbed me and pulled me away.

"It's all right," said one of the officers. "We're here to help you."

CHAPTER 13

In comparison to the humid Miami weather, the emergency room was refreshingly cool, and everything felt tranquil. The bed was soft. The pillow was soft. The walls were white. The sheets were white. The nurses and doctors were dressed in white. Until someone spoke to me, I felt at ease, but all it took was the sound of a human voice, and I was back on the defense.

"What is your name?" asked a male nurse.

I hesitated.

"What is your name, sir?"

"Benton Savage."

I immediately regretted giving my real name. This was the chance I had been hoping for to change my identity. I could have said any other name in the world, and they would have accepted it as the truth. I could have said Max, or John, or Jay. Anything would be better than Benton Savage. Now it was too late. I could not recover from my mistake. I had to make the best of being Benton Savage.

"All right, Mr. Savage. What were you doing on the deck? Were you going to jump off? Did you want to kill yourself, Mr. Savage?"

"No."

"Then why were you on the top of the parking deck?"

I didn't answer. I couldn't make another mistake if I didn't answer.

"How long has it been since you've eaten? You look dehydrated. We'll hook you up to an IV and pump saline into your system. That will help you sort things out."

A female nurse came to my bed and hooked the IV to my arm. She wore rubber gloves. I imagined that she didn't want to touch me with her exposed skin, that I was so disgusting, I was like a leper or even worse, that I had AIDS. I did feel weak, and due to all of the lithium blood tests, there was the possibility that someone had used a contaminated needle on me.

It didn't take long until I was absolutely convinced that I had AIDS. That's why

I felt so bad. That explained all the negative thoughts and the draining of my energy. I needed to tell the doctors. Not because I feared that I would die, but out of fear that I might spread it. When the doctor finally came, I told him my fears.

"Why do you think you have AIDS?" asked the doctor with a smile. I suppose he was trying to soothe me with his neutral bedside manner, but I took the smile as evil. He was condescending. He was a dirty doctor.

"I feel so weak."

"That's from not eating or drinking fluids," said the doctor. "You'll feel better once the saline gets in your system." The doctor tapped the bag of saline and smiled again before asking, "What were you doing on top of the parking deck? Were you going to kill yourself?"

After the nurse disconnected the IV, she brought a wheelchair around for me to ride in. When I protested, she explained that it was hospital policy to take a person from the emergency room to the mental health ward in a wheelchair. I thought of my homeless friend Carl. I imagined the nurse knew I had once made fun of Carl for having a wheelchair. I was now learning not to judge a person until I had walked in his shoes for a while.

Compared with the mental health wards in Atlanta and Palo Alto, this ward was tiny, consisting of a living area that doubled as the dining room and a single room with sixteen beds where all the patients slept. The patients here were unlike any I had ever seen. In the past, patients had been subdued and, for the most part, quiet. They didn't seem mentally ill. In this hospital there was no doubt.

First, everyone wore blue gowns patterned with tiny tic-tac-toe boards. To me this symbolized that there was no hope for us. Like a game of tic-tac-toe that never had a winner, there was no chance for us to be winners in the game of life. Despite my efforts to once again be Benton Savage, it was futile.

Signs posted around the room also took on special meanings for me. For example, atop the television was a sign that read, No one can touch the TV. Simple enough, it meant the staff controlled the television, and patients weren't allowed to change the channels. Unfortunately, I interpreted it to mean that no one could touch the transvestite. As a child, I had once dressed as a woman for Halloween. Now, just like being a beggar for life, I believed I had become a transvestite for life, and no one was allowed to touch me. This was a tough proposition for someone as obsessed with sex as I had become in the last year.

What bothered me most was, how was I supposed to know this? I had only been eight years old at the time. Why hadn't my parents told me that what I was doing was wrong? It was their job to tell me. This furthered my distrust of my mother and brought back bad memories of my father, who had always been "aggressive" in his discipline. In my youth it wasn't rare for my dad to slap me across the face when I misbehaved.

This brought me to the next sign taped to the wall: Abuse Counseling, 9:00 Monday. I took this to mean that all the patients had been abused by their parents and that group therapy was being offered so we could come to terms with the fact that it was beyond our control.

Though I had never considered my dad's harsh treatment abuse, this provided me with a ready scapegoat for my predicament. Instead of holding my deceased father on a pedestal, I now blamed him for my demise. He rattled my confidence when I was growing up with his overbearing personality. He made me ashamed of myself at a young age. Basically, he raised me to be an inadequate and insecure adult. Of course, this further fueled my suspicions about my mom, whom by this time I had spoken to only once in the last three months and had not even considered calling for a long time. I thought that my mom had a hand in placing me in the mental hospital, and I didn't know how I could go lower, but I knew I could. If my mom had put me in this mental hospital at her own will, she could certainly send me to another place even worse.

After being wheeled into the ward, I stepped out of the wheelchair and sat in a chair beside a man with bleached blond hair and a goatee. His mouth was curled, and his eyes appeared mischievous. His name was John Pryor. The staff called him simply Pryor. He had been in the unit for a while.

"Do you smoke?" Pryor asked.

"No."

"We get to smoke at ten o'clock. Can I have your cigarette?"

"They let you smoke in here?" I asked.

"Four times a day. Can I have yours?"

Though I smoked, I wasn't going to smoke in the hospital. I partly blamed my incarceration on my alcohol and tobacco use, but I also included other things, such as eating meat. I had never been a vegetarian, never even considered it in the past, but now I wanted to be one. If I was going to advance up the food chain, I needed to start at the bottom: respect not only the homeless but animals as well. I was desperately trying to climb the ladder, and there was a progression of steps I had to take, the lowest form being an albino ant, which, I reminded myself, started with the letter A. I would start with the albino ant and move up until I was once again "Benton Savage."

"Where's your socks?" asked a Haitian staff member.

I looked down at my bare feet. They were pink on top and blistered on the bottom. "I don't have any," I said.

"Here. Put these on," said the staff member.

He handed me some light-blue terrycloth socks with rubber traction on the bottom so I wouldn't slip on the smooth floor. I hesitated. My favorite bluegrass band was Turry and the Tellico Militia, and somehow I connected the terrycloth socks to the band's name. How did they know my favorite band? Or did Turry and the Tellico Militia know that I would one day be in the mental hospital and name their band for that reason? It was a dilemma. In the end I decided to split the difference: I put on one sock and left the spare one sitting on the floor.

"Chow time!" called a staff member. The place was filled with Haitian staff members. They spoke with accents, and their eyes and teeth gleamed like ivory against their dark skin.

The food was brought out on a cart, and trays were placed on the tables. We usually had two choices of meat, so the faster you moved to the dining area, the more likely you were to get your choice. By this time I had firmly decided I was no longer going to eat meat. I sat down and fiddled with my green beans, taking slow bites and chewing the food thoroughly before swallowing.

"Do you want your chicken?" asked another patient. "I'll give you my green beans for your chicken."

Without hesitation he reached over with his fork, stabbed the chicken breast, and brought it to his plate. "Do you want me to scrape my green beans onto your plate?" he asked.

"Thanks."

After giving away my chicken, I felt somewhat better. I felt that I was moving my way up the ladder. Beyond the fact that I was trying to respect all forms of life by not eating meat, it was more about sacrifice. Recovering from the hell I was in was not going to be easy. I began to think that if an action forced me to suffer, it was probably the right thing to do. It was about taking the road less traveled.

Only since I was locked in a sterile environment with little stimulus, besides the television and radio, could I prevent myself from being a threat to myself and others. There was very little conversation between the patients outside of what channel they wanted to watch on the television.

"When is smoke break?" asked Pryor.

"The same time as yesterday, Pryor," said the staff member.

"When was that? I forget."

"Three o'clock."

"What time is it now?"

"One-thirty."

Pryor dropped his head and began to pace the hallway; never looking up from the ground but moving fast. He seemed to have an enormous amount of energy. Five minutes later he started up again.

"What time is smoke break?" asked Pryor.

"The same time as I told you five minutes ago, Pryor," said the staff member.

"I forget. What time is that?"

"Three o'clock."

"Can I smoke mine now?"

"No, Pryor. You can smoke when everyone else does."

Pryor dropped his head and once again paced the hallway, walking from the locked front door to the locked back door. I watched him more carefully. I wondered if he was putting on some kind of act. No one could be so dumb that he forgot the question he had asked just five minutes before, and Pryor didn't seem dumb at all. On the contrary he seemed quick. Not normal, but quick. He spoke fast. He walked fast. His eyes moved fast.

I began to be suspicious of him. He was so irrational that I couldn't help but think he was pretending to be mentally ill. In fact, all the patients seemed to be pretending. They laughed too loudly, acted too silly, walked too funny, and sometimes even danced by themselves to no music. I was absolutely positive they were acting.

Why were they acting? I didn't know. Was I supposed to act too? What act was I supposed to do? I supposed it had to be original. I looked around the room. Each person was doing his own thing, independent of everyone else.

After smoke break the doctor called me in. He was a short, stocky man who looked like a bullfrog. He sat behind his desk. He wore a sport coat and mock shirt underneath. He told me to take a seat in the chair in front of his desk. He had a chart in his hand. He slid on his reading glasses, crossed his legs, and looked at the chart.

"I see that you have a history of bipolar," said Dr. Buchanan.

"I'm not bipolar," I said. I regretted divulging this information to the emergency room attendant. I felt that no one was bipolar. That this was some disease that had been conjured up by my mom and the doctors.

Not taking my personal diagnosis seriously, the doctor continued, "What medicines did you take in the past?"

"Lithium and Paxil."

"Were they helpful?"

"Obviously not. I'm here, aren't I?"

Dr. Buchanan smiled and took off his glasses. "Tell me. Why don't you think that you are bipolar?"

"I just don't."

"Can you explain why you were standing on the top of the parking deck? That is where they found you, isn't it?"

"They wouldn't check me in the hospital."

"Why did you want to check into the hospital? You must have thought there was something wrong with you. That is why most people check into a hospital."

I didn't say anything.

"I understand. It's hard to talk about," said the doctor.

"I don't want to take medicine."

"Why not?'

By this time, I had a new reason for not taking the medicine. Like I said, I wasn't sure that people really died--that many people simply went bankrupt and were removed from society and then placed in either jails or mental institutions. I got the term 'bankrupt' from Ernest Hemingway's book *The Sun Also Rises*. Hemingway was my favorite writer, and I somehow read messages into some of his writing. There was little doubt in my mind that I was bankrupt, just like all the other patients. I thought that the medicine just kept us alive longer, furthering our suffering. I truly wanted to die. I just didn't have the courage to commit suicide.

I believed the medicine kept you alive because of a term I learned in high-school chemistry called half-life. I didn't remember what it meant, and I doubt I had truly understood it when I studied it; I had probably just memorized the definition so I could answer the question on a test. I remembered that some half-lives could be as long as a million years, or even longer, or possibly much shorter; I was fuzzy on the subject. In any case, I believed the medicine stayed in the body far longer than the expected lifespan. I thought I would remain alive long after I had been buried. That was what I was thinking when I believed I would live forever. The more medicine I took, the longer I would have to suffer under the earth. Of course I didn't tell the doctor what I was thinking, after all, he was the enemy; he was trying to keep me alive. "You need medicine if you want to live a normal life," said the doctor.

"No. I don't."

The doctor leaned up in his chair and smiled again. "Why don't you just try the medicine and see if it helps? There are many different medicines. Some work better than others. It all depends on the person."

"Haven't you been listening to me? I'm not going to take medicine."

His smile disappeared. "That's your prerogative. But I must tell you. I'm not going to discharge you until you are medicine compliant."

"You can't keep me forever," I said.

"Yes. I can, and yes I will."

"Can I leave now?"

"Yes. You can. But just think about what I said. I'm sure that you want to leave here as soon as possible."

I returned to the recreation room where the other patients were watching TV.

"What time is snack break?" asked Pryor.

"The same time as yesterday, Pryor."

"I forget. What time is that?"

"Eight o'clock."

Pryor walked away but returned a short time later.

"What time is snack?" he asked again.

"The same time I told you just a minute ago, Pryor."

"Oh." Pryor dropped his head and walked away again.

I looked up at the television perched in the corner. It was turned to VH-1. Destiny's Child's 'I'm a Survivor' was playing. Some of the other patients maniacally danced to the song. I watched as their frantic limbs jutted out in all directions, and their smiles broadened. No one was dancing as a couple. When the song stopped and the next one was slow, they ignored the music and continued to dance at a fast pace.

I slumped down in my chair and closed my eyes. Then I came up with a new plan. I would just sit in this chair with my eyes closed for the rest of my life until I died. I wouldn't speak when I was spoken to. I wouldn't move when I was told to. I wouldn't eat when chow time was announced. I would sit there forever. Just like everyone else had their acts of lunacy so they could remain in the hospital, this was mine. I would stay as still as a statue. If they didn't like it, they could pick me up and carry me to a bed. I wasn't going to help or hinder anything they wanted to do with me. If they lowered me into a coffin, I wouldn't fight it. This was my final rest stop. My life was going to end here. I was giving up.

When bedtime was announced at nine o'clock. I remained motionless in the chair. I heard the other patients shuffle towards the sleeping quarters. Someone turned the television off. Even though my eyes were closed, I sensed that the recreation room lights had been turned off to signal the end of the day. Someone tapped me on the shoulder.

"It's time for bed," said the voice of a patient.

I didn't move.

"Hey man. It's time for bed." He shook me harder.

I ignored him.

"Mr. Rudy," called the voice to a staff member. "This guy won't get up from his chair and go to bed."

"Who?"

"You know. The one that never talks and never takes his medicine."

Mr. Rudy was a little ornerier than the rest of the staff. I heard the swishing of his steps as his scrub suit rubbed between his legs. His large hand grabbed my elbow.

"Hey, Jim Bob. It's time to get up."

I didn't say anything.

His hand shook me hard enough this time that my neck moved. Still not opening my eyes, I shifted my hand under my chin and placed my elbow on the armrest of the chair.

This time Mr. Rudy's voice was stronger and more ornery. "Get up, Jim Bob. I don't have time to mess with you."

I kept very still. I was nervous. I could feel his angry eyes bearing down on me. I wondered if I could hold out. This was going to be harder than I thought.

"Jim Bob, I'm going to ask you one last time. Get up and go to bed!"

Mr. Rudy placed his hands under my armpits and pulled me up. My legs remained limp, and when he let go I collapsed and sprawled out on the cold floor, my head turned to one side.

"I'm not going to mess with you anymore, Jim Bob. You can sleep there for all I care. I have a feeling you won't last long."

The voices trailed off until they were barely audible. I heard a couple of the staff members in the office adjacent to the recreation room; they were laughing. I assumed they were looking at me. I tried not to move, but I wasn't comfortable. I hadn't expected them to leave me lying on the floor like a complete buffoon. I had expected them to either leave me in the chair or carry me to my bed.

I don't know how long I lasted, but as time passed I grew more uncomfortable and felt ridiculous. The staff wasn't going to do anything about it. They were smarter than I had anticipated. They were going to let me conclude this on my own. No matter how hard I tried, I could not fake my death.

Finally I picked myself off the floor and slinked back to my bed. When I lay down, one of the patients laughed uncontrollably for at least five minutes. Every time he laughed, I thought he was laughing at me. He was always laughing like this. He never said a word. All he did was laugh. That was his act. Laughter in the loony bin is like a crying baby on an airplane—intolerable. Good God. I hated that bastard.

By morning I had a new plan. I would starve myself to death. It wasn't a hunger strike. I knew that they weren't going to let me go. I realized that I belonged, but I didn't want to live like this. I wanted to die. When breakfast was called, I remained in my seat as the other patients scrambled for food.

"Mr. Savage, you don't want your breakfast?" the staff member called.

I shook my head.

"C'mon, Mr. Savage. You must eat your breakfast. You will get weak if you don't eat your breakfast. You don't want to be weak, do you, Mr. Savage?"

I shrugged. I was not going to eat. Maybe I couldn't lie on the cold floor all night, but I sure as hell could control what I put into my mouth.

"Can I have his breakfast?" Pryor called.

"Can Pryor have your breakfast, Mr. Savage?" the staff member asked.

"Yes."

I heard my stomach growl. I was hungry. I knew this wasn't going to be easy. But no one said dying was a pleasurable experience.

A couple of days went by, and I still didn't eat. However, I did drink lots of water, not out of necessity but more out of boredom. Without food or cigarettes there was nothing to look forward to, and I grew weary. I didn't know if it was possible to starve yourself to death, nor did I know how long it would take. I figured two to three weeks.

The staff seemed indifferent. At mealtimes they asked me a couple of times if I wanted my food, and when I said I didn't they left it at that and gave my food to the other patients. They didn't seem the least bit concerned about my health. Though I wanted to be alone and left to my absurd thoughts, I couldn't deny that I craved some attention, whether it was being browbeaten to eat or anything else. It is difficult to have nothing pleasurable in one's life.

On the fourth day, I took my dinner plate. I picked up a roll and spread some butter on it. I took a bite. It was probably the most satisfying bite of food I ever tasted, but I felt guilty about it. If I were serious about dying, I would have gutted out the pain. But I comforted myself with the saying, "Man cannot live on bread and water alone." Maybe I was prolonging my life, but if I stuck to just bread and water, I would eventually die.

More days passed with my only source of nourishment being bread and water. I imagined that I was going to spend the rest of my life in this wing of the hospital. It seemed like no one was leaving. I wondered if all these people were going to remain here for the rest of their lives, just like me. I didn't know if I could hack it. I thought of calling my mom but tried to fight the urge. I was so bored. I needed someone to talk to, someone to love me, someone to care for me.

I wanted to die, but I couldn't seem to muster the strength to follow through. Sometimes I ate some of the vegetables on my plate but never the meat. Maybe I wasn't as serious as I thought I was about starving myself to death, but I was serious about climbing the ladder of the food chain, and I believed that to do so I couldn't eat other breathing organisms. I even refrained from drinking milk and stopped putting butter on my bread. I was a vegan. That was as low as I could muster.

Days passed. Pryor kept up his incessant questions. A new patient swore he was Muhammad Ali. Another woman who had eaten a few too many cheeseburgers talked to me about her life when she was a model. I remained almost catatonic. I didn't reciprocate in conversation. I didn't participate in the group exercises. I did nothing, and I was miserable.

As time wore on, I could no longer rationalize my behavior as heroic or even reasonable. If I wanted to remain in this hospital the rest of my life with no one knowing where I was, it was becoming clear that I could make this fantasy a reality. No one gave a damn. There was no rehabilitation. The questions about my nutrition lessened. If I didn't eat, they didn't care. If I showered once a week, that was enough. I didn't shave, and the staff didn't care, but the patients noticed.

"You trying to look like Jesus with that beard?" asked a young woman without boundaries who was constantly inquiring about other patients' lifestyles and habits.

"And who's asking? Mary Magdalene?" I said.

"Who's that?" the girl asked.

"His secret lover," I replied.

"Doesn't sound like much of a secret if you know about it. I thought Jesus was a virgin anyway," the girl said.

I didn't reply. The girl wasn't much to look at, and I was in no mood to discuss theology, a subject I knew little about. But the conversation stirred something inside of me. I had said precious few words in the past month, and the sudden outburst had me thinking about religion. What if Jesus was a symbol of a certain kind of person? What if I was that certain kind of person? What if I was in fact perfect? I knew that I wasn't, but I thought of words I had often heard in church when I was growing up: 'There was only one perfect man.'

I was only a child. I could still grow up to be perfect. But what event transformed a child into an adult? I determined it to be love. Since I had never been in love besides with Lane and that love had never been consummated, I decided that I was still a child. I wasn't proud of this fact, but it was true. A child isn't held responsible for his immature behavior. He knows nothing better.

Suddenly my spirit lifted. This line of reasoning gave me newfound optimism. If I wasn't responsible for my behavior, then I couldn't possibly be the devil. What a great burden to have removed from my persona. I wasn't even sure that I had to stay a vegan. Perhaps I wasn't lower than an albino ant. Perhaps everything that was going on in my head was a figment of my imagination. Perhaps I was some kind of beautiful freak of nature. The 27-year-old 'little boy.'

However, I wasn't positive. I didn't feel like a hero. I wasn't being treated like a hero, and to be honest, I wasn't acting like a hero. I wasn't sure what I was. Everything appeared gray instead of black and white, where there were only right and wrong answers. I wasn't sure what was going to happen in my life, but I knew it was time to leave the hospital, or at least make strides in that direction.

After months of not even considering calling my mom, I walked over to the phone and dialed her 1-800 number. The phone rang several times before going to voicemail. I immediately hung up. I was having second thoughts. What if I was wrong? I still wasn't sure if my mom was on my side.

I didn't have long to reconsider. Two minutes later a staff member called my name and said I had a phone call. It shouldn't have surprised me. I knew my mom had caller ID.

"Hello."

"Benton! Are you okay? Where are you? I've had a private investigator looking for you the last six weeks. I've been worried to death."

"I'm in a hospital in Miami."

"How long have you been there?"

"I'm not sure. Probably a month."

"Are they taking good care of you?"

"I guess so."

"How did you end up there?"

"It's a long story." I wasn't about to tell my mom the truth.

"I want to see you. I want to see that you are okay."

"That's fine. I'm not going anywhere."

"Do you want to see me?"

"Yes."

"Then I'll book a flight and come down as soon as possible."

"Thanks, Mom."

"I love you, Benton."

"I love you too, Mom."

When I hung up, I didn't know if I should have called her. I didn't know if I should leave the hospital. I didn't know what the future had in store for me, and I was petrified. Every action, every word, every response seemed of the utmost importance. If I ate, I felt guilty, people don't need to eat. If I slept, I felt lazy—people don't need to sleep. If I spoke, I felt needy. I didn't want people to feel sorry for me.

Two days later my mom arrived. She smiled and gave me a big hug. There wasn't a separate room for visitors, so we sat across from each other at one of the dining room tables. We could still hear the senseless drivel of the other patients in the open room beside us.

"You've lost weight. You look good," said my mom.

"I weigh a hundred sixty pounds."

"How high did you get?"

"About two hundred."

"How did you lose all that weight? Have you not been eating?"

"Not much."

"Do you not like the food? I can bring you some food. Do you want me to bring you some yogurt?"

"I'm fine."

"Have you been taking medicine?"

"No."

"I spoke with your doctor over the phone. He said you could leave once you start taking your medicine."

"I guess I should start."

Neither of us said anything for a minute. My mom looked at me, but not with judgment. She wasn't pressing me to take the medication.

"You just don't want to take the medicine under any circumstances, do you?" she asked.

"It's not so much that. I just don't know if I should."

My mom furrowed her eyebrows. "What do you mean, you don't know if you should?"

"It's hard to explain."

Once again, we were silent. I could tell that my mom was trying to avoid conflict, which I appreciated. I was going to have to ease myself back into society, and my mom was facilitating these efforts by not pressing for details.

"We do have some issues we need to talk about. I paid your taxes for the last quarter, but I have received a letter from the storage company that is holding your furniture. You haven't paid in six months, and they are going to cut the lock and take your furniture if you don't pay the rent within the next two weeks."

I didn't say anything.

"I wouldn't make such a big deal about this except that some of the furniture is mine, and they won't let me pay the bill without a power of attorney. I brought some paperwork for you to sign so I can take care of it."

"What's a power of attorney?" I asked.

"It simply states that if needed, I can take care of your affairs."

I didn't know what to say. It was obvious that if I signed these papers, I would be losing some of my autonomy. "I don't know," I finally replied.

"I'm just looking to protect you if you go on one of these tangents again. I am trying to take care of your valuables. If you do well for a couple of years, we can rip it up. I'm not looking for a power play, but this needs to be done, and it needs to be done right now, or else they are going to throw away that furniture."

"Let me think about it."

Mom stared at me. "You know, Benton. If you take your medicine, you can live a normal life and be whatever you want to be. You have such great potential. I hate to see you squandering this out of some issue of pride. It's just like a diabetic taking medicine to maintain their blood sugar level. You have a chemical imbalance."

"I know, but why me?"

"It's just the way things worked out. Just be glad that there is treatment."

"I know."

My mom stood up. "It's time for me to leave now, but I will come back tomorrow. Please think about signing these papers. I am doing this for your own good."

We hugged again, and I walked back to the TV room with all the other patients. I had to get out of here, I thought. This is no way to lead a life. I don't know what I was thinking, but this was ridiculous.

I asked one of the staff members if I could speak with the doctor. Five minutes later I was in the doctor's office sitting in a chair facing him.

"So, you want to start treatment," he said.

"Yes."

"Good for you. I guess your mom's visit went well?"

"Yes."

"I thought we would start you on a cocktail of lithium and Paxil. Both of which you were taking in California, I believe."

"Yes sir."

"I thought we would also start you on a dosage of Zyprexa. It is a new drug that I think will work well with your symptoms. It should help control the psychosis."

"That's fine with me. When can I leave?"

"First, let's get you stabilized, and then we'll talk about it."

With the addition of Zyprexa, my thoughts cleared rapidly, and by the time my mom visited the next day I was feeling much better. Don't get me wrong. It was not an instant cure, but there was finally a ray of sunshine in my otherwise dark universe. I signed the Power of Attorney statement, and my mom went back to Tennessee with us on good terms.

However, I still had no idea what I was going to do next. Where would I live? What kind of job I would seek? What would I do with my life? Despite the vast improvement I was in no shape to tackle a job in the real world.

Then a minor miracle came my way. My dad's brother called me at the hospital. I didn't know him that well, but I looked up to him. He was a bit different from my dad. Not better by any stretch, but different. More in tune with the earth, not consumed with money, and that was what I needed at this time in my life. A change of pace.

Uncle John told me he was building a log cabin in Saluda, North Carolina, a small settlement about an hour away from his home in Asheville. He offered me a job helping him build it. There was going to be no pay, but he offered me free room and board. I was delighted. This was exactly the situation I needed. A chance to work and get my head on straight without the stress of working in an office with deadlines and clients. Though I had absolutely no carpentry skills, I accepted the job.

Uncle John was an alcoholic who hadn't drunk in close to ten years. Though we weren't especially close, he knew enough to know that I drank too much. His only requirement was that I could not drink alcohol or use drugs while I lived with him. I had no problem with this request. I didn't look at this ultimatum as a burden but more as a blessing. I knew that if I was going to make a successful stab at life, I had to eliminate alcohol. A week later I took a Greyhound bus from Miami to Asheville. I had a second chance at life, and I was feeling optimistic for the first time in long while.

CHAPTER 14

I was not 'normal' just because I had been discharged from the hospital. It took me a long time to recover from the fall. The strange ideas that clouded my mind and judgment did not disappear overnight. Many lingered for years, and even then I was never entirely sure they were gone. The main difference was that I stopped talking about what was going on in my head, though the paranoia remained. I felt certain that Lane had been in California. In my mind, the signs were vivid and concrete. It would have helped to talk to a professional, but I preferred to work through these issues on my own terms.

My time with my uncle building the log cabin in North Carolina proved beneficial. I opened up to him somewhat—more than I had to anyone else. We joked about some of the wackier thoughts. One of our favorites was that anytime we sat down to take a break, someone would say, "Sitting on a park bench / Eyeing little girls with bad intent." *Aqualung* was a good one. I'm still amazed that the brain can conjure such ideas, and even more amazed that someone wrote a song about it.

There were serious moments as well. We talked about what was bothering me, and we talked about Lane. Uncle John told me that what I felt wasn't love but infatuation. He was probably right, but I hated to hear it. It made me feel as though I were incapable of love, a fear that still troubles me from time to time. I've heard that one symptom of insanity is an inability to love, and I worried that love was an emotion I might never experience.

Mostly, though, we enjoyed working on a project we both believed was meaningful. I held up my end of the bargain by not drinking or using drugs. We had productive discussions about sobriety while we worked, and at his request, I even attended a few AA meetings.

The change in medication turned out to be a godsend. I improved and felt better than I had since my initial diagnosis of bipolar disorder eighteen months earlier. I gained emotional strength each day, and the paranoia diminished. It had been ingrained in my mind for so long that I no longer recognized it as an unwelcome intruder. I accepted it as a fact of life. But since it had lessened, I brushed it off as a minor deterrent in my recovery and convinced myself I had it under control.

After a few months of taking my medication regularly, my thoughts grew clearer and more reasonable, but I still wasn't ready to rejoin the workforce. My life had changed drastically in the past year and a half. After all the mental anguish, I was only just beginning to have normal thoughts and reach sound conclusions, yet I wasn't prepared to handle a stressful job, or at the very least didn't want one. I rationalized that since I had already been doing so much walking, I could give my wandering a purpose. I decided to hike the Appalachian Trail.

I don't want to call it a life-altering experience, but the journey was certainly beneficial to my psyche. Those six months were a rebirth after a long, brutal stretch. It was the kind of uplifting experience I had hoped for when I moved to California. After living so long with the belief that the world was aligned against me, it was refreshing to become the recipient of so many acts of kindness. Whether it was a fellow hiker offering to fill my water bottle or a stranger leaving a cooler of sodas at a trailhead for thru-hikers, I was amazed by the humanity my fellow men and women showed each other.

The trek wasn't easy. There were days when I simply did not want to walk. Although only ten percent of the people who start the trail finish, never for a second did I consider quitting. I had set aside six months to complete this adventure, and that was exactly what I did. If I felt bad one morning after a restless night of sleep on the hard earth, I just thought to myself that it sure as hell beat working.

The sense of accomplishment I felt from completing the Appalachian Trail boosted my confidence. I believed I could do anything that I put my mind to. As strange as it may seem, after the solitary experience of hiking the Trail, I decided to go to the opposite extreme. I moved to New York City. This time my mom didn't protest.

Despite seven million people basically living on top of each other, New York can be a lonely place. I only knew a few people when I moved up there, and although my friends welcomed me wholeheartedly, they worked long hours at highly competitive and stressful jobs. Their time was limited except for weekends. This left me with a lot of idle time on my hands, and the devil got the best of me.

I walked the streets and saw that there was so much to do, and so much fun to be had, but the problem was, I had no one to share the experience with. It wasn't long before I started drinking again. Just like I had in California, I bellied up to a bar, ordered a beer, and talked with the person closest to me. I can't claim I was happy, but at least I wasn't bored or lonely.

Initially, I planned to be a fulltime writer and reasoned that since New York housed many publishers, it made sense to live near them. Shortly after my arrival, I took a writing course through New York University and continued to work on my novel about my experience with bipolar. The writing class humbled me enough to realize that I wasn't as close to being as polished a writer as I had hoped. I decided to place my writing goals on hold and find paying work.

I secured a job as a commercial real estate broker with a highly respected national real estate firm, primarily on the merits of my achievements in a similar position while I lived in Atlanta. In the beginning I enjoyed the work, even though it entailed being little more than a glorified telemarketer. I worked hard and closed four large deals in my first 18 months and felt like I had some direction in my life.

I continued to see a psychiatrist every two weeks. Though I lied to him about my alcohol abuse, he wrote my prescriptions, and I took the medication without exception. The only negative side effect from the medication was weight gain. Ninety percent of patients who take Zyprexa gain a substantial amount of weight. When I was originally diagnosed in 1998 with bipolar, I weighed 160 pounds. By 2003 I had ballooned to 230 pounds, and friends called me "Big Benton."

Growing up I had always been the skinny kid. Now I was as fat as Santa Claus after eating all those cookies on his Christmas run. It bothered me, to say the least. But at the time I accepted the harsh reality that this was what had to be done. Zyprexa was the only pharmaceutical that was effective. I developed a creed to make myself feel better. "Sanity before vanity."

The workplace moved fast both in and outside the office. We worked all day and played hard all night, usually congregating at the Irish bar across the street around six o'clock every evening. This wouldn't have been so bad if only alcohol was being abused, but soon cocaine entered the fray.

Cocaine is absolutely the worst thing that a bipolar person can put into their system. With the use of cocaine, the manic energy that had been slowed by the medication was now manifested artificially. I had used cocaine only sporadically before I moved to New York, mainly because I never had a direct relationship with a dealer. Because of that, I was never able to abuse it. This changed.

I secured the telephone number of the dealer. Unlike most places, where the customer has to go to the dealer's residence for the transaction, in New York City the dealer delivered it to my apartment or just as frequently he would drive up and meet me on a street corner. I would ride around the block with him and then return to the bar where I was drinking. Shortly thereafter, I tooted it in the bathroom stall.

The cocaine was hard on me. My problem-solving skills fell to ridiculously low levels. I could not focus long enough to figure things out. Using formulas to evaluate the values of properties proved difficult. Solving daily basic computer glitches proved impossible. I was becoming known as an unreliable person.

I never missed a day of work, but many times I showed up at ten or eleven o'clock, feeling worse than I looked. It didn't hinder me too much on the phone. I kept on dialing every day at a ferocious pace, figuring that if I threw enough shit on the wall, something would eventually stick. Sometimes it did.

By my second year in New York. I was using cocaine several times a week, but had upped the ante by buying more than I needed for the night, and frequently started the next day with a few lines to pull me through the morning. Many of my coworkers used a lot as well, but I was quickly running away with the prize. I was even keeping my habit from my closest friends. But I still took my medicine every day, and though I didn't look or feel healthy, I had not returned to a crisis situation, meaning I had not been admitted to a psyche ward.

Toward the end of my second year in real estate I received a call from my mom telling me that Lane Johnson had died. She fell from the balcony of her apartment in New York City in a tragic accident. Apparently she was pushing open the French doors leading to the outside and tripped and plunged to her death. I hadn't spoken to Lane in over four years and had progressed so far in my recovery that I had not even uttered her name to anyone during that time.

It was a difficult pill to swallow. The fact that she lived in New York, without my even knowing it, was especially troubling. Although I had accepted that Lane and I were never going to be together, I never fully experienced closure. Now I was forced to, and there would be no opportunity to express my regrets about the awkward position I had put her in.

It was the second loss of someone extremely important in my life. Learning from the death of my dad, I knew that I must mourn Lane's death early rather than carrying the baggage around for years until I became bitter. The next several months were extremely difficult. A couple of months before Lane's death, I had abstained from drinking alcohol and using cocaine. Their absence probably helped with the mourning, but at the same time it was hard to find any joy in the day-to-day routine. Unexpectedly, life without alcohol and drugs brought on depression when I was expecting the opposite to be true. I deemed the experiment without substances a failure, and three months later I was back on the bottle and making up for lost time.

At the end of my second year as a real estate broker, I'd had enough of the business. After toying with the idea of co-founding a real estate investment company with a coworker, I turned on a dime and decided that I no longer wanted to be involved in real estate in any form. I quit my job and once again began writing full time.

This was not a popular move with my mother, who realized better than I did that maintaining a regular schedule benefited me. However, I was steadfast in my belief that writing was the only thing that could provide me with the fulfillment I was seeking.

About that time I found a coke dealer who delivered twenty-four hours a day, 365 days a year. My previous dealer always quit at midnight; this inconvenience had limited my intake and kept me somewhat sane. My new dealer would make runs to my house at three in the morning, and I could call him three hours later; he would scrape himself out of bed once again to make another delivery. Sadly, he became practically my best friend.

Now I began going on two-, three-, or four-day binges, usually by myself, so coked out of my mind that I didn't even move. I was drowning in a sea of ridiculous thoughts that proved to be my downfall. For example, I once again believed that some people couldn't have sex because of mitigating circumstances, just like Jake Barnes in Hemingway's *The Sun Also Rises*. Like Jake, who became impotent because of an injury in the war, I thought that 'war' was a metaphor for the negotiations between men and women in the courtship process. Some men would lose the war and wouldn't be able to have sex. Therefore they were 'bankrupt.' I was bankrupt.

Shortly after moving to New York, I developed an attraction to Asian women. I had never considered dating an Asian woman while I lived in the South; there simply were not many to choose from. I could only remember going to school with a small handful. That notion changed when Cathy Turner walked into our real estate office. From the moment I saw her I was enraptured—her dark skin, almond eyes, and unobtrusive manner. I liked it all.

I pursued Cathy with the caution required, given that we worked together, and we became friends. I flirted with her the best I knew how without pushing the limits. In the end, things didn't work out with Cathy. If I ever had a chance with her, I blew it with my cocaine habit by making a series of mistakes that I couldn't undo.

But still, my mind wandered toward an old friend of mine named Edna Garret, who I had known in New York, but who was now attending law school in Athens, Georgia. I'm not saying that Edna and I were perfect together, but there was chemistry. Edna and I were similar in the sense that both of us knew a little about everything and liked to share our knowledge with others. Some people might call that kind of behavior nerdish, but it was who we were.

Around this time my psychiatrist and I decided to change my medication. My weight had leveled at around 220 pounds, and I felt uneasy being 'the fat guy." The doctor took me off the Zyprexa and lithium, both of which had significant side effects of weight gain, and we started me on Risperdol and Depakote, which were supposedly comparable drugs.

Although I slowly lost some weight, I also slowly lost my mind. Like the previous times, the metamorphosis was so gradual that I didn't even notice I was slipping back into mania. It didn't help that I was using cocaine at a rate that could kill a rhinoceros, but in my defense, I was only trying to battle the symptoms of the disease.

I was once again taking a writing course at NYU. The teacher gave us an assignment to write about the unhappiest time in our lives. Of course my time down in Miami immediately came to mind. Even with the bitterness about my father's early death ten years earlier, or the death of Lane in the past year, Miami was still the most brutal period of my life.

The class discussion shifted towards the different ways a person could commit suicide. It was intended to be a lighthearted discussion with no one taking it seriously. Everyone but me. When one student brought up the fact that taking a bottle of aspirin to kill themselves was one option, I immediately thought that the comment was directed toward me. Was I supposed to swallow a bottle of aspirin? Was I supposed to commit suicide? Surely not. But I was thinking about it.

I became forgetful. Three times I left my keys in my apartment and locked myself out of the building. Each time I buzzed a neighbor so they could allow me back in the apartment building. Each time the neighbor grew more frustrated. I thought this occurrence had special meaning. Like "three strikes" is an out, or three outs is an inning, I thought that I should be out of the building for good.

Everything was happening for a reason. When I locked myself out of my apartment building for a fourth time, I finally got the message. This was a sign from God. I was not supposed to be in my apartment. That was God's plan. I had no choice in the matter. This was not my destiny.

Still not convinced, I buzzed every unit in my apartment building. When no one answered, I looked down at my watch. It was eight o'clock in the morning. Without thinking about it longer than 15 seconds, I immediately decided that I should take a Greyhound bus down to Athens, Georgia, to tell Edna how I felt. I didn't even wait to get back into my apartment. I didn't take a change of clothes, toiletries, or anything. I took the subway down to the Port Authority and bought a ticket on the Greyhound.

When the bus stopped in the various stations on the long route southbound to Athens, I got out of the bus and paced the waiting area. I felt that everyone was watching me. Every word I overheard was a statement about me and my plight. By the time I reached the Tennessee-Georgia state line, I finally wondered if I was doing the right thing. It wasn't too late to turn back.

I ended walking from the bus station to Edna's apartment building. I looked up her number on the apartment directory. I buzzed her. She didn't answer. I stayed by the front door for about fifteen minutes. I went to a payphone and called. She didn't answer so I left a message.

I felt somewhat relaxed at this point. At least Edna would know that I was in town, and the trip wouldn't be completely wasted. I went to a downtown diner called 'The Grill' and ordered some food. About the time that my food was served, Edna walked up to the table. She was smiling with her goofy grin, happy to see me.

"I thought you might come to The Grill," said Edna.

"Are you surprised to see me?"

"Yeah."

"I got locked out of my apartment. I took it as a sign so I just turned around and took a bus down to see you. I hope you don't mind."

Poor Edna deserved better than this. Unlike the first time five years ago, when Edna led me along, I couldn't claim that excuse this time around. We both understood that we were just friends, and this had been a solid foundation for our friendship the past three years with neither of us expecting much from the other person besides honesty.

"I don't mind, but I do have some classes that I have to attend so you'll be on your own a little bit." Edna pulled out a pack of cigarettes.

"Can I have one?"

"Sure."

We smoked cigarettes and talked. That was the good thing about Edna. No matter how awkward she might have felt or how alarmed she might have been, she had a way of making a person feel comfortable with her lightheartedness and humorous way of looking at the world.

"How long do you plan on staying?" asked Edna with a cloud of smoke filtering out her nose and mouth.

"I don't know. Maybe Friday." It was Wednesday.

"Does anyone know that you came?"

"No. Like I said, I turned around and came straight here."

"Maybe you should call your mom. She might wonder where you are."

"I guess you're right."

We walked back to Edna's apartment. It was late March, and with the sun shining, it felt much warmer than the frigid weather I had left behind in New York.

"I don't have my medicine either," I said.

There were few people in this world I could talk to casually about my mental illness without making them uncomfortable, but Edna was one of them. In fact, we bonded over the subject.

"I hope you don't mind, but I have a lot of work to do over the next couple of days," Edna said.

"That's no problem. Do your own thing. I guess I should have called."

"That's all right. It's good to see you."

Over the next few minutes, Edna straightened her cluttered apartment while I called my doctor and my mother. Both sounded concerned, but I assured them everything was fine.

"After my appointment, I'll take you to the pharmacy. Take a nap if you want, I'm sure you didn't sleep much on the bus. I'll wake you up when I get back," said Edna.

After Edna left, I lay on her couch and tried to sleep. It didn't go well. I was extremely anxious. I had come to Georgia to tell Edna how I felt, and now I was having second thoughts. I didn't know if I could get up the nerve. And despite the fact that Edna had been more than congenial, I didn't sense any romance on the horizon.

In the meantime, since I couldn't sleep, I rinsed the dirty dishes in the sink and placed them in the dishwasher. I pulled *The Brothers Karamazov* from Edna's bookcase and sat on the couch to read. Granted, Dostoevsky would not be considered light reading by anyone, but my concentration was so shot I couldn't make it beyond the first page. I set the book on the coffee table and turned on the television. A few minutes later, Edna returned home.

"Thanks for cleaning up," she said.

"Just earning my keep," I replied.

Edna walked over and sat beside me on the couch.

"There's something I want to talk to you about," she said. I recognized her tone was serious. She looked me in the eye without a trace of a grin on her normally happy face. She cleared her throat. "Like I said, I'm very busy over the next couple of days with midterms coming up. I spoke with my therapist, and she didn't think it was unreasonable for me to tell you that I really need to study and won't be able to entertain you."

"You don't need to. I can entertain myself."

"Yeah. That's not exactly what I'm saying. You would be a distraction even if you were just hanging out in my apartment. I really need the place to myself so I can study."

"Oh. When do you need me to leave?"

"Tomorrow. I'm sorry. I hope you're not mad. I know you've come a long way, and it's truly great to see you, but it's a bad time. I need to study."

"No. No. I understand." And I did. Then I remembered the reason for the trip in the first place, and a shot of adrenaline raced through my body. I wasn't going to be able to put off my confession of true love for a couple of days while I courted her in the best way I knew how.

"I have a friend that I want you to meet," said Edna. "He's also bipolar. I think you will like him. He reminds me a lot of you."

"Sounds good. I'd love to pick his brain," I said.

Over the next couple of hours the two of us stayed in Edna's apartment and smoked pot. Edna was similar to me in her substance use. One week she quit everything; another week she drank alcohol. Sometimes she just smoked pot. I could relate to this. I was always searching for the right combination of substances that my troubled mind could handle while still allowing me to take care of my responsibilities.

"You need to find yourself a girlfriend," said Edna after we were tanked and laughing.

"I would like to have one. I just don't know how to go about it. I don't meet many new women in my line of work."

"You know what you need to do. You just need to do it. You're too picky."

"I don't think that's my problem," I replied.

"It's at least part of it. You need to accept the fact that you aren't going to marry some supermodel."

"Hey. I went out with you, didn't I?"

Edna laughed. It was hard to hurt her feelings. She was like a guy when it came to stuff like that. In fact, she always had more guy friends than girls.

"Hey! Where's your bipolar friend?" I asked.

"Probably got lost. He's just like you, he couldn't find his way out of a paper bag," said Edna, now lighting another cigarette.

We were both sitting on the couch looking at each other. She looked down at my jiggling leg.

"Why the hell are you bouncing your leg like that?" asked Edna.

"I haven't taken my medicine in two days. I get like this."

"Why didn't you say anything? I have some Klonopin you can take. It's for anxiety. It will relax you."

"How did you get those?" I asked.

"I have a very understanding doctor."

Edna poured two pills into my hand and filled a cup with ice and tap water. With the break in conversation, my mind wandered. Why was Edna giving me this medication? Was she trying to tell me something? I looked at the bottle of Klonopin still in her right hand. Was I supposed to swallow the entire bottle of pills and try to kill myself? Was that what Edna was telling me I 'needed to do?' I had come close to jumping off a bridge in Miami, but I had never actually tried to kill myself. Ever since a classmate's comment about eating a bottle of aspirin as a possible way of killing oneself, I had taken it seriously.

The buzzer rang. I was so jittery that I jumped out of my seat. "What was that? A fire alarm?"

Edna laughed. "No. It's the downstairs buzzer. It's obnoxious. I should have warned you. I'm sure that's Robert."

"Your bipolar friend?" I asked.

"Yeah."

I was intrigued about spending time with another bipolar person. In the hospitals I had never interacted with anyone who was bipolar, at least not anyone who admitted it. Even in this more enlightened era in the treatment of mental illness, some people still passed judgment.

Edna answered the door and let Robert in. He looked normal except for his shifty little eyes wandering across the room until they met mine. We introduced ourselves.

"Do you have any pot, Robert?" Edna asked.

"Of course."

Edna turned to me. "Robert has the most incorrigible pot. The dealer only sells one bag per customer; it is so good."

"I shouldn't even smoke pot," Robert said. "I'm bipolar."

That was an easy enough way of breaking the ice. I had wondered if Edna had told Robert about me the same way she had told me about him. Obviously she had. Not even the most reckless of the mentally ill divulge their illness before the first drink is served.

"I'm bipolar too," I said.

"How are you dealing with it?"

"Just grand," I said, and rolled my eyes.

Robert laughed. "My mouth has gotten me in so much trouble that I've practically been run out of a couple of towns. Fine with me. I just keep moving."

This comment alarmed me. Was I about to run myself out of New York?

"Where have you lived?" asked Robert.

"I live in New York right now," I replied, not wanting to elaborate, even though, if there was anyone in the world who wouldn't judge me, it was this guy.

"What are you doing down here?"

"I came to see Edna."

"Oh."

There was an awkward pause. I wondered if Robert and Edna had ever been a couple and whether that was why she had invited him over.

"If I give you some pot, will you give me a kiss?" Robert asked.

Edna turned to me. "You'll have to excuse Robert. We went out once, and he has never gotten over me."

I could tell she was joking, but when I looked at Robert, I sensed that he wasn't in on it. He reached up and scratched his nose, then wiped his mouth. He had odd mannerisms, just like me. I'm always biting my lip or popping my knuckles.

Watching Robert's habits, I began to wonder if my own mannerisms were just as irritating to others. Soon I was paranoid about every move I made.

"Is the only reason you invited me over here because you want me to sell you pot?" Robert asked.

"If you mind your manners, I'll smoke it with you," Edna said, reaching into a kitchen drawer and pulling out a glass pipe.

"And if I don't?" Robert asked. Robert.

"Then you can go home. I've got my own pot. It just isn't as good," Edna replied.

I thought the whole exchange was odd. The more I watched and listened to Robert, the more I feared I was just as annoying as he was. In my fragile state of mind, it felt like looking into a mirror—and I didn't like what I saw.

Robert turned to me. "You're not her boyfriend or anything, are you?"

"No. Just good friends," I said.replied.

"Then what's the problem, Edna? Just a little kiss."

"Why are you acting like this? I invited you over so you could meet Benton. I thought you two would be a hoot together with all your funny stories."

If Edna thought I would enjoy Robert's company, I couldn't imagine what that said about her opinion of me, because I didn't like him one bit.

"But I came to see you," Robert said.

"Have you been drinking?" Edna asked. Edna.

"A little," Robert admitted.

"A whole lot of a little," Edna shot back.

"What's the problem?" Robert asked.

Edna walked across the room and took him by the arm. "Why don't you leave for a while and come back when you've sobered up? I can't deal with you right now."

By this time she was escorting Robert to the door.

"Don't be like this, Edna."

"Robert, you can come back when you can behave. I'm not dealing with you right now."

The whole conversation was awkward, but I didn't sense animosity between them. It seemed more like a routine they had played out before. I supposed Edna hadn't changed much in the last five years. She was still leading guys on, even if she didn't mean to. It was just her nature.

"Sorry about that," said Edna after she had closed and locked the door. "He sometimes gets like that."

"Did you really think that I would enjoy that guy's conversation?"

"I don't know. He's not that bad. He just drinks too much sometimes."

"Do I act like that?"

"No. You are more functional than Robert."

"Good."

Edna pulled out a bag of pot from her purse and loaded the bowl. "Do you want to smoke?" she asked.

I knew that I shouldn't. I had come all the way from New York to profess my love, and smoking pot wasn't going to help matters any. I was already paranoid. I couldn't get that conversation in my writing class about eating the aspirin out of my mind. Somehow I knew that conversation was directed toward me. Edna offering me the Klonopin just strengthened this belief. I only had to try and kill myself, I thought, but it had to be an honest attempt. I couldn't take five aspirins and call it a go. I had to go all the way.

"Do you think that I was too hard on Robert?" asked Edna.

"No. I don't want that guy back over here."

"But should I call him and apologize? I feel bad. He just has a little crush on me."

"You shouldn't lead him on," I said.

"But I do like him as a friend."

I saw my opening. "Is that how you see me? Just as a friend."

"I am much better friends with you than I am with Robert."

I stood up and walked towards Edna. I grabbed her hands, looked her in the eye, and took a deep breath. "Edna. Don't you understand? I love you."

Edna was no longer smiling. "I love you too, Benton. But I'm not in love with you. Don't you understand?"

"No."

Edna walked toward me and gave me a hug. I tried to tilt my head so that I could kiss her. Not only was "Benton" below the biting stage, I was also below the pop kiss stage. I interpreted this gesture as a sign that the most physical intimacy I could have with a woman was a hug. What would be next, a handshake? Eye contact? How low could I go?

Suddenly Edna pulled away. "I need to smoke pot. This is serious. I'm going over to Robert's. I need to see him." Without hesitation Edna walked out the door.

I took it to mean that she was going over to Robert's house to have sex. Just like in the past with Lane, Edna was going to sleep with someone else besides me. I had to do something fast. I had to end this misery. Like Edna said, I knew what I had to do. I had to eat the bottle of Klonopin.

It wasn't hard to find. Edna had conveniently left it on the kitchen counter. Yes. This is what she wanted me to do. Yes. I had correctly interpreted what she meant to say. Yes. I would take these pills. This would convince Edna how I felt about her. That I could not live without her love, and I had to do it quick. At the same time, I didn't want her to find me lounging on her couch. I needed to go someplace else.

I opened the bottle of medicine. There were only nine pills. I hoped that was enough. I didn't know much about Klonopin, but I figured that Edna had left enough in the bottle so that I could kill myself. I swallowed the pills with a cup of tap water. I threw the empty bottle on the ground next to her couch so that Edna would see it when she returned. I wanted her to know what I had done even if I didn't want her to see my ultimate demise.

CHAPTER 15

I sprinted out the door so I would not see Edna if she returned quickly. I knew exactly where I was going. There was a Holiday Inn just off the UGA campus and only a couple of blocks from Edna's apartment. I ran past the intoxicated students who flood the streets of downtown Athens on most nights. No one seemed concerned about my plight, which surprised me. I felt the world was watching. I felt that the world wanted me to commit suicide. I felt I was doing the right thing. I rushed through the hotel lobby and tried to remain calm as I checked in. Privacy was of the utmost importance to me; I feared I might keel over and croak at any moment. I didn't want a bunch of people peering over me as I took my last breath. I wanted to curl up in bed and fall into a painless slumber.

I headed to my hotel room, stripped down to my boxers, and lay on the bed with the covers pulled over my head. I prepared for God to lift me to the promised land, whether to his kingdom above or Edna's bedroom below. I really didn't care at that point. I just wanted this horrible nightmare of a life that I had created to change, and change drastically. I could no longer manage my life. I could not deal with the pressures of society as they forced me toward my ultimate demise. I was finally succumbing to the desires of the world. The pain was finally going to be over.

It didn't take me long to figure out that neither was going to happen. I wasn't even more tired than usual. In fact, with my adrenaline flowing, it took me a while to fall asleep at all. The only effect I had from the overdose was a very deep sleep that was finally interrupted around eight the next morning when the phone rang. I hesitated, but after several rings I reluctantly answered. Edna's high-pitched voice was on the other end.

"Benton. I thought I might find you there. Are you okay?"

I hated that I was so predictable, but like I said, the Holiday Inn was the closest hotel.

"I'm fine," I replied, seething that I wasn't even the least bit ill from the attempted overdose.

"Are you mad at me? Why did you leave?"

I didn't know what to say. Could Edna possibly not know the reason for my anger?

"I had to get out of there," I finally said.

"Do you want to come back?"

"You don't want me there."

"We can go out to breakfast or something before you leave. I feel like you are mad at me. Are you?"

"I have to go now."

"But, but—"

I hung up. The phone rang again two minutes later. I didn't answer it. Now I knew that I was going to eat a bottle of aspirin. Nine measly Klonopins hadn't even made a dent in Edna's armor. But at this point it wasn't about Edna. I hated that I was being judged for mistakes that I didn't even know were wrong.

I wasn't sure where I was going to eat the aspirin, but it wasn't going to be at the same Holiday Inn. I checked out and walked down Broad Street toward the bus station. I was scared. I didn't want to live my life out with no one to love, but I was afraid it was too late. I couldn't change the past, but even as doomed as I felt, I was looking for a loophole. Maybe I didn't have to kill myself. I needed to talk to someone. Someone I felt comfortable with. But whom? A psychiatrist wasn't going to cut it.

My mind scrambled through all my friends. I had a couple of fraternity brothers still living in Athens, but I hadn't spoken to them since college. Trying to talk out my predicament with them would be pathetic to say the least. I thought of some of my friends living in Charlotte, but it had been years since I had talked to them either. Finally, I decided that my Uncle John in Asheville would be able to set me straight. He had been there for me the last time I was in trouble. I'd had frank conversations with him in the past. Much more so than I ever had with any of my psychiatrists through the years. Maybe I could live with him again as I recovered. Maybe I could live out my life by myself like a hermit in the log cabin we had built together. I could write a book similar to Thoreau's *Walden*.

I bought a one-way Greyhound ticket to Asheville. I wasn't planning on calling. I was just going to show up. For some reason I thought that my uncle would be expecting me. I thought he knew what was going on in my life. I thought that everyone knew what was happening in my life.

Suddenly I knew I had to quit smoking cigarettes and quit dipping snuff. If I was going to fight my way out of this downward spiral, I was going to have to quit all my nasty habits. Quitting cigarettes would bump me up to a pop kiss. Quitting snuff would move me up to a bite. Quitting alcohol would nudge me up to a French Kiss. Yes. I could move up the ladder this way. For once, all my nasty habits would prove beneficial. Quitting each of my addictions gave me the opportunity to climb up the ladder.

It wasn't going to be easy. I needed a tobacco fix with an urgency second only to my need for oxygen. But I'm a fighter, and I knew I had to make serious changes if I wanted to get what I desired out of life. I would do whatever it took. I knew that about myself. At the same time, though, I felt as if I had no control over my life, as if my outcome were already predestined.

I was raised in a Presbyterian church. I don't know the doctrine well anymore, or maybe I've simply forgotten what I learned since my confirmation, but I do remember something about predestination. As I understood it, predestination was meant to give believers assurance of their entrance into Heaven rather than fear of Hell. Unfortunately, I didn't see it that way.

Lane had once told me that everything in life works out the way it's supposed to. That sounded like predestination to me. Lane was an atheist, and I suppose this was her way of explaining the world without God. With the name *Benton* sounding like bitten, I believed I had no choice in the matter—that no matter what happened, the result was beyond my control. I found both solace and bitterness in that truism. So much for all men being created equal. To me, that was hogwash, like so much of the folklore passed down to me throughout my life.

My mind was so distracted by these abstract thoughts that I missed a transfer bus in Fayetteville and didn't arrive in Asheville until nine o'clock at night. It had been a long day, but I still wanted to reach my uncle's house before going to bed.

It would seem obvious that I should have taken a taxi and been there in no time. Instead, I decided to walk. I was entering a minimalist stage. I even feared that the bus driver might sleep with Edna since he had driven me to Asheville, but I hoped she would understand. There was no way I could walk from Athens to Asheville, but I could certainly walk from the bus station to my uncle's house. I didn't know the route, but that didn't stop me from trying. With only the vaguest idea of where I was going, I set off, trusting that God's will would lead me in the right direction.

After a couple of miles walking down a busy road, I finally came to my senses and stepped into a convenience store to consult a city map. I didn't want to talk to anyone, not even the clerk. I was on a secret mission and being judged on performance; asking a clerk would cost me points. It took several long minutes to figure out where I was on the map, and several more to locate the street where my uncle lived.

"Do you need some help?" the female clerk finally asked.

"No, I'm fine."

"Are you going to buy the map?"

"I don't have any money," I lied.

"Where are you trying to go?"

"I found it. Don't worry."

I had been walking in the right direction. Judging from the map, I was only a couple of miles away. But I made a serious error in judgment: in my shaken state of mind, I didn't remember the streets where I had to turn. I thought that once I reached the neighborhood, I would recognize the landmarks and guide myself from there. After all, I had lived in Asheville for six months a few years earlier.

Two hours later I found myself walking along the interstate, cars whizzing by. I had no idea where I was going. Exhausted, I lay down under a tree to rest my legs. The sweat that had kept me warm turned icy. As tired as I was, it seemed wiser to keep moving. I had to get off the interstate.

Eventually, I came across another convenience store. This time I didn't bother with a map. I had no idea where I was or what direction I needed to go. be going.

"Could you tell me where Old Winston Highway is?" I asked the male clerk.

Two exhausting hours later I arrived at my uncle's house. His two dogs greeted me by barking furiously. I hoped the noise would be enough to wake the household. My uncle's car was not in the driveway. Could it be possible that, after all this effort, Uncle John might not even be home?

I knocked on the back door. No one answered. I knocked again. Still nothing. Desperate now, I walked across the deck and tapped on his bedroom window. A light turned on. Thank God, I thought.

I walked back to the door.

"Who's there?" a woman's voice called out.

"Lin? It's Benton." Lin was my aunt.

"This isn't Lin. This is Cindy. Who are you?"

I was stuck. I didn't know anyone named Cindy.

"I'm John's nephew, Benton. Are they home?"

"No. I'm house-sitting. What are you doing here?" The door slowly opened and a woman with blonde hair peeked through the crack.

"I came to talk to John," I said.

"They went on a trip. They won't be back for a month. Where did you come from?" asked Cindy.

"Athens, Georgia."

"You used to live here with John and Lin, right?" Cindy never took her eyes off me.

"Yes. A few years ago."

"I thought John had mentioned you to me. Do you want me to try and call him or can it wait until morning?"

"It can wait until morning," I said.

"Do you want to come in? You look like you could use some sleep." There was caution in Cindy's voice, but at the same time it was soothing to hear kind words.

"Thank you. I'll leave in the morning. I'm sorry to have woken you."

"I go to work at eight tomorrow. Maybe I can take you somewhere."

"Yeah. That would be great."

As I lay down on the couch in the basement, I thought about taking the aspirin once again but knew I couldn't do it here. I couldn't put Cindy in the position of discovering me. I had to get back to New York. That's where my home was. That's where I wanted to die.

I slept hard for about four hours and was woken by the sound of Cindy's feet upstairs as she rummaged through the kitchen. Not wanting to make her late for work, I dragged myself off the couch and plodded up the stairs to the kitchen. She was talking with my Uncle John on his cellphone. After a brief chat explaining the situation, Cindy handed the phone to me.

"How are you doing, Benton?" asked John.

"Not good, John."

"What's happening?"

"I'm in big trouble."

"How do you mean? What have you done?"

"I've done some terrible things."

"Like what?"

"I tried to commit suicide," I said hesitantly. I was embarrassed to admit it, but at the same time I had to.

"How?"

"I swallowed some pills."

"Damn, Benton. What drove you to this point?"

"My life."

John was silent for a minute. "I don't know what to say, Benton. What do you think is going to happen to you because of this?" he asked.

"I don't know. I fear that I'm going to Hell."

"I don't believe that," John said. "What you did is not good, but I don't believe there is a hell for whatever you have done. Don't worry about that."

"I don't know. It's hard for me to understand anything right now."

"Are you taking your medicine?"

"No."

"Take your medicine. Have you been using drugs?"

"Not recently."

"Okay. Don't start up again. That won't help matters. I can assure you. Where are you planning on going?" asked John.

"I was hoping Cindy could take me to the bus station, and then I would go back to New York."

"I wish I was there so I could help you out, but I'm in Texas visiting John." John was his son. We called them 'Big John' and 'Little John.'

"That's alright. I feel better. I just needed someone to reassure me."

"Well good. I'm glad that I could help. Do me one little favor. Call your mom and tell her where you are."

"Thanks, John."

We hung up the phone. I looked at Cindy.

"I need to call my mom."

"That's fine," said Cindy. "Then I'll take you to the bus station."

My mom's voice was grave as we spoke on the phone. She told me to go see my psychiatrist. Go take my medicine. Do not drink alcohol and be careful. The last thing she said was that she loved me, and to call her when I arrived back in New York.

It was a solid 20-hour ride on the Greyhound back to New York. In that time my mind played out endless scenarios about my demise. I feared that I wouldn't be able to get into my apartment building. I didn't have a key. I would have to call either the super or buzz another resident to let me into the building. I decided that there was no way I was going to do this. I was scared that if they did let me in the building without a key, then I would never be able to leave. I had strange thoughts about being banished in my apartment like a dog in a cage, only coming out occasionally to eat meals, never being able to leave. I feared that I would spend my remaining days as a recluse with no friends to talk to and certainly no one to love. With no food I imagined myself eating my own flesh for nourishment. Slowly I would gnaw on my arm until it was gone and then move next to the other arm. That's why my last name was savage. This was my destiny. This was my ultimate demise.

It was six o'clock in the morning when I arrived at the Port Authority in New York City. By this time, I was definitely not going back to my apartment. I was never going to face that situation. I didn't care if I lost all my money in the investment. I could not go there. I thought of what Robert had said about running himself out of several towns. That's what I believed I had done. I felt not only was I unwelcome in my apartment building, but I also wasn't even welcome in New York City.

I stayed in the Port Authority. My mind was still stuck on buying a bottle of aspirin and finishing the job for real this time, but where could I do this? There was no way in hell I could do it in the bus station. I needed to find a hotel, but where? In the meantime, I tried to catch some shuteye. Every seat in the station had someone already sitting in it. It was a rough looking crew. These people didn't look like they had just finished 18 holes at the Country Club golf course. I found a spot in the corner, lay down, and tried to go to sleep. I was beyond any self-respect. I was just an old bum looking for a place to lay my head undisturbed. Five minutes later I was called out. "You can't sleep here," said a security guard.

Without saying anything, I rose to my feet and walked away. Though I was hungry and thirsty, I did not buy food or drink; all I wanted was to sleep. Finally I found a group of men standing just inside the station in a designated area where we could remain as long as we didn't sit down. If we left the building to smoke, we weren't allowed back inside, so I had little choice. The temperature outside was below freezing.

Homeless men surrounded me. As I looked around, feeling sorry for myself and not believing I deserved to be judged this way, I realized these men lived like this every hour of every day. There were no smiles on their faces and no conversation between us. The only happiness we felt was being temporarily sheltered from the freezing outdoors. That may seem minor, but it was all we had.

After standing for close to two hours, my feet were exhausted. Finally, I went to a drugstore, bought some aspirin, and paid for a hotel room down in Greenwich Village. Being as early in the morning as it was and not having any luggage, I feared I would be turned away as undesirable, but I wasn't.

In the room, I wasted no time. I filled a plastic cup with water and began swallowing handfuls of aspirin. After gobbling about twenty aspirin tablets, I felt nothing. I thought the result would be that I would grow very tired, fall into a deep sleep, and eventually lapse into a coma. I was not expecting pain; I expected extreme relaxation.

I swallowed pills as fast as I could, refilling my cup of water over and over. I was halfway through the bottle and still nothing had happened. This was bullshit. I wanted to die. Why wasn't this working? I went to my window and looked down. I was on the sixth floor. I wanted to jump.

However, I feared strangers looking at me. I wanted my privacy. Besides avoiding the pain, I didn't want people gawking as I lay splattered on the pavement. I wanted to fall asleep and have no thoughts.

I took more aspirin. Twenty minutes later I was three-quarters of the way through the bottle, which meant I had ingested approximately 150 aspirin tablets. Then I began to sweat. My stomach burned as the aspirin wedged in the lining. My heart began to beat faster and faster. Sweat gushed from my pores. This was not what I had expected. I was not going to sleep. In fact, the opposite was happening: the aspirin was acting as a stimulant.

I stumbled to the bathroom and tried to make myself vomit. Some of the pills landed in the toilet. I ran the sink and splashed water on my face to try to cool down, I was burning up. I took off my clothes to cool myself. My hands began to shake uncontrollably. I couldn't hold the cup anymore and dropped it to the floor. I tried to turn on the faucet but couldn't. I looked at my face in the mirror: my lips trembled; my entire body was shaking. My heart felt like it was beating two hundred times a minute. This was torture, but I knew I must not call 911. I must let myself die.

I lost all control of my motor skills. I could no longer hold a cup of water, and walking became difficult. My muscles failed me. My eyes were dilated and my lips were pale. I tried to lie on the bed and relax but couldn't, the pain was too much. I pulled the covers up, but that didn't help; I was shaking all over.

Once again I tried to make myself vomit but could not. This was hell. I wanted to die, but I didn't know how long I could endure the pain. My heart raced faster and faster. This was worse than death; this was hell on earth.

Finally, I couldn't take it anymore. I crawled to the phone and called 911.

"I've swallowed a bottle of aspirin!" I yelled into the phone.

"Where are you, sir?"

I gave the address and room number.

"I'm calling Poison Control," said the dispatcher.

I struggled to put my clothes back on. My hands shook uncontrollably, and my legs didn't cooperate either. I stumbled around the room. Oh Lord I was in pain. Nothing could be worse than this. Even in my state of shock, I planned to tell them that it was an accident. I was convulsing so badly that the only place I could hide the empty bottle was under the bed. About fifteen minutes later Poison Control showed up at the door. It felt like I had been waiting for days.

"What did you take?" asked one of the two men. His teeth were stained yellow. These two guys looked shadier than undertakers.

"Aspirin."

"How many?"

"About fifty?"

"Was it aspirin or Tylenol?"

"Aspirin."

"Are you sure?"

"Yes. Why?"

"Tylenol is much more lethal. Were you trying to kill yourself?"

"No."

"Then why did you take so many aspirin?"

"I had a headache that wouldn't go away."

The two men from Poison Control sat me in a wheelchair. We took the elevator down and went straight through the lobby. I tried to keep my head down. Even in my crazed condition, I felt shame. They placed me in the back of the ambulance and drove the few blocks to St. Vincent's Hospital.

There were many other patients in the emergency room. I stayed in the wheelchair and tried to act calm. I watched as other patients were wheeled in on stretchers. The different doctors and nurses quizzed me about whether I had tried to commit suicide. I continued to lie, but I was weakening. I felt worse and worse, and my tolerance for the pain was diminishing. If I told them I took closer to 200 aspirin, I would have to change my story. I couldn't do that. I didn't want to confess that I tried to kill myself. When they asked why I took so many aspirin, I said that the headache just got worse and worse. The more they asked, the more I believed that I would be persecuted if I admitted that I did this on purpose.

Eventually they gave me a bunk in the emergency room. They gave me a cup full of black tar to coat my stomach. It tasted terrible, and I regurgitated the black fluid onto my gown. I did this again, and then again. Nurses hustled around the room, but none seemed to care about the awful shape I was in. They didn't even bother to wipe my gown clean. I threw up again.

The next eighteen hours were the most painful of my life. They hooked me up to an IV and a heart monitor. I watched my heart rate on the monitor stay at 180 beats a minute for the next twelve hours before it finally started to slow. I squirmed. I cried out. I was so dehydrated. I demanded water. When they only gave me one cup, I demanded that they give me more. I was in sheer agony.

Every hour or so someone would come and talk with me. They asked me what mental health medicines I took. They asked me why I took so many aspirin. Where I got the resolve to maintain the lie, I do not know.

Twenty-four agonizing hours later they transferred me to the mental health unit.

CHAPTER 16

Over the next two years I continued to toy with the idea that maybe I could live a normal life without medication. I convinced myself I was just being weak, that my illness manifested because of my drug and alcohol abuse. Unfortunately, I usually reached that conclusion in the middle of a three-day cocaine binge, which would sap the serotonin levels of even the sanest person. The cocaine mentally crippled me to the point that I became delusional, creating problems that did not exist.

When I worked in commercial real estate in Atlanta, my boss's screensaver read 'Drink More Coke.' At the time I assumed he had invested a large portion of his wealth in Coca-Cola stock and was showing his spirit with that screensaver. I didn't think much of it then, but the phrase stuck in my mind. As with many things when I was off my medication, everything took on a different meaning than the one intended.

Though it had been ten years since I lived in Atlanta, my boss's screensaver now signaled that I should no longer smoke cigarettes, chew tobacco, drink coffee or beer, or use drugs. My sole vice would be Coca-Cola. Of course I took this too far. If I was supposed to drink Coke, by God there was not going to be any mistake about it. Once I bought 200 two-liter Coca-Colas and barricaded myself in my apartment with plans of not leaving until Christmas. It was August. I wasn't going to eat or drink anything but Coke. I figured whatever was in Coca-Cola's secret formula would keep me alive.

Sequestered in my apartment with 200 two-liter bottles piled in the corner of my bedroom, I didn't answer the door or the phone for ten days. I didn't even check my messages. Finally, my cousin, who also lived in New York City, called the police, fearing I was dead. Even when the police came to the door, I did not answer; I thought they would grow frustrated and go away. I was wrong. The police knocked down the door and found me relaxing on the couch with a two-liter Coke in my hand and wearing only my boxers. I spent three weeks in the mental hospital for that stunt.

Another time I ate only eggs for a month. I didn't tell anyone I was doing it, and I honestly can't remember what I hoped to accomplish.

A friend had joked that his friend would open a restaurant selling only omelets and would throw the scraps of everything else he ate into them, peanut butter, sausage, jelly, turkey, whatever. I took my friend's remark to mean I should eat nothing but omelets. So that's what I did.

After a month of eating only eggs with plenty of salt, I woke one morning so stiff I could barely move. An hour later I was catatonic, unable to move a muscle. With my last ounce of strength I somehow rolled across the room to the phone and called a doctor friend. I lay flat on my back for six hours waiting for his callback. When he finally called, I explained the situation and he told me to call 911. Paramedics carried me out of the building and into the ambulance. The diagnosis was potassium deficiency, most likely caused by the massive amounts of salt I had been dousing on my eggs. The doctor told me the lithium in my system probably saved my life.

Another time the police stopped me in the dead of winter while I was walking down the street carrying a suitcase, wearing socks but no shoes. In my suitcase were ten two-liter Cokes—nothing else. Once again it was straight to the mental hospital, where I refused medication. While I remained hospitalized with no hope of release until I took my medicine, I was taken to court and ordered to take medication. The court order meant nothing to me, and I refused. Each night for a week thereafter, security guards held me down while a nurse injected Haldol into my rump. Finally my spirit broke, and I began taking the medication voluntarily.

Then I went on a hunger strike in the hospital. It began on Valentine's Day and continued until February 24. The reason: during one of my father's final days before he died of cancer, he was so medicated that he had difficulty communicating. Even so, he asked me to get a calculator. He punched in the numbers $2 \times 2 = 4$ and asked if I understood. At the time I had no idea what it meant, and I'm not sure he did either. Seventeen years later, in the hospital, I believed I was not supposed to eat until February 24. I thought I had cracked the code and felt like a genius for figuring it out. I imagined how proud my father would be for remembering his symbolic gesture.

I thought my Filipino friend, Cathy Turner, would be waiting for me when this date was reached. I told no one the reason I was doing this. The doctors and staff kept trying to feed me and constantly questioned why I was fasting. It was my secret. That was the way the game was played; to me it was a game in which I connected independent moments from my past and contorted them into some purpose in my everyday life.

During this visit to the mental hospital my cat died. I was in the hospital for ten days and never called anyone to feed her. My cousin, who at that point had a key to my apartment, discovered my dead cat. My mother finally tracked me down by calling every hospital in Manhattan until she found me. When told that my cat had died, I didn't believe it; I didn't believe that anyone died—I thought we all just rested beneath the earth for eternity.

When I was finally released from the hospital and learned that my cat really was dead, I was devastated. I loved that cat. She was all mine, and I took the responsibility seriously. Now she was dead, and there was only me to blame.

By this time I was utterly isolated from the rest of the world. In the last couple of years I had lost touch with all of my real estate friends. The people I knew in New York City from high school and college had started families and either moved to the suburbs or back South. The only friends I had in New York were the people I met at neighborhood bars. For any kind of face-to-face interaction I had to go to the bars and belly up.

By the summer of 2007 my cocaine use had reached mythic proportions. My dealer was practically the only person I spoke to. Many days passed when the only words I uttered were to the clerk at the convenience store when I asked for a pack of cigarettes. I survived on staples such as McDonald's, Taco Bell, and pizza, all of which were within two blocks of my apartment.

The strange thoughts continued. I thought about my cat's death constantly. I felt that there had to be repercussions for my negligent behavior; surely I would be punished for this neglect. Through my escapades at the neighborhood bar, I met a man named Wallace. Immediately red flags went up: my sister had a cat named Wallace. I thought this Wallace had been sent to me as some kind of sign from God about what was going to happen to me because I had let my cat die.

Wallace was a good guy. We had a lot in common. He read a lot of books, and he liked to drink beer. He had recently gotten out of rehab for cocaine addiction, so of course we had that in common; it didn't take long for us to go back down that path. But what struck me most about Wallace, besides his name, was his phone number: 336-2122. The direction of the numbers from 21 to 22 had great meaning to me. The number 23 had special significance.

When I was a kid, I had bad acne. I used a cream containing benzoyl peroxide. I exercised ferociously when I was growing up, frequently doing push-ups and sit-ups in my bedroom. Because benzoyl peroxide stuck to my hands, doing push-ups bleached the blue carpet in my bedroom. It meant little to me, but my parents were not pleased. Dad came down to my room to discuss it. He counted the number of bleach marks on the rug. It came to 23. Dad wrote the number on a piece of paper and placed it on my dresser with a warning that I wouldn't be in any trouble if the number didn't increase. We never spoke on the subject again.

I thought about this incident off and on for years. The significance of it to me was that if I could reach the number 23 in other ways, then I would not be held accountable for my mistakes, including the death of my cat. My slate would be wiped clean. This included credit problems and unpaid bills; all debts and disservices would be forgotten. It was kind of like being a born-again Christian. It would be a new lease on life. So when Wallace's phone number had this progression, I thought that he had come with a message.

I didn't know if it meant 23 days or the 23rd day of a month, but I was leaning toward the date December 23. My dad's father died on December 23, 1982. Of course, I thought that people chose when they wanted to die, so I believed that some kind of message was being sent to me by both coincidences.

But what could the repercussions be for letting my cat die? I didn't really know, but of course I assumed the worst. My biggest fear in life, besides living forever, is being homeless. My time on the streets of Miami still haunts me. Never have I felt as alone or as scared as I did during those harrowing days. The thought of fighting the elements every day and having no one to talk to scares the hell out of me. I know that no one wants to be homeless. But I looked at it differently. I felt that homeless people had done something that sentenced them to this lifestyle. In my warped mind I determined that all homeless men had killed their cats.

How could I be held responsible? It was an accident. I was in the hospital. I didn't kill my cat with my bare hands or anything like that. It wasn't my fault. But that didn't matter to me, the blood was still on my hands. Of course, I kept these fears to myself. I believed that even mentioning the fact would sentence me to a life outdoors. Still, I was determined to be ready. If there was any chance at redemption, I was going to take it. I would do whatever it took. And I knew that whatever was going to happen, it would happen soon.

I was off my medication again and on another of my crazy dietary habits. This time I ate nothing but pizza. For a week, all I had each day was two slices of pepperoni pizza. The other twenty-three and a half hours I spent lying around my apartment reading books and avoiding television as much as possible. I wasn't fully cut off from the world, I was answering the phone, and I was honest with friends and family about not taking my medication. I told them I didn't need it. This time would be different. This time it would work out.

My mind was wandering everywhere. It was late July, and for the past three weeks Lane had resurfaced in my thoughts. It had been four years since her death. I rarely thought about her anymore; some days she didn't cross my mind at all. But along with my desperate hope that my cat was somehow still alive, I began to wonder if Lane was alive too. Maybe everyone told me she had died just to force her out of my mind. Eventually, I felt like a fool for having been duped by such a hoax. Everyone had gone to great lengths to convince me. There were even newspaper articles my mom had clipped and mailed to me in New York. There had been a wake, though I didn't attend. Other than my mom, I had never really spoken to anyone about her death. I knew if I brought it up with friends, it would make for an awkward conversation. So I decided the best way to handle the matter was not to handle it at all.

After a week on the pizza-only diet, my stomach was not in good shape. No matter what was going to happen, I obviously wasn't going to be able to eat only pizza for the rest of my life, no matter how good it tasted. To celebrate the awakening, I went out for a jog and came back to take a hot shower. I put on some fresh clothes, went to the convenience store, and searched for something that would be gentle on my stomach. I bought Special K cereal, a carton of milk, and a carton of orange juice. I ate several bowls of cereal and drank orange juice. I felt much better and began to relax.

I lay on the couch and watched a baseball game. At about ten o'clock that night, my coke dealer called. Like I said, he was practically family by this point. He called every so often if I didn't call him, checking to make sure that I was all right. We talked for a while. At the end of the conversation, he made a comment that caught my attention.

"Benton. I just want to tell you that I think you're a real special person."

"I appreciate that, Dee. You're all right too."

"Benton. Keep in touch."

I hung up the phone feeling good about myself. Though Dee didn't ask, he called to see if I needed some coke. He was looking to make a delivery. I was proud that I withstood the temptation. I wasn't going to snort coke that night.

The conversation stuck in my head. Dee telling me that he thought I was a 'special' person was an unusual comment. After all, we were men. We didn't display our affection in that way. Then it hit me. I had just bought Special K. Dee had called me "special." Though I've never done Special K, I knew that along with being a cereal, Special K is the street name for a recreational drug whose intended use is as a cat tranquilizer.

This was the sign that I had been waiting for. The clerk at the convenience store reported to Dee that I had bought Special K. The world had been watching me. All my greatest fears were happening. Dee telling me that he thought I was a 'special' person meant that he knew I was responsible for the death of my cat. I never once considered that this conversation was coincidental, and even if I had, I wasn't going to risk it. I was going to do whatever it took to make amends for the death of my cat.

It was August 3, 2007. I went into lockdown mode. I was too scared to move, too crazy to understand. I had to do something, but I was too scared to leave my apartment building. If I never left my apartment, then I could never be homeless. I didn't know how long this trial would last, but I was going to pass it no matter what it took.

The first thing I did was change clothes. Instead of shorts and a T-shirt, I wore the melancholiest clothes I owned: khaki pants and a light-blue button-down shirt. Once again, this change of clothes stemmed from a story my dad told me about a fraternity brother who wore khaki pants and a blue button-down every day of the week; his closet was filled with them.

I questioned every statement ever made to me. I did not believe anyone. I didn't believe the sky was blue. I didn't believe the grass was green. Everything ever said to me led to this point. This was what Kafka meant when he wrote *The Trial*. I never believed I was alone in this scenario. I thought everyone went through an informal trial at some point in life, but I believed that my trial had more at stake. Under no circumstances did I want to become homeless.

This stinking thinking carried over into other aspects of my life as well. I wear contact lenses, just as my mom does. Only my mom frequently wears just one lens, which I have always thought strange. I took my mom's wearing one contact as a sign that I should wear only one contact, too. Then I tried to figure out why. The reason I came up with was that, in fact, the eye doctor had somehow contaminated my eye; that was how doctors made their money. They weren't trying to help the patients. They were trying to make money off the patients. I was stunned by the hypocrisy of the world.

I took this one step further. I thought about dentists. It was pure propaganda that we had to brush our teeth to prevent cavities, so I just stopped. I even thought that toothpaste gave people cavities and yellow teeth, bad complexion, yellow teeth.

I didn't need soap or shampoo. I thought that shampoo was what made a person bald. What did humans do before soap and shampoo were invented? Their bodies adjusted. Nor did I need to shave. Hair grows faster after it's cut, that's a fact. If I quit shaving, eventually my whiskers would quit growing. Just another example of how big business manipulated society for monetary gain.

I had only half a box of Special K and half a carton of orange juice. I decided that this would last me ten days. I ate small bites of cereal and sipped the orange juice so that I would consume roughly the same amount each day. At the same time, I slowly weaned myself off water, believing that the body didn't require water to survive.

On the third day, I cut off the air conditioning. It was August. Within hours, my apartment was eighty-five degrees and humid. I lay on my sweat-stained sheets and remained as strong as possible. Even though it was humid and I needed more fluids, I abstained from drinking water as long as possible, eventually making it up to twenty-four miserable hours. When I did drink water, I drank out of a cereal bowl like the one I used to give my cat. I imagined the misery my cat went through as she struggled to stay alive with no food or water.

On the eleventh day, I went to the convenience store and bought another carton of orange juice. I did not take the elevator; I took the stairs. I did not check my mail for unpaid bills; I wasn't worried about penalties. If I could make it to the twenty-third day, my delinquency would be forgiven. If I made it to the twenty-fifth day, because of the secret alarm code at my mom's house, I would have Lane. My dad said he would kill me if I punched "1225" as a joke. Symbolically, this meant that under no circumstances should I eat regular meals until after the twenty-fifth day. No matter how bad it got, I had to do this for my dad. It was his dying wish, and I was not going to let him down.

The phone rang. The buzzer to my door went off. I didn't answer, but I left the door unlocked just in case the police came. Under no circumstances was I going to let my door be knocked down again. On the thirteenth day, I unplugged every light and appliance in the apartment. I was going as low as I possibly could: no AC, no lights, no clock radio, nothing.

I imagined all sorts of scenarios. Who would pick me up? What should I do next? What would I say? I looked at it as some kind of obstacle course and believed that someone was going to pick me up, drive me to Tennessee, and then I would finish the saga by running five miles across town to Lane's house, where there would be our wedding, once again completing the greatest story ever told.

On the fifteenth day, the orange juice tasted sour. I learned later that, since the only thing with substance I'd had to drink all that time was orange juice, my colon had gone rotten. My eyes turned red and itched as if I'd somehow contracted pink eye. This inconvenience convinced me that I was doing the right thing.

On the sixteenth day my mom and stepfather walked through the door. It was a Saturday around noon. They had flown up from Tennessee. I was lying on the couch.

"All right, Benton. What's going on here?" my mom asked.

"Nothing," I said.

"Obviously there is something going on. You haven't answered the phone in over two weeks."

I didn't say anything.

My mom looked around the apartment. "And why is everything unplugged?" she asked.

I didn't say anything. I wanted them to leave. My mom was keeping me away from Lane.

"Obviously you haven't been taking your medicine."

"No."

"Where is it?" my mom asked.

"I flushed it down the toilet."

"And why did you do that?"

"I don't need it."

My mom glared at me. By this time, my stepfather was going around the room, plugging everything back into the outlets.

"When was the last time you ate?" she asked.

"Today," I replied. I had been very meticulous about eating every day, even if it was just a few flakes of Special K. For some reason it was important that I ate or drank something every day.

"Just cereal? No milk?" she asked.

I didn't say anything.

For everything my mom said, I assumed the opposite. I felt that people had different ways of communicating; I believed some people communicated with lies. I thought my mom was lying to me. This was a strange revelation, because my mom is, without a doubt, one of the most honest people I know, she rarely even bends the truth. But at that time I felt she was lying. I wasn't sure whether she was doing it with malice or whether this was just the way a mother communicates with a son; in any case, she wasn't being straightforward with me.

My mom and stepfather returned an hour later with groceries. I remained on the bed. My mom emptied the grocery bag in front of me so I could see what she had bought: cereal, oatmeal, Pop-Tarts, milk, orange juice, peanut butter, a loaf of bread, and a quiche, which my mom immediately placed in the oven.

As the smell of the baking quiche swept through the apartment, I thought immediately of the famous book *Real Men Don't Eat Quiche.* Yes, my mom was trying to tell me something. No matter that she was cooking quiche; I was not supposed to eat quiche nor any of the other things my mom had bought. I was going to be a real man. Lane wouldn't be satisfied with anything but a real man.

I went further into lockdown mode, I quit answering questions. I certainly didn't eat. I didn't do anything. I didn't know what to do.

"If you don't answer my questions, I'm going to have to take you to the hospital. I can't leave you like this. You'll eventually die if you don't eat," my mom said.

I didn't answer.

"You leave me no choice."

Half an hour later, the paramedics arrived. I remained on the bed with my eyes closed. I heard my mom explain to the paramedics that I was bipolar and that I hadn't been taking my medicine. She told them I was a writer and that I had written a book about a boy ending up on the streets.

"I fear that he's going to end up on the streets, and we'll lose him if we don't get him back on the medication," she said.

Two male paramedics came into my room.

"Can you stand up?" one of them asked.

I didn't answer.

"We'll help you, then."

The paramedics picked me up and set me in a wheelchair. I kept my eyes closed as they wheeled me out of my apartment, down the elevator, and outside, where they once again lifted me and loaded me into the back of the ambulance.

I didn't know what was happening, but I thought it was all some kind of test, and at the time I believed I was doing exceptionally well. I still wasn't taking my medication, and, just as importantly, I hadn't eaten the quiche.

At the hospital, they placed me on a cot and took me to the mental health unit of the emergency room. There were two other patients in the room. My eyes were in excruciating pain from having drunk only orange juice. The fluorescent lights only exacerbated the condition. I kept my eyes closed as much as possible to alleviate the pain.

The nurses took my vital signs and asked the standard questions, what kind of medication I was taking, why I was here, and why I had not been eating. My answers were short and combative. I wasn't eating because I did not want to eat. I wasn't planning on explaining my answer to these stiffs. At the same time, I wondered whether these doctors were really doctors. I imagined that they were mental-health patients who worked for the government in order to control other mental-health patients. The exceptionally smart mental-health patients played the role of doctors. The next tier of intelligence were nurses, all the way down to the imbeciles who acted as patients in this charade. It was some kind of elaborate joke, and I wasn't going to be suckered into their game.

I remained on the cot, trying not to get angry. I wasn't going to help matters by losing my temper. A short time later, a meal was brought to me. I hadn't had a real meal in over two weeks. I was trying to make up my mind. I knew that it would be normal to eat. I looked over at another patient.

"Go on—eat," said the patient.

Reluctantly, I picked the plastic top off the steaming plate and took a bite of the country-fried steak. It tasted great. I practically swallowed the food without chewing. I did this several more times until I realized that the food was not going all the way down my esophagus. It was stuck. I tried to wash it down with water, but I could feel the water being blocked. I swallowed. Nothing moved. I knew that I was in trouble. I swallowed some more water. Same thing. Finally, after another sip, the water came gushing out of my mouth and onto the floor beside the cot.

"What the hell are you doing?" called a nurse. "Go to the bathroom if you're going to do that."

I walked to the bathroom and stuck my finger down my throat until I threw it all up. I flushed the commode and walked humbly back to the room with the other patients.

"Now we need to take your blood," said a nurse.

"No."

The nurse glared at me. "And why not?"

"Because I don't want to."

A young doctor with sideburns approached. "What seems to be the problem?" he asked.

"He won't let me take his blood," replied the nurse.

"Why not?" asked the doctor.

"I don't belong here."

"Your mom must have called the hospital for some reason."

"She shouldn't have. She shouldn't have even been in my apartment."

"Why not?" asked the doctor.

"Because I didn't invite her."

The doctor looked at me with a straight face. "I see we have some things to work through."

I didn't say anything.

"Tell me what's going on," said the doctor, pressing his stethoscope to my chest.

"Nothing. My mom called the ambulance and now I'm here."

"Have you stopped taking your medication?"

"Yes."

"Why?"

"Because I don't need it."

"Hmm."

I walked to one of the three rooms surrounding the holding area and lay down on a cot. Another patient walked back there with a newspaper in his hand.

"Do you want to look at the newspaper?" he asked.

"No."

Once again I thought of Kafka's classic *The Trial*. Every time something was offered to me, whether food, drugs, or medical assistance, I refused. I could see the frustration on the doctors' and nurses' faces. In my skewed state of mind I thought that meant I was doing well. After all, along with my mother, the doctor was the enemy. They had created this illness. The medication in my system only exacerbated the condition.

When I arrived there were only three patients in the room. Over the next 24 hours, at least 20 more people were admitted, and the room became very crowded. I thought these people were from the CIA. I imagined someone in a room spying on me through a hidden camera—calling in members of the CIA to see what I was up to, to see if I was dangerous. When a young black man with cornrows entered the room wearing an O.J. Simpson throwback jersey, I couldn't help but laugh. Who would even manufacture an O.J. Simpson throwback jersey? These people were just trying to scare me, and I began to feel confident that I could handle whatever they threw at me.

Then a young man with a beard and beaten jeans entered. "I am the Antichrist, and I have come to save the world!" he called, hands raised above his head. He took a seat two spaces away from me. He was a hippie and smelled like patchouli. The knuckles of his right hand bore a green tattoo of the number 666.

This was getting crazy. Who were these people? Why were they here? Where did they come from? Not that I was scared or even nervous. Like I said, I was having fun acting like a badass in front of these people by refusing food and medicine. I was on top of the world, and no one could stop me. Several times a staff member asked if they could take my blood pressure. I refused that, too. An EKG? No, I wouldn't do that either.

I grew more confident by the second, my head swelling to match my pride. I thought seeing Lane was in my immediate future. I wondered how it would happen. What would I do when I finally saw her after so many years apart? Would there be a celebration with all our friends and family? Would we get married immediately? And how was I going to get out of this hospital? I imagined myself naked, running down the street to the nearest bar, where we would have a wedding party. It was supposed to be a surprise party, but I was too smart. I was on to them. This was just a game to see if I was ready, and boy howdy, was I ever.

Feeling cocky, I moved over a slot so I could sit directly beside the "666"-tattooed man. I wanted to be close to his evil. I wanted to show that I wasn't afraid of his deceptive ways or the fear he was trying to instill in me. Good would triumph over evil. Despite his proclamation that he had come to save the world, he wasn't fooling me.

Still not talking to anyone, the hippie took off his shoes. I could see the holes in his white tube socks. He sat very still with his hands on his knees. I wondered what 666 really meant. Years earlier I'd thought that I was 666 and had been ashamed. Now this fellow trumpeted the fact.

Believing that I was going to see Lane in a matter of minutes, I was practically shedding tears of joy when a female doctor walked into the room. A group of other people followed closely behind. Without my contacts I could barely see who it was, but I assumed she was about to release me. There was nothing left for me to prove. I had withstood the temptation of taking handouts in the form of food, and I had stared evil directly in the face by not allowing myself to be intimidated by the hippie or the man with cornrows and the O. J. Simpson–throwback jersey.

"Mr. Savage, can I speak to you?" said the doctor with a foreign accent.

"Sure." This was the first time I had done anything agreeable since I had been in the holding area. I didn't know if I should see her; I feared she was going to make me take medication. I cautiously followed her back to the office. At the same time, I tried to judge the doctor's motivation for seeing me. The seven or eight other people followed closely behind. They didn't say anything, but even without my contacts I felt their eyes on me. I imagined them as the jury in my trial.

I was in such a euphoric state that I couldn't stop wiggling in my chair. I was laughing and crying at the same time. My destiny was here. The trial was over. Now all I had to do was listen to some last-minute instructions about my life, and then it would be a direct path to paradise.

"Mr. Savage, these other people are resident physicians. They are just here for observation. My name is Dr. Salinger."

"All right."

"Tell me how you are feeling right now?" asked the doctor.

"I feel great."

"Is that because you are in a manic state?"

"No. It's because I'm in a good mood."

"Why are you in a good mood?"

"You know. I'm excited about my future."

"That is good. Why don't you tell us what happens when you are in a manic state of mind?"

I paused. This was not the line of questioning I expected. I wanted to leave immediately, and it was becoming clear that wasn't about to happen.

"When I'm manic, I can't sleep," I finally said, but it was in a much lower and serious voice than earlier.

"Is that what's happening to you right now? You can't sleep?"

"No. I can sleep. I just don't want to."

"What about when you are depressed?"

I didn't answer. I was not happy.

The doctor walked over to me and placed her hand on my shoulder. "That's okay, Benton. We'll talk about it later. Just try to stay calm and get some rest. I'm sure you are tired."

I walked back into the holding area, confused. Had I made some horrible mistake? Was I supposed to ignore this doctor's request like I did everyone else? If I wasn't leaving, what were they going to do with me? I sat beside the hippie. A moment later a nurse gave him a tablet of Zyprexa. He swallowed the pill with water and smiled.

"Come with me," the nurse said to the hippie.

I thought this exchange had something to do with me. Did that mean I was now 666? I didn't know, but then I remembered an independent movie I had seen called *Buffalo '66*. I immediately felt better. Since the hippie left, I had lost a 6. I wasn't 666. I was 66. But what did that mean? It had to be good. That was why everyone was coming down on me. They were jealous because I was 66.

I immediately thought of the number of children Lane and I would have together. Then I thought of grandchildren. I dreamed that we would have ten children: eight boys and two girls. The eight boys would have seven children apiece, and the two girls would have none. The total number of children and grandchildren would be 66. Wow, I thought. I had never considered how many children we would have, and now Lane and I were having ten. It was set in stone. That's the way things had to be.

But what did 666 mean? I decided that the hippie had been greedy and wanted 666 children and grandchildren, and God punished him for his greed by making him sterile, perhaps even impotent. Now I was going to be rewarded for my righteousness with fertility. I grew in strength, thinking about all the pain Lane would have to go through bearing ten children. My plight seemed easy in comparison. I wasn't going to let Lane down. I was going to remain strong.

Over the next several hours, the emergency room cleared out until I was the only one remaining. I felt that the trial was over; I felt triumphant. I had done well.

Even the staff had left. It was after midnight, and the only people remaining in the room were the security guard and an obese black woman behind the counter. I was suspicious of the woman.

I thought back to my father's death. My mother, sister, and I were all beside him when he took his last breath. The last hours were hard as he became weaker and weaker. He said things that didn't quite make sense, but I felt he was trying to tell me something. He struggled to catch his breath, so we held his hands to let him know we were with him, that he was not dying alone. In his last painful words as he approached death, he finally said, "I've come to the gate."

"That's good, Dad. Go on through," my sister said.

"There's a big black woman standing in the way," he said, with a puzzled look on his face.

"Push her out of the way!" the three of us said in unison.

My father's eyes closed, and he stopped breathing. I assumed he pushed the woman aside and entered the kingdom of heaven.

For years I had wondered about those last words. Very strange indeed. But what did they mean? Was he trying to tell me something? At that moment in the psychiatric emergency room, I imagined that this obese black woman was going to try to seduce me. It was like the last temptation of Christ, a test, and my dad's last words were a warning. I was to push this woman out of the way. Only then would I be allowed into the kingdom of heaven, which in my mind meant a life with Lane.

My forecast seemed even more plausible when the woman finally told me to go to one of the rooms and try to get some sleep. So this was how it happened. I was too smart for that. I was prepared.

I didn't lie down on one of the cots. I wasn't playing their game. I paced the room, always keeping an eye on the woman just in case she decided to jump me. She was quite a bit bigger than I was, but I wasn't overly concerned. God was on my side.

CHAPTER 17

Morning came, and the black woman didn't try to seduce me. Instead, she transferred me out of the emergency room to one of the mental health units on the upper floors of the hospital. After a Q&A with a staff member about how I ended up there and what medication I had taken, she led me to a room with a bed in each corner. The lights were out, and there were patients in the three remaining beds. I heard one stir as I lay down to rest.

"Who's your favorite superhero?" asked a voice. A young man with a shaved skull pulled himself up on his bed and looked at me with a chipped-tooth smile.

"I don't know. Maybe Green Lantern," I replied.

"Good choice."

"Who's yours?" I asked.

"Batman," replied the young man.

"I also like Apache Chief," I said, thinking about my childhood days when I worshipped these heroes.

"Talk about racism," said another voice. "They sold the farm when they came up with that superhero."

"I wonder what happened to the actor who played him?" I asked.

"Probably doing some low-rent porn," the first man said.

The second man got down on the floor and did a set of push-ups. I heard him grunt after each one. Then he stopped and sat back down on the bed.

"How many did you do?" I asked.

"Twenty-five. I try to do one hundred a day. It's hard to stay in shape in here."

Suddenly I stopped talking as I realized how ridiculous the conversation was. "Who's my favorite superhero?" Give me a break. These guys were here to test me, just like everyone else. They were spies. That was why they had kept me in the emergency room so long. The CIA had to call all these people, place them in the rooms, and go over each of their roles. I wasn't going to have any part of it. They weren't going to play head games with me.

Though I was angry about the manipulation, I felt somewhat sorry for them. I imagined these people were going to live forever because they took medication. Their role was to convince me to take medication so I would be sentenced to the same misery. Rather than face the horrors of an ordinary life, these people had sold out and agreed to take medication. Their only responsibility was to come to the mental hospital when they were summoned.

"What's your favorite food?" the young man asked me.

I said nothing. Instead I turned onto my stomach and tried to sleep. They knew I was the enemy. The only way I could win the game was not to play at all. For three days I remained in bed. I didn't go for food when called, and I didn't drink water. The only movement I made was to go to the bathroom, which was not often since I was neither eating nor drinking.

By the fourth day the doctors and staff had grown concerned. A nurse came to my room and wanted to draw my blood.

"We can't allow you to do nothing. You have to eat. You have to drink. I must take your blood to ensure your safety. Please let me see your arm. It will only take a minute."

I refused.

"Mr. Savage, come with us. If you won't take your medication, we must take you to the observation room," a doctor said.

I followed the doctor down the hallway into a room adjacent to the administrative desk called the Observation Room. A cot with white sheets had been set up in the corner. There was a square window in the door so staff could watch my every move. Since it was August 23, my sins and misgivings had been forgiven and erased from my permanent record, but that was not enough for me. I wanted paradise. What were two more days of torture in the big scheme of things? I had to make it to August 25. Then I would eat, but not until then. Nothing was going to stop me.

On August 24, a group of doctors, nurses, and staff members came into my room. They surrounded me. The head of the psychiatric department introduced himself, an older, distinguished-looking man with white hair and loose skin at his neck. I supposed that was why he got to play the role of doctor in this ongoing charade.

"You have to eat, Mr. Savage," the doctor said.

I didn't answer.

A nurse interrupted. "I can go to McDonald's and get you pizza. Just tell us what you want. I will get you anything, but you have to eat!"

I was tempted to eat a cheeseburger, but I only shook my head.

"Okay. You leave us no choice," the doctor said.

Suddenly six bodies closed in. Chaos ensued as they grabbed my arms and someone attempted to pry my mouth open. I kept my mouth shut. I felt apple juice trickle down my throat through my clenched teeth.

"Swallow, Mr. Savage! You need to swallow!" they shouted.

I didn't. After a moment they stopped wrestling with me.

"He won't swallow. All right. You leave us no choice. We're going to tie you up and force-feed you," the doctor said.

I laughed to myself. If they believed I was going to buy that fat lie, they must have thought I was weaker than expected. There was no way they were going to tie me up. But sure enough, five staff members surrounded me and flexed their forearms as they knotted both my wrists and ankles to the bedpost with white hospital sheets. I was completely immobilized. I looked at them and smiled like I was the biggest badass in the world. I was not going to give up. But when they left the room except for the doctor, I grew nervous. What if they never untied me? What if they were going to spoon-feed me for the rest of my life? I was working in a world of absolutes, and there was no turning back. For the first time I was scared. First I panicked, then I hyperventilated. When I regained my breath, I cried like a baby. They had finally broken me, and I became as helpless as a newborn.

"Please untie me," I said. "Please untie me."

The doctor didn't even look up from his clipboard.

"Please untie me. I'll eat. I'll take the medicine. I'll do whatever you want. Just please untie me."

"Do you promise to eat and take your medicine?" asked the doctor.

"Yes. Just please untie me."

"Okay. I will."

He untied me and handed me two Zyprexas. I swallowed them with water. A few minutes later a nurse escorted me to the dining area. A plate of food was waiting for me, and I ate every bit.

After the meal, a staff member wrapped a hospital identification bracelet around my left wrist. There were several different numbers. The first one was 1600 2 50. Immediately I thought of 1600 Pennsylvania Avenue. Did this mean that if I did well I could be president of the United States? Not only that, did the 2 50 mean two terms and me winning all fifty states? Yes. That's exactly what it meant. This brought me great cheer. All that suffering was worth something. It suddenly seemed like a small price to pay to become the most powerful person in the free world. But I also realized that there was no way the president could be on psychiatric medicine. I had to be free of the medicine, but how?

The second group of numbers read 2799723. The "27" symbolized the twenty-seven outs in a baseball game, therefore indicating the day I would die. The "99" indicated how many years I would live, ninety-nine years, and the "723" specified the exact day, which would make it the day before my one-hundredth birthday: July 23, 2072.

With this interpretation of what was going to happen in my grandiose life, my ambitions and desires ran wild. The problem was that I had so little control over my environment. I had to go to bed at a certain time. I had to get up when they told me. I took the medicines at the same time every day, and I had to eat three meals a day.

But suddenly I noticed the different colors of clothing that some of the female patients were wearing and where they were stationed on the ward. It started with a woman wearing a red T-shirt who was sitting directly beside the water fountain. I thought the red shirt signaled me to stop drinking water, but I wasn't sure. How could that be? Everything I had ever read indicated we should drink eight glasses of water a day. Now I was not supposed to drink water at all?

I decided to ignore it, but for the next few days this woman in red remained in that chair by the water fountain. Finally, I took it seriously. She was not the enemy; she was trying to help me, sacrificing her time to tell me not to drink water. I determined that drinking water was going to shorten my life, or at least render me unhealthy. Drinking water was just a scheme perpetrated by the medical establishment so the public would remain ill. Despite everything I had learned in life, water was, in fact, bad for me. This woman had sacrificed five days of her life to tell me this. I wanted her to get back to her own life. As much for her as for me, I quit drinking water to show my appreciation for her gesture. After a couple of days of my abstaining from water, the woman changed clothes and no longer sat beside the water fountain. I took this to mean that I was doing the right thing. It was one more notch in my progression up the food chain.

I noticed other women patients wearing yellow hospital jackets. Unlike the red, which obviously meant stop what I was doing, I deemed that the yellow meant caution, but what was I supposed to be cautious about? These women changed into regular clothes between meals but always wore the yellow when we dined. I tried to understand what it meant. I believed there must be some pattern to their behavior, which is how my brain was working. It was like playing a game in which every behavior was analyzed.

I thought about the food being served. I felt that I should not be taking handouts; that was no way for the future president of the United States to act, but I had already traveled that beaten path and wasn't about to go back there.

Then I observed how the food was served. On the tray were five options separated by a container. First, milk was served in a carton; second, a main course on a plastic plate with a cover to keep it warm; third, coffee or tea in a Styrofoam cup; fourth, a slice of bread, wrapped in plastic; and fifth, a dessert in a plastic cup. Breakfast was similar, except that juice was also served.

I thought of the Jackson 5 song "ABC"—"easy as 1–2–3." To me, that signaled a routine: one decaffeinated coffee at breakfast; two, milk and a main course, at lunch; and three, milk, a main course, and decaffeinated coffee, at dinner. That meant I was not eating salads, starches, or desserts, a sacrifice, but one that made complete sense to me. The other foods weren't necessary, and by the next morning at breakfast the women no longer wore yellow robes. Once again, I had cracked the code. Immortality was within my grasp.

Not long after I incorporated this eating pattern into my daily routine, my mother called. It was the Sunday after the first weekend of the college football season. We had spoken a few times since my admission; obviously she was concerned, but the news she brought was different from what I expected: she asked whether I had followed the football games over the weekend. This was unusual, my mother had about as much interest in football as I did in one of her passions, gardening.

"Did you hear about Georgia Tech beating Notre Dame?" my mom asked. "No." "I'm sure that Mark and Harold are happy. They went to the game in South Bend," she said.

Mark and Harold were my cousin and uncle, both of whom had attended Georgia Tech.

"And did you hear about Appalachian State beating Michigan?" my mom asked.

"No."

I had another cousin who attended Appalachian State. I took both of these major upsets as signs from God that my "123" eating habits were correct. Georgia Tech defeating Notre Dame was believable, but Appalachian State beating Michigan was about as close to a divine miracle as changing water into wine. There was no doubt in my mind that my behavior had influenced the outcome of these games.

I felt good about the way things were shaping up. This eating habit was just a form of self-control. I could handle it, and I could stand losing the weight. In July I weighed 210 pounds. By September I was down to 180 and still dropping on what couldn't have been much more than a 1,000-calorie-a-day diet. It was tough, and the side effects of Zyprexa didn't help, but no one said the road to Lane's heart would be without speed bumps, nor did I expect the path to the White House to be a cakewalk. The thing was, I didn't even want to be president. I had never seriously considered politics.

Hell, I wasn't even a registered voter. But that's the way it was. It would be selfish of me not to sacrifice my God-given talent for my country. It was my patriotic duty to fulfill this prophecy. I had to be president.

I continued this eating pattern for ten more days, one day for each of the ten children Lane and I were going to have. My children's future successes were determined by what I ate. They would be given the same opportunity as me. Despite my pathetic circumstances, I felt like the luckiest man in the world. Someday I would spend the rest of my life with Lane, and someday I would be the most powerful man in the free world.

The days passed slowly in the psych ward. There is an odd combination of tension and calmness present in all the psych wards I have spent time in. Many patients seem to make it a second home by playing games, watching television, and generally attempting to befriend other patients. On the other hand, some patients scarcely talk. Instead, they roam the hallways with their heads down, barely speaking.

On this occasion I was all business. This was how the future President of the United States should act. I rarely spoke with anyone and frequently was a complete ass to anyone who attempted to enter my bubble. For example, a regular activity in all psychiatric wards is the trading or sharing of food. Often people don't want a particular item on their tray, so a voice calls out, "Salad for your dessert!" and the deal is sealed.

Just as frequently, scavengers will do anything for extra food, attempting to get it for nothing. In my past visits I had always been forthcoming with giving away my food, but this time I steadfastly refused, which made me unpopular with many of the other patients. Why I did this I'm not exactly sure, but it stemmed from my not getting anything in return; it was not a fair trade. Though I was never a very strong negotiator even in my days as a commercial real estate agent, I was trying to improve and felt that this was a small step in that direction. It was about being firm about what was rightfully mine. One time, after I refused to give away my food, someone said, "I can tell that you aren't going to vote for Obama."

To leave the hospital, I had to be compliant with my medication. The average patient probably just lied and said they would take medication when released. On the other hand, I was trying to be honest, how else would the future President of the United States act? The hospital took me to court, which was held on a weekly basis right in the hospital for patients who demanded their release or refused to take medication. However, I was different. I wasn't either demanding my release or refusing my medication. I made it abundantly clear that I would stay in the hospital indefinitely until they released me on my own recognizance. No President could be on mental-health medication.

I was taken in front of the judge, who, as expected, did not release me under these circumstances. I didn't protest; I simply went back to my bed and lay down. It wasn't going to be easy, but I was determined to get my way. There was no way that I could win Lane's heart nor be President if I was on medication. In my mind, that was just the way it was.

However, there were obstacles. The hospital could not release me due to the Mental Hygiene Law, commonly referred to as "Kendra's Law," named for Kendra Dale, a young woman who died in 1999 after being pushed in front of a New York City subway train by a person living in the community at the time but not receiving treatment for his mental illness.

A compromise was sought. I was to be discharged under the supervision of the Assisted Outpatient Treatment Program (AOT). I would report to the program six times a month by attending biweekly meetings at the hospital; if I didn't participate, the doctor and/or social worker would visit my apartment to make sure I was still sane. I didn't like it, but I did appreciate the flexibility that everyone was showing me, and, to be honest, I wasn't positive that I could maintain my life without medication, but I wanted one last try. If it didn't work out, I swore that I would take my medication until the end of time. After spending an additional two weeks in the hospital, I was admitted into the program and discharged on October 15, 2007.

CHAPTER 18

I f I were going to be President of the United States, I needed to distinguish myself in other ways than just being a fiction writer. Ernest Hemingway may be the most intriguing writer in American history, but I've never heard anyone say that he should have been the president. Though writing was how I wanted to spend my life, I've always felt that to be a successful writer I needed plenty of outside stimulus. My undergraduate degree from the University of Georgia is in business administration. My first ten years out of college I primarily worked in marketing. I thought possibly I could work for the family business, a steel fabrication plant in Cleveland, Tennessee.

However, this was not my decision. I am a shareholder, but the business is on my mother's side of the family. In my warped mind I imagined myself working as the right-hand man to my cousin Mark White, and then we would flip-flop when I became President of the United States and he became vice president. It smelled like nepotism, but all the rules were off. I was Benton Savage, dammit!

But all of that was out of my control. Despite my long-term ambitions, I needed to focus on the present. I needed to focus on the things I could control, and I felt that my frugality would be rewarded by future wealth. After all, I was being judged. Every move I made outside my apartment was being watched by society. Inside my apartment,

Lane had somehow installed hidden cameras and was judging me in my private life. I can't tell you how stressful it was to live under those conditions. Every single action I took was being watched and analyzed. It drove me mad—the restrictions I imposed on myself. But in my mind all these sacrifices meant that I was doing well. I believed that I had cracked the code. I believed I was acing the test.

Even though I didn't think I was truly bipolar, there was no doubt in my mind that I was wired a little differently from the average person. Obviously, I could no longer take drugs. I also decided to give up alcohol, and, reluctantly, cigarettes as well. Even one cigarette could kill my dreams. The main reason was that some people called them "cowboy killers." That was how I viewed myself, as a cowboy, and once again I had the crazy thought that I could not have sex with Lane if I didn't live a clean and sober life. One slipup, and it would be a life without sex. I had dug myself a hole, and being perfect was the only way out. I wasn't even planning on drinking regular coffee; it was only decaf for me. Coca-Cola was to be my only vice, and I was only going to drink two a day: one at lunch and one at dinner, with one decaf coffee at breakfast and one after dinner. This behavior stemmed from my boss's screensaver reading "Drink More Coke," and my dad showing me 2 × 2 = 4 on the calculator shortly before he died. Though I convinced the hospital at the time of my release that I was sane, I was not.

I was trying to become the richest man in the world. I had to do things a little bit differently to reach this dream. I bought the cheapest cleaning products for my house, including the cheapest detergent, Ajax. I figured every product was basically the same anyway. Money spent on advertising is what drove up the price. I bought the cheapest toilet paper. I didn't turn on my heat. The fall can be cold in New York, but instead of using heat, I wore a coat. I didn't use shampoo. I used bar soap to wash my hair. I rarely brushed my teeth. I wore the same clothes every day—blue button down and khaki pants. Just like only having two Cokes and two coffees a day, I only watched two shows a day. The local and national news. Given my future, I figured the least that I could do was follow current events.

I only listened to two CDs, Jimmy Buffett and Jack Johnson. Serious rock and roll was out. The messages from that kind of music could shake my future children's values. I don't know why I believed that, but my best guess is I watched the movie 'Footloose' too many times. The lyrics to Jimmy Buffett affected me as well. I had grown up on Buffett. That was practically the only music my dad listened to. I had not liked it growing up. But when I told my dad this, he replied, "Trust me, son. Someday you will."

As I listened to Buffett's Greatest Hits album, I once again heard eerie similarities in my lifestyle to his songs. For instance, in 'Cheeseburger in Paradise' the words read:

> Tried to amend my carnivorous habits
>
> Made it nearly <u>seventy days</u>
>
> <u>Losin' weight without speed, eatin' sunflower seeds</u>
>
> <u>Drinkin' lots of carrot juice and soakin' up rays</u>
>
> But at night I'd have these wonderful dreams
>
> Some kind of sensuous treat
>
> Not zucchini, fettucini, or bulgar wheat
>
> But a big warm bun and a huge hunk of meat
>
> Cheeseburger in paradise
>
> Heaven on Earth, with an onion slice
>
> Not too particular, not too precise
>
> I'm just a cheeseburger in paradise
>
> <u>Heard about the oldtime sailor men</u>

<u>They eat the same thing again and again</u>

<u>Warm beer and bread they said could raise the dead</u>

Well it reminds me of the menu at a Holiday Inn

But times change, sailors these days

When I'm in port I get what I need

Not just havanas or bananas or daquiris

But the American creation on which I feed

The last verse reads:

Worth every damn bit of sacrifice to get a

Cheeseburger in Paradise

I had been discharged from the hospital on October 15, which meant there were seventy days until December 25. In my mind, I had already etched Christmas as the day when Lane and I would be together, and this song only reinforced it. I would be tested for seventy days. This was too much of a coincidence to overlook. I was not alone. Other people had gone through the same situation. The difference was that I was going to do better than anyone else. I was going to be the best of all time.

I listened more closely to the song. I had never really paid attention to the lyrics, even though I had heard it hundreds of times growing up. When Buffett sings about "the old-time sailor men" who "eat the same thing again and again," I thought about how, for three weeks at that point, I had eaten almost nothing but taco salads. This was before I made the connection with the lyrics. I had eaten only one thing by instinct. I thought this was genius. Buffett had found himself in the same position as me, but instead of eating taco salads, he ate sunflower seeds and drank carrot juice. He had not told anyone else about his future wife at the time, so he was trying to win her heart all by himself.

Instead of considering himself a "cowboy," like me, he related to the "sailor men." I thought it was safe to say that sailors and cowboys came from the same mold, just from different geographic locations.

Suddenly, I didn't feel sorry for myself anymore. Taco salads and Coca-Cola were much more nourishing than carrot juice and sunflower seeds. Then a thought came to mind: maybe to break the code, I was supposed to eat a cheeseburger. I had been dreaming about paradise. Maybe it was "worth every bit of sacrifice to get a cheeseburger in paradise." Maybe I didn't have to wait until Christmas. Maybe this was the exact reason my dad listened to Jimmy Buffett—he was trying to help me. I felt great pride in having such a great dad. I was not going to let him down.

I grabbed my wallet and bolted for the closest McDonald's. I ordered a double quarter pounder with cheese and expected to see Lane at any moment. Of course, when I finished, Lane had not arrived. Disappointed, I slinked back to my apartment. Then another thought came to mind: maybe I was supposed to eat cheeseburgers at every meal until Christmas. It sounded disgusting, to be honest. I had recently seen the documentary *Super Size Me*, which told the story of a man who ate only from the McDonald's menu for a month and what happened to his body and health.

However, I went back for dinner. Only problem was, the soda fountain was down, so they could only serve noncarbonated Fruitopia, no Coca-Cola. That stopped me in my tracks. I had been drinking only Coca-Cola and decaf coffee for three weeks: no water, no juice, not even a Dr Pepper, my favorite soft drink. Could this be a sign that I should not be at McDonald's? Could Lane have known what I was up to and gotten McDonald's in cahoots so that I would stop eating there? I ordered a burger to go and walked back to my apartment, freaked out.

A few minutes after finishing the burger I received a call from my mom. "How are you doing, Benton?" she asked.

"Good," I said hesitantly. I was still nervous about my mom standing in my way of sheer bliss.

"How's the weight?" she asked.

"Good, I guess. I haven't weighed myself recently."

"What did you have for dinner?"

"McDonald's."

"McDonald's! Why's that?"

"Just felt like it."

"You certainly aren't going to stay thin on that diet."

A few minutes later I hung up. All right, I get it. Lane had been watching me and called my mom to tell her what I was up to. Then I had another thought: maybe my mom was on my side. If she and Lane had been conspiring together, they had to be on the same side. This felt good. People communicated in different ways; I just had to learn how a person communicated. That idea was right up my alley. I had been reading things into what people said for years. I was on the right track.

I had only eaten at McDonald's twice. Three times would have been too many, just like in baseball: three strikes and you're out. I learned from my mistake and went back to eating taco salad. Not much different, they're both hamburger meat.

In the second week of November, my sister was throwing a birthday party for my nephew in Bethesda, Maryland. His birthday fell on November 11. The numbers 11/11 held special meaning for me, so I thought my sister had planned the date as a sign. She had scheduled a preplanned labor induction for that day two years earlier when Wells was born, so she had chosen the birth date.

As I mentioned, I thought I was 66, which meant ten children and fifty-six grandchildren. Now I moved it up a notch. With the date 11/11, I believed I would have eleven children, and each of my children would have eleven children. This made complete sense to me. When I had asked Lane to marry me, I had joked that she probably wanted a football team of boys. Despite the joke, that was exactly what I thought would happen.

The weekend at my sister's went exceptionally well. It had been four weeks since my release from the hospital, and I was at the peak of my mania. I was funny, energetic, and sharp. In short, I was a joy to be around, and everyone complimented me on how well I was doing. Outwardly, I appeared to be doing well, but in reality my version of events was becoming completely distorted.

As I sat in a chair waiting for my train at Union Station in Washington, D.C., the screen reporting arrivals and departures showed that my train was running thirty-five minutes late. I took this as a sign, since a person must be thirty-five years old to run for president, and that was exactly my age. The significance of this was compounded by the fact that Amtrak trains only sold Pepsi products. I felt my candidacy would be compromised if I drank anything other than Coca-Cola, so I refrained from drinking sodas for the entire trip back to New York.

My mind wandered from thoughts of spending the rest of my life with Lane to greedier considerations. If I was going to be the richest man in the world, how was I going to make all that money? I wasn't worried, it was a foregone conclusion, but I was curious. Since the family business was in steel fabrication, I had many options for generating vast wealth. My mind immediately turned to the troubled American automobile industry, which clearly fell under the umbrella of steel fabrication. I pictured us buying out Chrysler and transforming it into something as great as Mercedes-Benz, thereby bringing automobile manufacturing back to the United States.

We could also make refrigerators, stoves, dishwashers, washers, dryers, blenders, microwaves, radios, and televisions. We would be like General Electric and General Motors combined. But even that wasn't enough. I also included Coca-Cola. I didn't know if aluminum fabrication fell under the category of steel fabrication, but I gave us the benefit of the doubt.

So now we were going to be bigger than GE, GM, and Coke. But that wasn't enough. I wanted more. I wanted to create an empire that would never topple. I wanted a company big enough so that all my eleven children could work and make a difference. I wanted a place where all of my one hundred twenty-one grandchildren could work. I wanted to create a world where Savages spanned the globe. I wanted the last person living to be a Savage. I thought that sounded like a great joke. Savages running the world!

When I received a letter from the New York Finance Department with a tax bill requesting payment, I read the enclosed information closely. At the top of the page it read, "Save Water." I wondered what it meant. I thought it was another sign. Yes, that was it. Along with steel fabrication, the family could monopolize the water supply. Pipes may be cast iron, but I figured, what the hell—I had already included aluminum in our company's future plans. Water was certainly an industry that was never going to die. But I wondered: how could I weasel my way into controlling the water supply? I was no longer drinking water, which I believed was a step in the right direction. Not even ice with my Cokes. Then I had an idea. I would stop using water altogether, or at least as little as humanly possible. No more showers. No more brushing my teeth. No more running the dishwasher. Only wash dishes with as little water as possible. Then I came up with the big one. No more flushing the toilet. This was the final step in my mastering of the universal business world. These things were done. On the eighth day I rested.

My financial advisor called the week before Thanksgiving. We were going to have our semiannual get-together to sit down and discuss finances. We were to meet at his Midtown office. I wondered if he knew that I was going to be the richest man in the world someday. When this day came, it would certainly affect his lifestyle and income as well. I thought of how not only I was going to be extraordinarily wealthy, I was also going to make those close to me rich as well. Beautiful woman. Eleven children. One hundred twenty-one grandchildren. Richest man in the world. Tons of friends who appreciated what I had done to improve their lives. Nobel Prize–winning author. President of the United States. It was good to be Benton Savage. But still I wanted more.

At the meeting with my financial advisor, who was very good at what he did, we decided to transfer a substantial amount of my money into bonds rather than stocks, and this was at a time when the Dow Jones had peaked at 14,000. We talked a while, and I asked a lot of questions. Though I considered myself an astute investor, mainly because I had read about the world economy consistently for the past ten years, I was no match for my advisor's knowledge, so I enjoyed picking his brain. I needed to learn more, and he was patient when I asked him everything I could think of. After all, the richest man in the world needs to be prudent, right? Toward the end of the meeting, I looked at his desk and saw a fraternity magazine with Warren Buffett on the cover.

"Warren Buffett was in my fraternity," said John.

"He went to Penn State?" I asked.

"No. He went somewhere else, but we're still brothers."

"Interesting."

When I returned from the meeting, a solicitation letter from Washington Mutual in Omaha, Nebraska, was in the mail. Warren Buffett is known as the Oracle of Omaha, and I took this as a sign that I was doing well, that someday I would replace him as the richest man in the United States. Of course, "Washington Mutual" had meaning too. I could have received mail from any credit card company, but Washington Mutual was a sign from Lane that she wanted me to be president of the United States. Lane was sending messages through my mail. It was "mutual."

I wondered how I was going to manage the world, be a good husband, raise eleven children, write all my books, and still have time for my favorite leisure activity, which was reading good literature. No doubt I was going to be busy, but I assumed I would hire good people and make only the important decisions. Not bad for a guy who had barely graduated from college and who at one time was thought to have an acute mental disorder. I was proving the doubters wrong.

I spent Thanksgiving by myself. My mom traveled to spend time with my stepfather's family, and my sister had plans as well. I didn't even eat turkey. Instead, I had a taco salad, which surprisingly was not getting old. I heaped piles of cheese, sour cream, tomatoes, lettuce, onions, and green peppers onto my plate.

By the weekend after Thanksgiving, my mind was all over the place. I was making lists, doing chores, organizing my file cabinet, paying bills, and still working frantically on my novel, which I hoped to complete by Christmas. I wanted to hit the ground running by the time Lane and I were reunited.

I was trying to cover all my bases. Then I thought of an area in my life I had been neglecting. This whole time I hadn't gone to church. In fact, I had never been to church since moving to New York. Religion is not a popular subject in the Big Apple, at least not in my circle of friends. However, I had noted a Presbyterian church in my neighborhood, and that Sunday I walked several blocks to the church and took a seat in a pew.

I was so wound up I could barely follow the service. When Communion was served, I took part. Then I thought about what Communion meant. I knew I wasn't God or the Second Coming, mainly because when I was much younger, there had been a young man at my church who believed at one time that he was Jesus Christ. I remembered how ridiculous I thought that was, and I didn't want to be thought of in the same way. Still, everything I was seeing seemed to push me in that direction. I didn't want to believe it. I knew it wasn't right, but still . . .

After church I realized I needed to have my own Communion. I needed to cook something and serve Coca-Cola. I imagined my disciples as my close friends, my groomsmen at our wedding. I searched through my cookbook for the perfect dish to serve. Finally, I found a recipe for maple brown sugar turkey that served twelve. I immediately went to the grocery store, bought a turkey, and stored it in my refrigerator. I didn't know when I would cook it, but I was confident that I would see the sign when the time came.

The next few days I was in frantic preparation as I tried to tie up all the loose ends in my life. During my three months locked away in the mental hospital, I hadn't paid some bills and was getting letters from collectors. Obviously, I had to straighten this out. Who had ever heard of the richest man in the world having credit problems? At the same time, I believed my credit problems would be erased because I hit the number 23, or had I already? It was difficult to tell. I wasn't sure. I checked my credit online. It was in shambles.

As I went through the information on my computer screen, I stumbled across a segment showing that I had a J. Crew credit card. I didn't even remember ever shopping at J. Crew, but I immediately saw it as a sign. Lane's last name was Johnson, which of course began with J. This signaled to me that Lane still wasn't convinced I was completely on board, that I wasn't fully committed to being part of the "J. Crew."

I looked up J. Crew in the phone book and found the closest store. Without wasting a moment, I took a taxi down to Midtown and bought J. Crew plaid button-downs, J. Crew corduroy pants, a J. Crew belt, and J. Crew socks. I don't think they carried underwear, though I'm not sure. I wore Banana Republic boxers, which I thought was a solid choice, at least it was my personal touch.

Now that I was officially the winner of the "Geek of the Year" award by becoming an outstanding member of the J. Crew, I felt settled. But still, where was Lane? What did I have to do to convince her? I could always cook the turkey, but what day? For some reason I decided on Thursday. It was Monday at this point.

I also wanted to give Lane something special, a personal touch from me, something I had never done for another girl, something that would show her she was more important than all the accolades I was going to receive in my triumphant life.

I decided I would write her a poem telling her how I felt. I had never written a poem for a girl; for that matter, I didn't recall ever writing a poem at all. I didn't even understand poetry, but that made no difference. Surely I could write one measly poem professing my love for Lane.

I went to the Public Library on 39th Street to read some examples of good poetry that I could incorporate into my own work. I had been going to the library rather than the bookstore for my reading material. I feared that I couldn't buy books from the bookstore anymore. I was afraid that if I bought books at the bookstore, eventually I wouldn't be allowed to read. I thought writers didn't read books. I believed one of the rules of being a writer was that you couldn't surf other people's literature in search of story ideas. I didn't like this, but I didn't write the rules; I just tried to play by them.

Of course, I was only going to check out two collections. I was doing everything in twos by this point. If I had a selection of three items to choose from, I always took the second option. I thought of it as being on a team. There were ones. Others like myself were twos. And then there were also threes and fours.

I chose poetry by Sylvia Plath and Charles Bukowski. Both were two of my favorite prose writers, and I had wanted to read their poetry for some time but had just never gotten around to it. As I flipped through the pages of both books, I quickly realized that I couldn't have picked more opposite poets. I should have figured as much judging from their prose, but I really wasn't thinking.

I couldn't even vaguely understand what Sylvia Plath was trying to say. I suppose that was part of her genius, but I simply did not get it. As for Bukowski, I liked his work right away. His poetry was everything I liked. It wasn't even really like poetry but more like quick anecdotes that often made me laugh or at least smile. I planned to use a combination of the two. For one, I wanted my poetry to rhyme. I'm not talking limericks, but I wanted a rhythm to my work.

I put off writing the poem until the end of the day, after I had done absolutely everything possible to avoid it. Finally, I laid down the book and got to work.

Resurrection

Driving down the road not sure when it happened

Talking and contrasting the difference between sin and religion

To everyone else it seemed like I was bent

As for me I believed that you were Heaven sent

Then you left and studied across the sea

In my heart this brought misery

I moved to Atlanta and tried harder to find the meaning of love

So when my time came you would think that I came from above

Things warped in my state of mind

I was sure that we were meant to be together until the end of time

Showed up at your apartment and nothing else was hidden

Next thing I know I was snake bitten

In the following days chaos reigned supreme

I sunk so low that I was sure I lost the dream

When I didn't see you for many a year

I felt no regret I didn't shed a tear

Don't remember the exact date but it was the first week of July

When I realized my goddess may have returned from the sky

In the beginning I felt like such a fool

Knowing that all my friends knew from the old school

Now I know what is important to me

To spend as much time with you and my family.

I chose eleven stanzas for the poem to signal the number of children we were going to have and two lines per stanza to represent the next generation of grandchildren. It wasn't great, I realized that—but at least it was completed, and I thought I could sleep well. However, my mind was ticking like a clock and kept coming up with rhymes. In my tattered state of mind, I began to understand why so many poets committed suicide. It was driving me crazy, and I had only written one, and not even a good one at that.

Over the next two days I wrote fourteen more poems on many different subjects, but all contained nuggets of information I wanted to share with Lane. When I finally exhausted all my ideas, I realized the fifteen poems represented the number of kids we were going to have. I had to stop myself. Fifteen kids were enough. What was I going to put this woman through for the sake of my own ego? I tried to sleep, but I couldn't stop thinking about poetry. Though in reality my work wasn't very good, I thought it was a good start and added "Poet Laureate" to the list of accolades I hoped to attain in my lifetime.

It was now Thursday. It was time to cook the turkey. I was positive I had done enough. All I had to do was cook this fifteen-pound turkey. I imagined Lane ringing my bell at exactly five o'clock on Friday, but I also had to clean up the apartment and needed to get an enormous pot so I could marinate the turkey. I went to the "everything" store across the street and bought a pot that appropriately said *My Land* on it. Yes, that was the one for me. Then I realized this was going to be a formal dinner with Lane. I needed to buy cloth napkins. After mulling over the choices for at least fifteen minutes, I decided on purple and green napkins with green placemats. I thought green and purple were the colors of royalty. I was pleased with my decision. I added the syrup and brown sugar to the pot and dropped the turkey into it so it could soak up the ingredients. I placed the turkey back into the refrigerator. It would be ready to cook the next day.

I thought more about the poems and how I planned to be both president and poet. Maybe I was only going to be a poet. Then I thought about lower forms of expression. Puns came to mind. Then a mime entered my head as well. Maybe I was supposed to go lower to show my love. Maybe that was what it was all about. I tried to come up with a pun. My mind was racing so fast that it only took a minute to come up with the perfect one.

We will be together until the end of time.

Lane. You are the best friend of mime.

Yes. That was the ticket.

I cleaned my apartment. I needed to free some room in my apartment if Lane was going to move in with me. I looked through my clothes. My weight had dropped down to 165 pounds. The extra-large shirts I wore when I weighed 220 were obviously not needed. I didn't need the large sizes either, but it had been so long since I had been at this weight, I had no mediums. I would have to make do.

As I was looking at the tags, I noted that most of my clothing had been made in China or Malaysia. I thought about my penchant for Asian women. Lane would be jealous if I was wearing clothes manufactured in these countries. Was I supposed to throw these clothes out? Was Lane really that sensitive? I didn't know, but I figured that I should be on the safe side. I began stuffing my clothes into trash bags, and then I stopped halfway. I was being ridiculous. Obviously, I was going to have to use products made in different countries.

I sat on the couch. The phone rang. It was my mom.

"How's everything going, Benton?"

"Going well," I replied.

"Have you done your Christmas shopping?"

"A little."

"I know what I want," said my mom. That was the way I did Christmas with my mom. She told me what she wanted, and I just went out and bought it.

"What's that?"

"There's a perfume that I saw at Neiman Marcus called 'Prada.' I want a five-ounce bottle."

"All right."

"I don't know if you even want to go to Neiman Marcus. Maybe you can get it somewhere else."

"Would you mind if I got you something else altogether?" I asked.

"Well. . .At least tell me if you don't want to get me the perfume so Don can give it to me."

"All right. I'll let you know."

This conversation had messages at many levels. First, the movie *The Devil Wears Prada* came to mind. Was my mom representing the devil? On any account, she was obviously trying to tell me something. I hate to shop, and my mom knew that. But even more important was the fact that she told me to go to Neiman Marcus. Lane and I had never really talked about past love interests that much, but she had mentioned that she had once dated an heir to Neiman Marcus. Yes—I got the picture. Yes, I was not supposed to buy Prada at Neiman Marcus, just as I wasn't supposed to wear clothes that were made in China.

I was becoming extremely territorial. If Lane didn't want me wearing clothing made in Asian countries, then there were probably other things that she didn't want me to have. At the same time, I was trying to balance my presidential ambitions so that I could ensure the United States would remain the most powerful country in the world for the next 1,000 years, which, I might remind you, was Hitler's goal for Germany before World War II. My thoughts immediately moved toward Russia. Though Russia may have seen better days, it was an ambitious country, and Russians were brooding over having been left behind.

I could stop their progress by purging myself of all my Russian literature. I went through my bookshelves and found Tolstoy, Dostoevsky, and Turgenev, picked them up, and shoved them down the trash chute in the hall. Then I moved toward my music, grabbed Tchaikovsky, and threw him down the chute as well. And just like that, I had eliminated Russia as a threat for the next 1,000 years.

On Friday I placed the turkey in the oven at 2:00 p.m. Afterwards I frantically cleaned my apartment. I vacuumed. I dusted. I mopped and wiped down the kitchen and bathroom. Everything was going to be just perfect. Around 4:00 p.m. I admired my apartment, but as I looked around I was not completely satisfied. I saw my No. 34 University of Georgia Herschel Walker helmet. I love Herschel Walker. He's my favorite football player of all time, and he probably had as much influence over my attending the University of Georgia as anything else. But now, as I looked at this helmet displayed in my living room, I no longer revered Herschel. I now looked at him as a threat. I didn't want the gear of a rival on display right in front of Lane. I imagined Herschel kissing Lane in front of me. This is ridiculous, I thought. How could Herschel possibly kiss Lane? But I wasn't taking any chances. I picked up the helmet, marched out the door, down the steps, and to the trashcans in the basement. I hated doing this to Herschel, but it just had to be done. I couldn't have Lane thinking I admired Herschel more than myself.

At five o'clock I took the turkey out of the oven. Still there was no Lane. Was it possible that I had been wrong again? Was it possible that she wasn't going to show? The idea was becoming more real. However, I carved the turkey. I imagined myself surrounded by my beautiful wife and fifteen children on Thanksgiving. I did not even take a bite of the turkey as I worked, so I wouldn't have eaten before Lane arrived. At seven o'clock I finished. I boiled some broccoli and ate the turkey, which I must admit tasted divine. I was so tired from all of the work that I lay on my couch and finally turned on the television. Strangely, I was not depressed in the least. I had no doubt that Lane and I were edging our way closer to a lifetime of bliss. If it wasn't today, it would start tomorrow. If it wasn't tomorrow, it would be the next day. Just like a regular Thanksgiving, an hour later I grew sleepy and soon fell sound asleep.

CHAPTER 19

The next couple of days were filled with football and eating fifteen pounds of turkey, which I ate with no vegetables and only Coca-Cola. By this time I was drinking regular coffee, mainly because Lane loved coffee. I thought it would be our daily ritual to drink coffee together every morning at eight o'clock after we had taken our kids to school. It would be our time together. We would drink our coffee and discuss the day's calendar.

I was positive that Lane was watching my every move. Somehow Lane had wired into my computer so that she was even reading what I wrote. I began to have silent conversations with her over the computer, telling her what I was thinking as I typed. I wrote about how I wanted to spend my life and my days. With fifteen kids, it seemed we would never have time for each other. I wanted us to set aside a specific time of day when we could devote uninterrupted time to just the two of us.

My mind was racing all over the place. Everything I saw was another sign. I went to the drugstore to pick up cleaning products. Walking through the store, I came upon a twenty-pack roll of paper towels called "Sparkle." I took this to mean that I was supposed to clean my apartment until it "sparkled." I picked up the jumbo pack of paper towels and then hunted for more cleaning supplies. I came across the sponges. Scotch-Brite stuck out to me as well. Lane had studied in

Scotland when she was in college. Had she been planning for this exact moment since she was in college? Had she known that someday I would be living in New York trying to get my apartment to "sparkle" using a Scotch-Brite sponge? Yes. That was exactly it.

I bought supplies as if I were preparing to house fifteen children, and, of course, man and wife. I went back to my apartment, ate some more turkey, and brewed a cup of coffee. I imagined Lane and me sitting around a table the size one finds in a Fortune 500 boardroom with our fifteen children, sipping our coffees as we finished our dinner.

I noticed that my lips had begun to chap and wondered why, but decided I was probably licking them because of the intense pressure I had placed on myself. To offset the pain, I began to clean. This time I was fine-tuning my cleaning. I cleaned the stove, refrigerator, and dishwasher with the Scotch-Brite sponges. I believed I was gaining monetary value by cleaning all the products we would sell from our steel-fabrication business.

As I looked around the apartment, I realized I had all kinds of items produced by other men: my collection of compact discs, my many books. I liked to read every night just before I went to bed, but I couldn't read Ernest Hemingway while I was lying beside Lane. That would be practically as bad as bringing a third party to our nocturnal activities, activities I imagined would last several hours each night, since people didn't sleep the entire night. There would be no fake sleep for us. We were going to slave to fulfill each other's lusts.

I stuffed my books and compact discs into trash bags and placed them in the corner. This was difficult; I did not want to throw my books away. Once again, I looked around the apartment. Since I hated to shop, Mom had bought me all kinds of clothes. They would not do either. I was only going to wear J. Crew. And just like that I started stuffing my clothes into more trash bags, sparing nothing—not even underwear. Since I didn't have any J. Crew underwear, I was going commando.

But what was I going to do with all these things? I couldn't just stack them in the corner of my room; that would look like I was only playing a game, that I was not serious about starting my life fresh, that I really wanted to keep these things. I decided the next morning to take my clothes to the Salvation Army just down the street. If I gave my clothes to the Salvation Army, then the family business could pursue clothing lines. We would become as big and respected as Brooks Brothers. Our greatness knew no boundaries.

And just like that I was clearing out my entire apartment. Everything had to go. Everything reminded me of my past life. I pulled pictures off the wall and stacked them in a corner of my den. Then I wrapped my glasses, silverware, and plates in clothes so they wouldn't cut the garbage men or my superintendent. I worked at a furious pace. Lane was watching. The quicker I finished the job, the quicker I would be with Lane.

At the same time, I didn't want my neighbors to know what I was up to. I waited until after midnight to haul my things down to the trash in the basement. Instead of taking the elevator like a sane person, I walked the three flights of stairs carrying bags in each hand. I thought that if I didn't take the elevator, we could get into the elevator business. I piled the trash bags in the basement, wondering what the super would think when he found them, but I wasn't concerned. The entire time I was doing this, all I could think about was how I had done the same thing in California nine years before. Instead of remembering the futility and the pain that came with that behavior, I could only think of how close I had been to winning Lane last time. If I had only finished the job then, I wouldn't have had to wait nine more years. But this time it would work. Nothing would stop me. Halfway finished, and after using forty trash bags, I plunged into bed for a deep sleep.

Sleep did nothing to slow my ambitions. I woke with a burst of energy and continued working. I went to the Salvation Army and dropped off the clothes. Whoever got them had hit the jackpot. I had some nice suits and shirts that I reluctantly gave away. Even the workers at the store gave me a strange look. I must have looked like an animal in heat, probably the eye of the tiger.

That night I sat down for dinner. It was Tuesday. Five days after I had cooked the bird, I still had tons left. I decided I needed to finish it. Since my silverware was packed away, I stuffed my face with my bare hands and washed it down with Coke. I decided to cheat a little. Up to this point I had never drunk more than two canned Cokes in a day. Instead of drinking two cans, I bought two two-liter Cokes. I sat at my dinner table, forced the turkey down my throat, and swilled the two large Cokes until I felt like I was going to pop.

By this time I needed to get everything I could out of my apartment. Nothing could be spared but fixtures and things I couldn't move on my own, like the couch and bed. Everything I owned was either at the Salvation Army or in the basement. No one could even reach the three recycling bins down there because of the seventy trash bags I had piled on top of each other. Practically the only thing I had not deposited was my computer, which, of course, stored nine years of writing. Then it came to me: I had to erase what I had written. I couldn't take intellectual property with me either.

Giving the notion no more than fifteen seconds of consideration, I marched over and deleted all the files from my computer, then emptied the trash bin as well. Two completed books were gone, along with three partial books and, of course, the poems I had written for Lane. They were gone forever, but I must admit that since I believed Lane was reading what I wrote, I assumed she had probably saved the files. This was the only game I played in this scenario. It was one thing to dispose of material goods. Money could buy them back. But my writing, that was blood, sweat, and tears. After erasing my work, I lay down on my bed. I had seriously raised the bar. Lane, you'd better have my back, I thought.

I woke up late on Thursday, angry at myself for oversleeping. What would it take for me to grow up and quit wasting time in bed? I guessed I wasn't there yet. I walked down to the basement to see if the superintendent had moved the bags outside for the city to pick up, but he had not. As I stared at the pile, I realized I was inconveniencing Manuel with this stunt. He didn't want to move that stuff, and I didn't want him to have to do it. Just like that, I carried all the garbage bags back up three flights of stairs and stacked them along the side of the living room so I'd still have room to walk. I was so focused it didn't even feel tiring. I was in the zone.

I made myself a cup of coffee, sat down at the table, and relaxed. My lips were so chapped it hurt to open my mouth. In the bathroom mirror I saw they were swollen and starting to scab. Surely this couldn't have happened just from licking them to ease the tension. Then I thought about the Arabian coffee I was drinking. It must have been poisoned. Lane had set me up to tell me I shouldn't be doing business with the Arabs, whether by drinking their coffee or buying my morning paper at the Pakistani-owned bodega down the block. I grabbed the bag of coffee and tossed it into the trash. Imagine me, the future President of the United States, drinking Arabian coffee. I might as well have been supporting terrorists.

I went back to the grocery store to find more coffee. I scanned the shelves, trying to decide which to buy. I wanted something good. Lane liked coffee, and I pictured it being our ritual, enjoying a cup together while reminiscing about how we had the world by the balls. Finally, I settled on Taster's Choice. Not because I thought instant coffee was any good, but because it was the most expensive. Naturally, I bought two jars.

The instant coffee was awful, but I forced it down and decided we could figure out the brand later. I had bigger fish to fry, like deciding what to do next. First, I needed to eat, but I had already thrown all my food and cooking utensils into bags. I wasn't about to dig through seventy garbage bags to find them.

Bored, with nothing to do or even look at in my apartment, I went back to the basement to see if Manuel had cleared out the recycling and trash. Sure enough, he had. In their place sat a Ray's Pizza box with a plastic bag draped over it that read "Thank You." That was the sign I'd been waiting for. Ray's Pizza was where I was supposed to eat, and I had made a friend out of Manuel by not forcing him to lug all my junk to the curb.

The pepperoni pizza at Ray's cost $15.50. Not surprisingly, I took the fifteen to signify the number of kids we would have. I sat down at my table, ate two slices, and thought about what to do next. I wanted everything to be perfect. Over the next few hours I dotted the i's and crossed the t's, erasing everyone from my email list and disposing of my contact lenses, opting for eyeglasses instead. Then I looked at the brand of my cellphone. It was an LG, made in Korea. That wouldn't do. I pounded the phone on the kitchen counter until it was unusable, then threw it in the trash.

What was left to do? The only things in my apartment that were not in trash bags, besides appliances, were a picture of my mom and stepdad, a DVD of my sister's wedding, and two Bibles still sitting on my bookcase. Lane may have been an atheist, but I knew enough about this country to realize the president of the United States must at least pretend he believes in God.

That evening I checked the messages on my home phone: I had missed a call from my coke dealer. What did it mean? He lived in Harlem. I took that to mean I was supposed to walk north toward Harlem, Lane would pick me up in the car, and then we would dash off into the sunset. Without wasting a minute, I walked outside with only my keys and wallet.

Despite living on the cusp of Spanish Harlem, I had never walked through Upper Manhattan. I had no idea where I was going, but I knew that I had to do it. As I wandered the streets heading north, I felt that the whole world was watching me. This idea was cemented by the odd looks I was receiving from the inhabitants. Though I didn't think of it at the time, of course I was getting strange looks, I was the only piece of white bread on the street.

For some reason, the entire time I couldn't dispose of the notion that maybe I could end this game by setting my keys and wallet on the tire of a car. I believed Lane would recognize this gesture and, in turn, reward me for my bravery by picking me up in her car. But I was scared. I wasn't positive I had to do this. It was only a notion, and I had seen no sign to indicate I should try to conquer the world on my own without any money or identification. It was after midnight by the time I reached 200th Street. I had walked roughly five miles. Realizing the futility of my efforts, I finally gave up, turned around, and walked back. I was exhausted and fell fast asleep.

The next day was December 7, the anniversary of the bombing of Pearl Harbor. Once again I slept late. I ate two slices of pizza and looked out my window to see what the weather was like. Parked right in front of the apartment was a white van that said "Lucky Plumbing," with several sevens in the posted phone number. Yup, that was the sign I was looking for. Without a doubt I was supposed to place my keys and wallet on the back left tire and walk out into the world with only my J.Crew apparel. I waited an hour to make sure this was the right move. When the van didn't move, I knew I had to do it. There wasn't any doubt this had to be done.

At 1:15 on the dot, I walked out the front door of my apartment and placed my keys and wallet on the back left tire of the Lucky Plumbing van. I was free. I had nothing left except the clothes on my back. It felt exhilarating.

Instead of heading north toward Harlem, I walked south on Second Avenue, having no idea how far I would have to go but knowing it didn't matter. I was playing for keeps. I thought of all the places that lay in my path to where Lane might be. I hoped it wouldn't be too far. My feet were aching, and I knew that wasn't a good sign. By the time I walked through Midtown, I was growing weary, but I was still confident. My movements were being monitored, and if anything bad happened, I would certainly be rescued.

Then I came up with a thought: what if I urinated on myself? It could happen. I had no idea where the closest public restroom was. Maybe that was what I was supposed to do. I thought of the lyrics to a song. The phrase "Golden Shower of Devotion" came to mind. Was this a way to show my love, by holding it until I could hold it no longer? I didn't know, but I sure as hell wasn't going to pee on myself until I absolutely had to.

I needed rest. I decided to walk to the intersection of First Avenue and First Street. It sounded like as good a place as any to wait for Lane. There was a subway station at the intersection and a small park with benches to sit on. Yes, this was the place. The search was over. If it wasn't, I didn't care. I wasn't moving any farther. I planned on sitting there until the end of time if I had to. I was out of tricks.

Five minutes later, a man walked up the stairs from the subway and announced that the park was closed. Everyone had to leave. I sat there a minute longer. I thought that, given my status, maybe I was exempt from this condition.

"Get along, fellow," said the gatekeeper.

Reluctantly I stood up and walked away. Now I was nervous. Where should I go? A cousin had given me a gift card from Land's End that I had never used and that was still in my apartment. It sounded like as good a place as any. I headed south with the intention of finding the southern tip of Manhattan. That would be the place. Hopefully there would be a bench. I knew from past experience that the biggest problem about being homeless is that there is nowhere to sit. Someone always comes along and shoos you away.

As I walked further, the streets were no longer numbered, and it was getting dark. After a few turns in the New York University area, I had no idea which direction I was heading. I looked for a landmark to signal where to walk next, but it really didn't matter. I didn't know the neighborhood well. I had only been this far Downtown a handful of times in my seven years in New York, and that was for jury duty or to take a real estate exam. I didn't know any of the streets.

The logical thing to do would have been to ask someone for directions, but I absolutely was not going to do that. I feared talking to someone would completely ruin this operation. I didn't go to the bathroom in a restaurant because I didn't want to speak to anyone. I didn't even say excuse me to anyone I bumped into on the crowded streets.

I tried to look at the buildings on the horizon to see if I could figure out which way was north. I was hoping that I could find the Empire State building and walk towards it, but the surrounding buildings were too high. Then I started walking to find the West Side Highway, which runs along the Hudson River on the west side of Manhattan. If I found it, then I knew that I could determine which way was north.

I continued to wander in circles. I saw some of the same buildings more than once. When I got back to Greenwich Village, I regained some of my bearings, but began to wonder what I was going to do. The most reasonable possibility was to call my cousin, who lived in New York City, and retrieve the spare set of keys she was holding, but that was out of the question. Then I came up with a plan. It was the thing that would surely get Lane's attention. There would be denial of that fact.

Finally, I started back north. It was probably around nine o'clock at night, and I had at least five more miles to walk. I decided which bar I would go to. Merrion Square was an Irish bar right across the street from my apartment. At this moment, Merrion Square was a play on the words 'marrying square,' meaning marrying and not using drugs, alcohol, or cigarettes. Had this bar been founded for my sole purpose? I did not know, but it was worth a try. It sure as hell beat my second choice, a bar called the Village Idiot.

As I walked by my apartment, I checked to see if the Lucky Plumbing van was still there, but it wasn't. I didn't even pause to see if my wallet had landed unfound on the street beside it. I walked into Merrion Square. The bar was crowded. I wedged myself into a corner at the bar nearest to the door, which was essential to my plan. It was an Irish bar, and I knew the owner. I had been banned from the premises because I had made fun of the Irish. A slight thorn in my plan, but I wasn't planning on staying long so I wasn't worried.

"Give me two Cokes with no ice," I told the bartender. I was a little concerned about not having any money, but I figured I could just put off the bartender if he asked, which he didn't. The owner walked over. He looked weary of seeing me.

"How's it going, Benton?" he asked.

"Couldn't be better," I replied.

The owner walked away. I moved quickly, guzzling the two Cokes because I knew that if I put off what had to be done, I might lose my nerve. After drinking the Cokes, I unbuttoned my shirt, laid it on the counter, slid off my shoes, took off my pants, laid them on the counter, pushed my boxers around my ankles, and set my eyeglasses on the bar. I was stark naked except for my dark J. Crew socks.

I heard a loud gasp, then laughter, as I quickly walked toward the door. Outside, I was greeted by the bitter cold, but it didn't slow me down. I headed north. Surely Lane would pull up beside me any minute. I imagined her picking me up and us driving away, perhaps to Gatlinburg, Tennessee, to get married. I figured I would leave my socks at the New York–New Jersey state line. Maybe I would even take my long-awaited pee break in a Gatorade bottle and place it on the state line as well. I was taking nothing with me. I was leaving this godforsaken state behind. I imagined winning the presidential election by carrying every state except New York, where I would be so despised that I wouldn't even get one vote, much to the delight of the rest of the country.

As I continued north, I figured I might have to walk to 125th Street, the heart of Harlem. I heard someone on the street yell, "Oh my God! This guy's naked!" I did not turn my head. I walked down the sidewalk on the toes of my socked feet. It was freezing. When I reached Metropolitan Hospital, three blocks up Second Avenue, a cop grabbed me. I was completely caught off guard. It had never crossed my mind that I would be arrested. The only thing that went through my head was not to fight back. Just let things happen. Just go with the flow. I am not in charge. There is a power greater than me.

CHAPTER 20

"What are you doing?" asked the police officer as he grabbed my arm.

I didn't say anything. A second policeman arrived. They hooked my elbows on each side and, without a word, led me into the hospital. The next thing I remember is the officer wrapping a hospital gown around me and seating me in front of a nurse with a computer. I didn't look around, but out of the corner of my eye I sensed many people staring at me.

"What's your name?" the nurse asked.

I knew I had to lie. I could not tell them who I was. Just like that, I answered, "Notneb," which is Benton spelled backward. I had not planned this in the least, it simply popped into my head. The name came from a personalized children's book my parents gave me when I was young. It told the story of Notneb and his pet giraffe traveling around the world together. I had often wondered about the underlying meaning of the book, but now I assumed I was about to find out. The book had been given to me for a reason, and that reason was now. There was only one correct name to give, and that name was Notneb.

"How do you spell it?"

"N-O-T-N-E-B."

"When is your birthday?"

The first lie that came to mind was 6-6-66. But I didn't want that, so I said, "6-6-76."

"What's your address?"

I didn't answer. I didn't want to tell any more lies. If I didn't speak, I couldn't lie.

"What's your last name?"

I remained silent. This went on for a couple of minutes before they gave up and took me to the mental health unit of the emergency room. This was the third time I had been admitted to Metropolitan Hospital in the last ten months. I recognized the security guard but not the nurse at the counter. They told me to sit on a cot.

"We need a urine sample," said the nurse, holding out a clear cup.

"No," I said.

"You're not going to give us urine?" she asked.

"No." I wasn't going to give them anything—not even my urine.

"Then we'll have to strap you down and use a catheter."

I didn't reply. Two minutes later, a male nurse returned with her, carrying leather straps.

"Okay, I'll give urine," I said, hopping down from the cot.

I wasn't about to let myself get tied down. Been there, done that. I walked across the room. Without my glasses I couldn't see the other patients, but I knew the routine.

"I can tell that guy is an asshole," one of the patients said, referring to me.

I blew it off. I wasn't going to be provoked into playing their reindeer games.

Despite my protests, it was nice to go to the bathroom. I had been holding it for a long time.

"That asshole had to use the bathroom the entire time," said the same guy when I left the bathroom.

I went back and sat on the cot. A couple of doctors came by and spoke with me, but I did not answer anything but my name, 'Notneb.' I wouldn't even tell them my fake birthday again because I didn't want to lie. The nurse performed an EKG after shaving part of my hairy chest. The only words I said the entire time were 'Thank you' when the nurse finally lowered the bed so I could lie flat on my back.

Around 4 a.m. they transferred me to the mental health unit. I was greeted by the night staff, a Black man and a White woman, both of whom had treated me on my previous two visits.

"What is your name?" asked the woman.

"Notneb."

"Are you sure your name isn't Benton?" asked the man.

I didn't say anything.

"He's buggin,'" said the man.

"What is your last name?"

I did not answer.

"When is your birthday?"

I did not answer.

"Take him to his room. We'll try tomorrow," said the woman.

"C'mon, Notneb," said the man with reproach in his voice.

A couple of hours later I woke and needed to use the bathroom again. I stumbled over and relieved myself but did not flush. When breakfast was called two hours later, a young Black man whom I recognized from my last visit two months prior walked out of the room wearing a yellow robe. My other two roommates followed soon after. One was Hispanic, and the other was of Middle Eastern descent. Except for Asian, all the races were represented in my room. I thought back to how I had been admitted on December 7. Did the omission of Asians in my room have anything to do with the anniversary of Pearl Harbor? Of course it did. That was part of the grand plan. Single-handedly, I was supposed to put the Asians in their place. The war was not forgotten.

But whose plan was this? Clearly I was not in control; I was merely a pawn in some master plan. It had to be someone in my family. I thought back to my deceased grandmother, who had lost her beloved brother in World War II. She always compared me to him. Of course it was a compliment, but was she trying to tell me more? I didn't know, but I was not going to let my grandmother down.

I went to breakfast. I drank milk instead of coffee; I feared that, just like the Arabian coffee, I might be allergic to the hospital's coffee as well. Though I had bought ChapStick, my lips were still scabbed and blistered. I went back to the sleeping quarters. What did the yellow robe mean? Then it came to me: I wasn't supposed to go to the bathroom. I was to hold it until I couldn't bear it any longer, and then I would open up the floodgates. Yes—that was what I was supposed to do: "The Golden Shower of Devotion." My instinct had been right the whole time.

Lunch was served. Instead of eating with the plastic knife and fork, I ate with my hands. I picked up this idea from the natives I met on a trip to Nepal in 2005. They eat their food with their hands. I was trying to go as low as possible, and I was doing a fine job regressing back to infancy by eating with my hands and wetting myself. I did not drink the milk; that would make me have to go to the bathroom sooner.

It was hard to deal with knowing I had to pee on myself. I didn't want to do it, but I had to, and I was angry about it. When dinner was called, once again I ate my food with my hands. After finishing my meal and not touching milk, I stood up and pushed the tray to the ground; the leftover food splattered across the floor.

"Notneb!" one of the staff members called. "Why did you do this?"

I didn't answer. I didn't look back. I kept walking to the sleeping quarters. I lay down and looked up at the ceiling. How the hell did I end up here again? I wasn't crazy. Everything I did made perfect sense. I had no regrets. The signs showed me the way.

When the young black man entered the room again, he was wearing a red T-shirt. Instead of the women wearing clothes to show that I shouldn't do something, now the men were. Since the man was wearing a red shirt, I gathered that I was not supposed to be dropping my tray at dinner. To pay penance I skipped breakfast and lunch the next day and finally dragged my famished body out to the dining area when dinner was called.

It is good that you are eating, Notneb. We are very worried about you."

They were going along with my charade. Even my hospital bracelet said "Notneb," with the last name listed as "Unknown." Everyone called me Notneb, and everyone knew exactly who I was. After all, I had been a patient two months before, not only in the same hospital, but the same wing. Several patients had remained in the hospital during my two months of freedom. Not even they said anything to me. Even when the staff called me Notneb, I usually didn't answer. The only thing I did was eat my meals and lie down on my bed. Once a staff member called me by the name "Benton," and I didn't move to get my food. The staff member looked straight at me, not amused in the least. "Notneb. Come get your food." I walked over and picked up my tray.

It was just a game I was playing. I believed that Lane had hidden cameras in the hospital and was watching my every move. I was no longer concerned about what society thought of me; this was all for Lane. After 40 hours of agony holding my urine, I finally wet myself. I did this for Lane. I thought she would be proud of me. For some reason I believed it would affect the behavior of our future children, that by wetting myself, our children would be ready to be potty trained earlier. I was trying to make things easier for Lane.

By this time I was up to 20 children, because I was not wearing my glasses or contact lenses. By not wearing corrective lenses, I was making it possible for all of my children to be 20/20 and never have to wear glasses. This was a major pain in the neck. I was almost completely blind without my glasses, but I was doing it for my family. I wanted my unborn children to have a better life than I had. I wanted them to be perfect. And if it inconvenienced me, I could handle it.

So with 20 children and 400 grandchildren, the magic number was up to 420, which I have always recognized as "International Burn Time." Meaning that at 4:20 p.m. around the world, it is the time to start smoking pot, kind of like Happy Hour in a bar. I once heard that the origin of the magic number 420 came from police jargon: "We have a 420 in progress," or something to that effect.

But I took "International Burn Time" to a new level. As there was a Black man, a Hispanic man, and a Middle Eastern man in my room, I thought they would be the groundskeepers of the vast farm where we would live. With all these little ones I was planning, we were going to need a lot of space, not to mention some help in raising them. These men's wives, or future wives, would act as the children's nannies. I loved the idea of being exposed to different cultures and was very pleased with this arrangement. There was little doubt that this would occur.

The question arises: how is a thirty-year-old woman going to have time to bear twenty children? Just as the doctors could give me bad eyesight, they could make it possible for Lane to have ten sets of twins, all boys. Though I was bitter toward the doctors for all the ailments I had, this gift of twenty children almost set the record straight. However, I couldn't be too careful. When the nurses took my vital signs twice a week, blood pressure, heart rate, and weight, I was convinced this was a way of giving a person high blood pressure or something else that could lead to a heart attack. But I was too smart. I always refused, which made them angry. This negative reaction only fueled my suspicions. I was on to them. It was just a game between me and the doctors.

But where was Lane? How was this game going to end? I was convinced that she was going to be admitted as a patient. I imagined a big party in our wing of the hospital, with all the nurses, patients, and doctors attending. Then Lane and I would slip out and begin our life together. But when?

I played with all kinds of numbers in my head to see if I could pick the date. My room number was L18, so I thought Lane would show up on December 18. But that day passed, and I was very sad and very angry. What did I have to do?

My mom called on the nineteenth. The patients used the pay phone in the hallway. One of them came in and said, "Benton. You have a phone call."

I didn't move.

"Benton. You have a phone call!"

I didn't move.

"Notneb. You have a phone call!"

I got up and answered the phone.

"Benton. Are you all right? We're worried sick," my mom said.

Without answering, I hung up. I was not talking to my mom. I was not taking phone calls. I walked back to my room. One of the nurses stopped me.

"Why did you hang up the phone?" she asked.

"It wasn't for me," I called as I continued walking back to my room. I thought this was clever. I wasn't lying, my mom didn't call me Notneb.

All this time I was refusing medication. Three times a day the other patients lined up for their medication. I never did. After everyone else had taken their medication, the nurse would call my name.

"Notneb. You need to take your medicine."

Usually I just shook my head. If they pressed me further, occasionally I would give a stern "No." This usually worked, and the staff would back off. In the meantime, the doctors continued to tell me that I was going to have to go to court on January 3 if I didn't take my medication. I was not concerned. Surely Lane would show up by then. When Christmas Day came and there was no Lane, I was deeply hurt. I had done everything perfectly. I had not eaten any dessert, coffee, tea, nor any of the holiday snacks that were offered, like cake and eggnog, both of which I was practically drooling over, but had abstained. My future depended on it. That's where my head was, not in the past, not in the present, only the future. The irritation I was going through now would be worth it for the grand future that was in store for me.

I had not showered since I entered the hospital, nor had I brushed my teeth or shaved. I was still playing games with the water. The shower in my room was out of order, and no one seemed to be in any rush to fix it. I took this as a sign that I was doing the right thing. People didn't need to shower or brush their teeth. This was just propaganda made up by industry so that we would spend money on their products.

More people called. When I heard my sister's voice on the phone, I simply replied that she had the wrong number. When my cousin or a couple of my other friends called, I wouldn't go to the phone. I couldn't make up my mind who was on my side and who wasn't. Just to play it safe, I spoke to no one.

Sometime around Christmas, I began to read messages into the food and drink that was served. It started with a frozen apple juice served for a snack. I thought this was done on purpose. I thought Lane was rewarding me for doing well. I determined that I was so cool I was ice. From that moment on, I strove to receive every drink frozen solid. If I accidentally dropped my guard and spoke to another patient, undoubtedly I was served a juice with no ice, or, worst of all, had my milk served warm. Then I knew that I had really screwed up, and no matter what, I could always come up with something that pinpointed my mistake. I would feel bad about it and brood over this minor inconvenience. I felt like I had let Lane down.

This fixation on food went further. If chicken was served, I showed fear. If carrots were served, which my mother always said were good for the eyes, I was supposed to look around and see what my mistake was. If I lost my temper, chocolate pudding came with my meal, and to me this meant control. If I received blueberries, it meant that I was acting immature, since my favorite dessert when I was a kid was blueberry pie. The ultimate was when the tray felt ice cold. That meant I was doing great.

Christmas passed, and I wondered how much longer I could hold out. My lifestyle was wearing me down. My weight dropped to 155 pounds. I was only eating about 1,000 calories a day. Never bread. Never dessert. Not even salad. Nothing but what was served hot as the main dish. The doctors pleaded with me to eat. They claimed they were worried, but I judged by their tone that they were just saying this because they had to. I imagined the doctors reading a script on how to deal with me. If I did this, they would react by doing that. Everything was by the book, and the more frustrated they became, the more steadfast I became in my resolve.

My mom came to the hospital on December 28. I had been expecting her. I was happy to see her, if for no other reason than to break up the routine. I had reduced myself to sitting in the same seat all day long, just staring at the television, which I couldn't see without my glasses. On occasions when I did stand up or went back to my room to lie down, my juice would not be frozen or my milk would be warm, both signs that I wasn't doing well. This would infuriate me until the next meal when I hopefully redeemed myself.

My mom was wearing red. This immediately made me cautious. I felt like she was trying to tell me something with her clothes, which she probably picked out to be in the holiday spirit, but of course I took it otherwise.

"Hey, Benton," my mom said and gave me a hug.

I didn't say anything, but I could feel tears coming on. I was sad because I knew I wasn't going to talk to her. I was sad because I was going to hurt her feelings. I was sad because I had to go through this.

"I brought you a present." She pulled a gift out of her purse, wrapped in red paper. More caution. "Your cousin Mark made a family cookbook with all the recipes he and Teresa made with their boys this year. He gave one to each family member."

I was still standing, but my back ached from sitting still in those damn chairs every hour, day after day. I began to cry. Not hard, but there was no denying it.

"Why are you crying?" my mom asked.

I stared back at her, trying to figure out why she was doing this. I was looking for any kind of hint from her that I was doing the right thing. That she understood why I was acting like this. That I was doing this for Lane. That I was doing it for our family so we would be rich. That I was doing it so that one day I could be the president of the United States. I didn't get the feeling that she understood.

She sat down in a chair in the visitor room.

"You can sit down too, if you'd like," she said.

I sat down and faced her. She made an ugly face and scooted over a seat. She had smelled the breath of a man who hadn't brushed his teeth in two months, but she didn't say anything. Instead, she began to read from the cookbook. I remained beside her, not listening, just trying to hold back my tears. Every once in a while she would stop and ask me a question or tell me some family news. She was being so nice it made me sick to act like that, but I wasn't tempted to stop.

A half hour later my mom got up to leave.

"I'll come back this evening. I hope you'll talk to me then."

I walked back to my room, brooding over the fact that I had even gone to meet her, but I couldn't help myself. I was curious about what she would say, curious what sign she would give. But I read nothing from her. I didn't walk away with knowledge, only sadness.

When she visited after dinner, she had a Coke in her hand. Obviously, with my history with the almighty soft drink, this was a peace offering. But I wasn't going to be tricked. I wasn't taking anything from her. She sat down at the table. The nurse brought a spiral notebook and told me to sign in before I returned to the ward. I didn't know if I was going to sign "Notneb" or not. For some reason I didn't want any written record of my deceit.

"I'm not going to just sit here all night if you won't talk to me," said my mom.

I said nothing.

"How about this. Blink once if you want to say yes. Blink twice if you want to say no."

Now even I realized how ridiculous this was getting, and I kind of laughed."You seem to be in better spirits than you were this afternoon. Are you going to talk to me?"

I accidentally blinked.

"Benton. Does that mean yes?"

I didn't want to smile, but I couldn't help it, even if I was mad that she called me Benton.

"Does that mean no?" My mom was smiling as well at me at this point. "I know you can understand me. That's why you're laughing."

I placed my fingers on my eyes and held them open wide to indicate that I wasn't blinking.

"I went by your apartment. Why are all of your things packed up? Benton, you must have planned this."

I didn't say anything. I looked down at the sign-in sheet. Why did she keep calling me Benton? Didn't she understand that if she kept calling me Benton, I would have to walk away? I couldn't have anyone knowing that I would respond to Benton.

"Where do you want to go?"I didn't say anything.

"I brought you some clothes." She handed a bag over the table. There was a red shirt on top. That was the sign. I looked at the sign-in sheet. I couldn't sign my name. In a sudden burst of energy, I stood up and walked away. My mom didn't try to stop me.

When I returned to the TV room, a few of the other patients were looking at me. A scraggly fellow named Rodney sat down beside me. He was always talking about something crazy. I normally eavesdropped on his conversations for amusement.

"Did you know that Pablo Escobar is the richest man in the world?" Rodney said to no one in particular.

"I thought Bill Gates was the richest man in the world," said another patient.

"No. No. It's Pablo Escobar."

Significance of this conversation: Pablo Escobar is head of the largest Columbian cocaine cartel. Since I had refused the Coca-Cola, I was going to be the richest man in the world. A smile spread across my face, but looking back, there is no doubt that Rodney was screwing with my head. How he knew I was scheming to be the richest man in the world when I hadn't told anyone about it, I do not know. Rodney was crafty like that. My only assumption is that all brains work similarly, and he had been in the same position once himself.

CHAPTER 21

"Today is your court date, Mr. Savage," said an Asian staff member. "You must get out of bed and go see the judge."

It was January 3. I did not move. I did not answer.

"Get up, Mr. Savage."

I wasn't going to move unless they called me Notneb. I expected them to drag me in front of the judge, but it wouldn't have mattered. I wasn't going to talk. I wasn't going to do anything they told me to do.

"Here are the clothes your mom brought you to wear. Put them on and come to court and see the judge."

I remained lying on the bed with my head propped up against the pillow. Our eyes met. He wasn't angry or upset; there was no emotion in his voice. He just stared at me. Then, without saying anything else, he left the room.

I walked over to the brown paper bag filled with the clothes my mom had brought me. Not even looking to see what was inside, I picked up the bag and stuffed it into the trash can. I wasn't wearing any of those clothes. I wasn't taking anything from anyone. I wouldn't have even worn the damn hospital uniform if I didn't have to. I didn't hear any more about skipping my court date until around seven o'clock that evening, when two staff members and two security guards entered my room.

"Since you won't take pills orally, we must inject you," said the Asian staff member.

I knew the drill. I had gone through this exact same routine eleven months prior. I did not resist. I rolled over onto my stomach. The security guards placed their hands on my back, but there was no pressure; it was just a precautionary measure. I felt my pajama bottoms being pulled down and then the sharp stick of a needle into my left buttock. I tried to relax until the needle was removed. I felt the hands pull away. The security guards walked out of the room.

"It would be much easier if you took the medicine orally. I know this must hurt. You don't have to go through this."

I didn't say anything. This scenario went on for another ten days. In the meantime I developed my own routine. I was trying to simulate how my days would be filled when I left the hospital. From 8 a.m. until 6 p.m. I remained in my room and only came out for meals; this was to show that I planned to work during the day. From 6 p.m. until 9 p.m. I watched TV; this was to symbolize the time I would spend with our twenty children. At 9 p.m. on the dot I retired for the evening, and my day would end. That was my schedule for the weekdays, and I believed that Lane approved. At least I was receiving frozen juices, and my milk was served cold.

During the weekends I remained in the TV room all day, which showed that during this time I planned to spend time with our children. This seemed to suffice as well, and I was quite comfortable with this setup. I believed it was the right mixture of work and play, but despite the routine my body felt like it was falling apart. No longer was it just my mind that was cracking up; I was uncomfortable physically. I could no longer sit still. It felt like bugs were crawling all over my body, and I squirmed in my chair like a hyperactive kindergartener who hadn't taken his Ritalin.

Finally, out of desperation I ate everything on my tray except for the coffee. I knew that was taboo. I couldn't have a vice, but surely from time to time I could eat a little extra. I felt guilty about it, though, and believe me it is a strange mindset when a man feels guilty about eating a salad without even a drop of dressing. But that's how I felt. However, the supplementary food did not relieve the symptoms of mania. I continued to feel worse.

On a Tuesday in the second week of January I overheard one of the staff members talking about poetry. I didn't catch the conversation but just the word 'poetry.' Immediately I thought I was supposed to write poetry. I welcomed this. I had been doing next to nothing for close to a month now, and I was bored out of my mind. By this time I was speaking to the doctors and staff. I asked the staff member I had overheard talking about poetry if I could have pen and paper, went back to my room, and began to write with a goal of 40 poems. 20 + 20. I did not rewrite the poems I had erased earlier from my computer. Lane had saved my collection of novels, short stories, and poems. So I wrote new poems.

I can only write poetry when I'm not taking my medicine. Something about the rhythm just clicks when I am in a manic state of mind. But the injections of Haldol weren't the same as my usual meds. Over the next three days I wrote forty poems. Only a few were any good at all, but I felt better that I had at least completed the task. But still I felt terrible. I could not sit still. I could not sleep. The addition of all of the food did not help. Nothing that I could think of made me happy. Finally, I considered calling my mom. She could give me advice. She could make me feel better.

Don't do it, I thought. *Don't do it!* But I had to do it. I could not put up with what had become not only mental anguish but physical agony as well. *Don't do it*, I thought again. *Don't call.* But I had to. I picked up my bed pillow and slammed it against the wall. *Don't do it*, I thought. Nothing good could come of calling my mom, but I was in such pain.

I slammed the pillow against the wall again. Then I thought of Lane watching me. She would not be pleased with the temper tantrum. Finally I walked over to the payphone, took a deep breath, and dialed my mom's 800 number.

"Hello."

"It's me."

"Who is this?" my mom asked.

"It's Benton."

"Oh."

"Mom. I need your help."

"What?" My mom was being short with me.

"I feel terrible."

"Are you taking your medicine?"

"No."

"You know they're never going to let you leave until you take your medicine."

"I'm starting to realize that." I thought my mom would ask why I gave her the silent treatment when she visited, but she didn't.

"If you're serious about getting better, you'll go talk to the doctor and get yourself back on Zyprexa."

"I guess you're right," I said.

"You know, Benton. I can't get you out of there. You have to start taking medicine if you want to get out the hospital, and you have to keep taking the medicine if you want to stay out."

"I know."

"Go talk to your doctor and call me back."

I immediately went looking for my doctor. Despite having been in the hospital for over a month, I didn't even know my doctor's name. In the meantime she had quit trying to speak with me. But finally I was ready to make amends. Clearly I was in too miserable a condition to go any further without a serious change. I remember it was a Friday. If I didn't catch the doctor before she left for the weekend, there would be nothing I could do until Monday. That was out of the question. I could not fathom putting up with this discomfort for another day, much less an entire weekend.

I put out the word to the staff behind the desk that I wanted to see the doctor and found out she was on a different ward. It was three o'clock. I was nervous the staff wouldn't tell her. I stayed right by the desk, waiting for the doctor. Around four o'clock the doctor strolled back into the ward.

"Doctor, can I speak with you?"

"What is it, Mr. Savage?" She was not at all amused with my antics.

"I was wondering if I could start back on my regular meds?"

"But you'll just quit taking them as soon as you leave," said the doctor.

"Listen. I am in serious pain. I cannot go another day on Haldol injections. My skin is crawling. I need to be back on Zyprexa."

"We'll talk about it Monday."

"Come on, doctor. I don't think I can last until Monday. I know I haven't been the best patient, but I'm trying to change."

"Okay. I'll put you back on the Zyprexa, but you have to promise you will shower every day, change clothes every day, and start brushing your teeth every day. The staff is very concerned about your personal hygiene. If you'll agree to this, I'll put you back on Zyprexa."

"Thank you very much."

"And remember, I will be checking up on you to make sure that you are taking care of your end of the deal."

"Thank you, doctor."

I immediately grabbed a towel off the rack in the hallway and walked to the shower. Despite my behavior, I wanted to take a shower, but I feared taking a shower was the wrong thing to do. I don't remember exactly what I feared. Maybe I was doing it for Lane. Maybe it was because I wanted to control the world water supply. Maybe I felt omnipotent and that by not taking a shower I could end severe rain droughts, therefore preventing world hunger.

That evening I took 20 milligrams of Zyprexa. This was the same dosage I had been on since my trip to Miami in 1999. Immediately I felt better. By bedtime much of my anxiety had dissipated, but I still didn't feel good about it. I thought I was being weak. I thought that all of my wild dreams were now in limbo. I thought I was letting down Lane.

Just before I went to shower on Monday, the fire alarm sounded, and we all filed into the dining area and prepared to evacuate. Of course it was only a test, but I took it otherwise. I thought it was a sign that I wasn't supposed to shower. I couldn't make up my mind, but I was trying to stay within the lines of my agreement with the doctor. Finally, I grabbed a towel and went to the shower. When I opened the door leading to the shower, an older patient was masturbating.

'Close the door," he said, but he didn't seem embarrassed. He didn't even stop what he was doing.

I took this as a not so subtle sign that I wasn't supposed to take a shower. I placed my towel back on the rack and went to my room and lay down. What was I supposed to do? I was trapped between doing what I thought was right for Lane, and what would be right in the eyes of the doctor. On Wednesday I saw the doctor again.

"Mr. Savage. You promised that you would shower every day if I gave you Zyprexa. You aren't holding up your end of the deal," she said.

"I'll go take one right now."

"I think we should bump your Zyprexa intake up to 30 milligrams a day."

"Don't do that. I'm fine. It was just a little bump in the road."

"Just the same I'm going to up the dosage."

This infuriated me. I did not want to be on a higher dose of medication. I thought I was doing just fine. Now I was angry. I thought it was time I should be discharged. After taking my shower I sought out the social worker for the ward. Though it was the doctor who made the final decision, I decided to try and solicit someone else for my cause. The social worker had told me earlier in my stay that I could go home when I started taking my medication. I decided I would put the squeeze on her to see if she was telling the truth.

"Cathy. I was wondering when I was leaving," I said.

"I don't know. Maybe a couple of weeks. We'll see how you are doing."

"A couple of weeks!" I shouted. "I'm taking my medicine. I'm showering. I'm doing everything that is asked of me."

"There is no reason to shout, Mr. Savage. Perhaps you don't remember, but you urinated on yourself when you first arrived, and then slept in it for several days."

"I had to do that. I didn't want to. I had to. The guy was wearing the yellow shirt. I know what that means."

"I don't know if we should be talking about this right in front of everyone," said Cathy.

"You're a liar! I did not sleep in my urine for several days! I immediately took a shower. You're a liar!"

"There is no reason for you to raise your voice," Cathy said calmly.

"I can't trust you anymore. You said that if I took my medicine, I could leave."

"You will leave eventually."

I walked back to my room and lay down. How much longer was I going to have to stay in the hospital? By this time my weight had dropped below 150 pounds. I had resumed my '123' diet plan, but with the addition of Zyprexa, my hunger grew more menacing, and it was difficult to restrain myself from eating more food.

The last week of January my mom and stepdad came to visit me. I had been talking to my mom on the phone every couple of days. I had also spoken to my sister. Neither said anything about the silent treatment I had given them just a month earlier. I appreciated this gesture. I did not know how to explain it. I still believed Lane was alive, but there was now a sliver of doubt. There was no way I could ask my mom if it was true. It was too ridiculous a situation to even admit, but it was just realistic enough for me to believe.

"I've paid most of your bills and your taxes," said my mom.

"Thanks," I replied though I was not happy. I had gotten it into my head that I didn't have to pay my bills or taxes. Since I had certainly passed the number '23,' I felt exonerated from this responsibility. I felt everyone in the world knew what was going on. I thought that my mom knew I was one day going to be president of the United States. I thought that she was just playing along. That's fine, I thought. I'll just play along with her.

"What about your glasses?" my mom asked. "I couldn't find them in your apartment."

"Really?" I wasn't about to tell her where I left them. As far as I knew, my mom had no idea I had been brought to the hospital wearing only socks.

"Would you like me to get you another pair? I'm sure that you are miserable not being able to see."

This brought a dilemma. I was miserable not being able to see, but at the same time I felt if I wore glasses, then my children would have to wear glasses too. I hadn't gone through two months of hell only to be derailed at the last minute.

"I want to pick out my own frames. Besides I'm getting out in the next couple of days," I finally said.

"Who told you that you that you were getting out?" my mom asked.

"The social worker."

"I hope you're right. What do you plan on doing when you get out? How are you going to keep yourself busy?"

"I guess I'll go back to writing."

"Are you sure that's a good idea? Don't you think it's time you got a job? You need some kind of structure in your life, or else the same thing will happen again. Do you think that you will have to come back to the hospital in the future?"

"No."

"What's going to be different?"

"It just will be."

"But you've said that before."

"If I thought that I was coming back to the hospital, then I shouldn't leave in the first place, is the way that I see it. Doesn't that make sense to you?"

"I don't know, Benton. I can't go through this again. You don't know how hard it is on me and your sister. The whole family for that matter."

I snorted. "If you think it's hard on you, imagine how hard is it on me."

"But you're in control. All you have to do is take your medicine, and this won't happen again, but we have to watch you suffer, and there is nothing we can do."

"I know. I'm sorry."

Another week passed by. I maintained my eating regimen. I took my medicine. I took showers. I brushed my teeth. Out of concern that I may have done permanent damage to my teeth, the doctor scheduled a visit with the hospital dentist, but the dentist found nothing more than irritated gums.

Still, I wanted out now. I could not stand to be in the hospital any longer. Tomorrow wasn't soon enough. Never mind a couple of weeks. Finally I realized what could get me out sooner rather than later. It came in the form of a sign, just like everything else did. I walked into the recreation room where the patients were playing 'Bingo.' Just like that, it was 'Bingo' for me as well. I knew what I had to do. I had to attend groups. Throughout my nine years of mental hospital visits, I had never attended groups regularly. I always thought they were so childish. We did juvenile things like making beaded bracelets or pasting collages and sometimes painting with watercolors. But I decided that it had to be done, and to be honest this therapy did help. It gave my mind something else to think about, and the anxiety lessened.

After I started attending groups, I noticed there was a shift in the clothing the other patients were wearing. More and more people wore blue. I took this as a good sign, but I didn't know exactly what it meant. Then I came up with it. My ultimate dream in life was *The Blue Lagoon*. I wanted to live on a deserted island with Lane. In fact Lane even kind of looked like Brooke Shields did in this movie.

With each passing day, more and more patients wore blue. I don't know where they got the clothing, perhaps the hospital had extra clothes to hand out. No matter. I knew I was doing well. With pleasure, my eyes traversed the room, and I marveled at the sea of blue I had created. When one girl wore a red-and-white striped shirt with blue pants, I took it to represent the American flag. I believed she was signaling that one day I would be president. Yes, I was certainly on the right track. Everyone knew it.

Finally, my release was scheduled for February 26. Once again, I was to be part of the Assisted Outpatient Treatment (AOT) program, in which the hospital would check on me six times a month. The only difference this time was that I agreed to take my medication.

On the day I was discharged, almost the entire ward, including patients and staff, wore blue. A couple of staff members wore brown, which I concluded meant I was full of shit. They were right. I had no intention of taking my medicine. I had only played along with their charade so I could get out of the hospital. That conviction only strengthened when they handed me a bottle of medicine labeled "Notneb." Since the label carried the wrong name, I took it as a sign that I wasn't supposed to take it. Even the doctors, I thought, believed I shouldn't be medicated. By placing me in the AOT program, they were just covering their asses. They knew I wasn't going to take medication. They knew I didn't need it.

As I walked out of the hospital for the first time in three months, I hoped Lane would pick me up and that we'd jet down the road toward our great future together, but of course she didn't. Still, nothing was going to dampen my happiness. This hospital stay had been the toughest stint since Miami. Under no circumstances did I want to return.

The biggest obstacle facing me was that, since I had thrown away my wallet with all my credit cards and photo identification, I couldn't even write checks. My mom had offered me money, but that was out of the question. I wanted no debts. I planned to tackle the world on my own terms, and one of the most important steps was cutting the umbilical cord. However, the AOT program agreed to loan me money until I received new cards in the mail. In the meantime, I had about fifty dollars in loose change at my apartment. That would have to hold me over for the next couple of days.

It felt odd returning to my apartment. My mom and stepdad had unpacked everything for me. As I was practically blind, I was grateful. The first thing I did was go to the grocery store and buy two chicken breasts, rice, broccoli, a twelve-pack of Cokes, and two bottles of apple juice. I planned to drink two Cokes a day, and for my second beverage I planned to drink hot apple cider. At the time I believed that I could have only two drinks, and no substitutes. I chose apple juice because once, when I drank only orange juice with no other fluids, my eyes became red and itchy. The other time, when I drank only coffee and Coke, my lips chapped. After both instances, apple juice had remedied my colon woes, and the symptoms disappeared. I guessed there was some truth to the saying, "An apple a day keeps the doctor away." I paid for all my groceries with quarters and dimes that I had stockpiled in my apartment. For some reason I had not thrown away my spare change before my admission to the hospital.

The next day I reported to the hospital to check in with the ACT team, a subsidiary of the Assisted Outpatient Treatment Program. I planned on securing a $200 loan so I could buy groceries while I waited to receive my credit cards in the mail. As I sat in the hospital lobby, I began to get paranoid. I watched as the different staff members moved about the office, but none came to speak with me. I must have waited fifteen minutes. All I wanted was to pick up my money and get the hell out of there. I was apprehensive about borrowing the money. I had wrestled with the idea for a couple of weeks while I was still in the hospital. It had troubled me greatly, but it was better than taking money from my mother. At least it wasn't going to be a handout. It was a loan, but someone was helping me, and I didn't feel good about it.

Suddenly I had a thought: they weren't going to loan me the money. That's why they were virtually ignoring me. They were waiting to see how long it would take me to realize this. Without hesitation I stood up and walked out of the office, realizing that had been a close call. I had almost asked for a handout, which would have foiled my entire body of work up to that point.

By the time I returned to my apartment, I had a new plan. Once again, it originated from the idea that 2*2=4. I decided that for the next ten days I would eat nothing. The only things I would drink every day were two Cokes and two hot apple ciders. No food, and certainly no other beverages.

I knew this would be tough. In fact, I didn't know if I could do it. My weight when I left the hospital had dropped to 139 pounds, so there wasn't much fat to burn for energy, but I knew that I had to try. I had to go as low as I could possibly muster. Eating no food for ten days, I thought, would suffice.

In preparation I made one last humongous bowl of rice with hopes that it would hold me over for a couple of days. Then I hunkered down. I wasn't going to shower. I wasn't going to shave. I wasn't going to brush my teeth. I wasn't going to listen to music. I wasn't going to read the newspaper. I wasn't going to check my mail. I wasn't going to watch TV. The last two would have major impact on my future. I determined that the last obstacle standing in my way of the presidency was that I should not check my mail for the entire ten days. I imagined that I should not take anything from the government. Then I would definitely be president someday. The same held true for watching TV. If I didn't watch TV for the entire ten days, my family could add a television station to our arsenal, just like General Electric owned NBC.

I spent my days writing. I averaged five pages a day on a new novel. I still held out hope that Lane had saved my other work and felt confident that this was true. There was no way I could keep my sanity if I believed otherwise. In between I read books, but I felt guilty about it. I feared that this luxury would be taken from me as well, but I did not care. I had to do something to keep my mind busy and more importantly to keep the demons at bay.   Every five days I returned to the grocery store and bought more Cokes and apple juice.

On the eighth day I received a visit from my doctor and social worker. I wasn't expecting them. I thought that the entire A.O.T. program was a scam, and that they would never show up, but of course once again I was wrong. I let them in my apartment. We sat around my dining room table.

"How's everything going?" asked Dr. Salinger.

"Good."

"Have you been eating?" asked Ron, the social worker.

"Yes."

"Have you been taking your medicine?"

"Yes." I lied. I had not taken my medicine. I had no plans to take my medicine.

"Are you sure? I hope that you are telling us the truth. It would be a shame if you had to go back to the hospital," said Dr. Salinger.

"Really. I'm fine."

"What about your glasses? I thought you said that you couldn't see without your glasses," said Ron.

"I'm going tomorrow."

"For real?"

"Yes. I promise."

"Have you really been eating?"

"Yes."

"Do you mind if I look in your refrigerator?" asked Dr. Salinger.

"Sure," I replied, but I was apprehensive. There was only Cokes and apple juice in there.

Dr. Salinger opened the fridge.

"Sodas and apple juice does not constitute a meal," she said.

"What have you been eating?" asked Ron.

"Chicken, rice, broccoli. That sort of thing." I wasn't lying. That was the last thing I ate. I didn't mention the fact that it was eight days ago.

"You look like you have lost more weight," said Dr. Salinger.

"Really?"

Ron picked up a book and handed it to me. "Read this."

I grabbed the book and read the first page.

"Okay. That's enough. I just wanted to see how bad your eyesight was."

"You know, Benton. We are here to help you. Do you understand that?"

"Yes."

"We can get you money for food. You need to eat," said Dr. Salinger.

"Yes, Benton. There is no shame in asking for money if you have no food. Everyone has to eat," echoed Ron.

"Really. I'm fine. My credit cards should be in the mail any day now," I said.

Dr. Salinger and Ron looked at each other.

"I feel bad leaving you with no food," said Dr. Salinger.

"I'm fine. You don't have to worry about me." I was trying to shuffle them out the door.

"Benton. You know you have an appointment down at Bellevue Hospital scheduled for next Friday, don't you?" said Ron.

"Yeah. What's that all about?"

"They'll just go over the rules and regulations of the A.O.T. program. If you aren't taking your medicine, they may admit you back to the hospital."

"I'm fine. Trust me."

Dr. Salinger and Ron left. Fifteen minutes later my buzzer rang. It was them again. I let them in the building. Their hands were filled with groceries.

"I couldn't stand to leave you with no food, so we bought you some," said Dr. Salinger.

They emptied the bags with milk, cereal, orange juice, oatmeal, peanut butter, bread, jelly, nuts, and I'm sure there were other things that I can't remember.

"You didn't have to do that," I said. I was scared they were going to stick around until I ate something, but they didn't. They left soon afterward.

Even though the gift was generous, I felt like this food represented the last temptation of Christ. I only had two more days to go, but they were also the hardest. The build-up to once again being able to eat food was so great that I was practically ready to chew on my arm. I was at the grocery store when the doors opened at seven o'clock in the morning on Sunday the eleventh day. I barely had five dollars left in change. I bought a box of rice and nothing else. That was the most bang I could get for the bucks. I filled a pot with rice and water and boiled. I did this several times throughout the day. That was Sunday. Still, there was no Lane. When was she going to show up?

I emerged from my shell slowly. I didn't want to make a mistake. On Monday I finally checked my mail. My debit card was in there. I went to the grocery store and bought spaghetti. My mind was absolutely consumed with food, and I felt guilty about eating it, but I was beaten down. I could hold out no longer.

On Tuesday I went out for a jog. My muscles had atrophied from the inactivity of being immobile in the hospital. I could only run for five minutes before I stopped, hunched over, too tired to take another step.

On Wednesday I finally drank some of the milk the doctor had bought for me, but I felt extremely guilty about it. I shouldn't have drunk milk. I felt I should only drink apple cider and Cokes. People didn't need calcium for strong bones. That was just an old wives' tale perpetrated by the dairy industry.

On Thursday I went to the optician and ordered some glasses. I still feared my children might have to wear glasses, but it had to be done. I had to see again. My glasses were ready two hours later. I went home and shaved, and then went to the barber and got my hair cut. I wanted to look my best when I went to the Bellevue Hospital the next day. I had decided I was going to be honest and tell them that I was not taking the medicine. I knew that I would have to answer a lot of questions, but I was prepared. I thought I was doing well.

I took the train down to the hospital with one of the social workers from the hospital. He came along for moral support. I did not tell him I wasn't taking medication. He did not ask. As we waited for close to an hour in the lobby, I couldn't help but realize I wasn't doing well. I felt terrible, but I had to push on. At the same time I feared that they would put me back in the hospital if I told them the truth.

The doctor called me. He was about my age. The social worker, David, came with me. All three of us sat down in an office that was no bigger than a walk-in closet. The doctor spoke first.

"You understand that you can have an attorney present during this interview if you choose to do so," said the doctor.

I didn't know it but said I did to expedite the process. But I grew nervous. This interview was more serious than I had imagined. I thought that I would be able to talk my way out of taking the medication. I thought I would show them the light.

"What medicines are you currently taking?" asked the doctor.

"I'm not taking medication right now," I replied.

The doctor and David looked at each other. They were caught off guard.

"Did you know this?" the doctor asked David.

"No. I did not. I need to use the phone and call back to the hospital to notify them." David stood up and left the room.

The doctor turned to me with a serious expression on his face. "Can you tell me why you're not taking your medication?" asked the doctor.

"I don't need it."

"What were the circumstances before your last admission to the hospital?"

"I was walking down the street with no clothes on."

"And you think that was normal?"

"Yes. I had to do that."

"Tell me what you think is the definition of bipolar disorder?"

"Someone who has wild mood swings."

"Does this apply to you?"

"Sometimes."

"You understand that it is a chemical imbalance. The only way to control these mood swings is through proper medication."

"I don't believe that."

Though I had heard what the doctor was telling me numerous times in the last ten years, for some reason it was different this time. I was actually listening. The recollection of all the self-induced torture I had put myself through for years was painful. However, those trials meant nothing. The success or failure of all of those actions meant nothing. They were all a figment of my imagination.

"How many times have you been admitted to the psych ward?"

"I don't know. Probably about ten."

"And you still don't think that you are bipolar?"

I hesitated.

"How do you think we should treat your illness if you don't take medication?"

Once again I didn't answer.

"You do realize we can readmit you to the hospital for a 24-hour evaluation?"

The first thought that came to my mind was my mother. I had promised her everything was going to be okay. For the past month she had been pressing to admit me to a private hospital where I could receive better care. There were even discussions of electroshock treatment. I didn't want that. I told her I had everything under control.

Suddenly a light went on in my head. I had been wrong about everything. Lane was dead. The doctors had been trying to help me the entire time. It didn't matter that I took psychiatric medication. I could still have sex. I could still work a job. I wasn't going to be president, but I never really wanted to be president anyway. Besides, there were advantages to all of this. I could drink a root beer instead of a Coke. I could drink water. I could eat salads and desserts. I could do anything I wanted, but I had to take medication. If I didn't take medication, I was breaking the law. I could be sent back to the mental hospital against my will.

There was no way in hell I wanted to go back to the hospital. The best thing to do was admit my mistake and hope the doctor believed me.

"I'll start taking my medication," I finally said, relief rushing through my body. I was not going to have to go through all of this paranoia again. The fear that everyone, including family and doctors, was out to get me was false. The war was over. I had finally surrendered to the wickedness of the disease rather than fighting the weapons that were there to help me.

"I don't think we need to check you into the hospital, but if this happens again, I won't hesitate to do so. Do you understand me?" asked the doctor.

"Yes, sir. I do."

They say everyone has to reach their lowest point before they come to terms with the illness, and this was mine. It was either take my medication or spend the rest of my life in a mental hospital. After all those years of struggling, I now understood that I was helpless against the disease.

I have the Assisted Care Treatment program to thank for that. Just by being kept under someone's eye before I once again hit the point of no return, I was saved from the demons that haunt me. I have no idea what would have happened to me if I had been allowed to leave the hospital that time without supervision, but it no doubt would not have been good.

Of course my well-being didn't change overnight, but this was the moment when I first saw the light at the end of the tunnel. It was still a month or so before I drank anything but Coke and apple cider. It was about a month before the paranoia of being spied on finally dissipated, which was about the same time I realized for good that I was not going to be president of the United States.

Sometimes I laugh at the crazy ideas that popped into my head that I believed. Other times I cringe when I think about Lane. But mostly I feel relief. It is still a struggle, but on the medication my life gets better each day. I hope that one day I will be able to go a day without thinking about the nightmare my life had become. Though I wholeheartedly believed I would never go a day without taking my medication, sure enough a month later I was back to my old tricks. The disease is relentless, and it is in my best interest to never think I have it licked.

Coming to terms with this illness was the biggest obstacle I have had to overcome in my life. Looking back, it is so simple: take the medicine. It may seem unbelievable that my ultimate recovery plan triggered in my mind the way it did in a matter of seconds, but that is how it happened. It was a revelation. A defining moment. After fighting a losing battle with the disease for the better part of ten years, I finally surrendered. This doesn't mean that people with bipolar disorder, or their family and loved ones, should hold out for what seemed like an effortless resolution, but patients should take it on faith and stay on the medication; and if the medications stop working, adjust them. This disease is managed, not cured. It will never be easy for me, but it is like insulin for a diabetic: you have to keep at it for the rest of your life.

EPILOGUE

The adage, "History has a way of repeating itself," has proven accurate in my experience with mental illness. I felt as if I was caught in a loop, echoing the same struggles a decade later. But by 2019, things were different: I had a car. Mobility meant my peculiarities could travel with me, rather than being confined to endless walks or Greyhound buses. In those last ten years since, I stayed true to my word. I took my medication every day... It helped.

I was in a four-year relationship with Seul Kee, a Korean woman, living together for three years. We left New York City and settled in Montauk, where we owned a house and she tended a vegetable garden. My move was for a long-term future with her, not for romantic adventures.

I had never talked to Seul Kee about Lane Johnson, or anything related to her, so it was understandable that she was taken aback when I suddenly ended our four-year relationship without giving any reason. I had a reason though. I believed Lane Johnson was still alive. The day before, I believed I had come to terms with Lane's passing and rarely thought of her. No one even mentioned her name to me. I just chalked it up as a mental health moment in time. I had moved on, and I wasn't looking back.

My initial sense of being followed was ambiguous and resembled prior experiences associated with Lane; at first, Lane's involvement did not occur to me. Afterall, it was 2014. Lane had been dead since 2003. Or was she dead? Back to the suspicions and paranoia that I thought I vanquished five years prior.

Understand. I was positive I was bipolar. I didn't even question it in my mind. I took my Zyprexa and Paxil every single day for five years. I worked for two summers as whitewater river rafting guide during that time. I had written numerous short stories and three books including 'Wrong Side Out: The Bipolar Experience" back in 2010. It wasn't published, but my psychiatrist liked my book so much, she asked me to hold a forum and speak about my experiences with bipolar disorder with her colleagues who assembled in an auditorium.

Don't get me wrong. I wasn't doing great, but I was not hospitalized either. Zyprexa kept me out of trouble, but I was struggling in most other aspects of my life. Singing my same old sad songs. Abusing alcohol once again. Sometimes pot. Occasionally cocaine. But my infatuation with Lane was nonexistent. It wasn't even an issue.

I remember the moment I felt something was array. I joined Rotary Club shortly after moving to Montauk. I attended the weekly meetings at a local restaurant and performed civic work in the community. Christmas parties and camaraderie. At a weekly Rotary meeting I was listening to a conversation. I wasn't even involved. I barely knew the Rotary member, but I listened as he described the twenty-thousand dollars of dental work he just had done. My ears perked. The reason: I have bad teeth, and I had dental work done in Flushing by a Korean dentist. Much more inexpensive. Convenient. I hadn't thought much of it. But at the moment, I believed beyond a shadow of a doubt this stranger was sending me a message that I shouldn't be going to Korean dentists.

This is hard to write about, but reading messages into other people's innocent comments has been a huge problem for the last twenty years.

My mom and sister are scared to speak around me because they fear I might take it the wrong way. I can't deny it.

From the moment of that innocent remark in 2014 until September 2020 when I was finally checked myself to a psych ward, I believed Lane Johnson was spying/stalking/following, whatever you want to call it. I'm not talking about hidden cameras in my bedroom. I felt like Jim Carey in the movie "The Truman Show" and I was being watched by the entire world for their amusement. It was terrifying.

I digress because this is a crucial aspect of the illness, and to explain mental illness is what this book is about. Specifically, paranoid schizophrenia, coupled with a severe case of obsessive-compulsive disorder, is my current diagnosis. Right now, at 10:29 on October 25, 2025, I believe somebody is secretly watching me as I type on the computer. In fact, I believe somebody is reading what I am typing right now. I know it's insane, but that brings me to the therapists I eventually saw in Key West.

My arrival in Key West marked the beginning of another disaster. Barely settled into my seasonal rental, paranoia crept in: I was certain my house was bugged, convinced Lane was watching me in my apartment, and that everyone—including my landlord—was part of some elaborate plot. My despair grew. I kept my suspicions to myself, telling only my mom and sister that I believed Lane was not only alive but spying on me every hour of every day. I didn't confide in anyone else; it was my secret, and Lane had upped the ante by apparently following me all the way to Key West. Feeling surrounded, I realized I had to speak up about what was happening inside my mind.

The secret I'd guarded more closely than Rumpelstiltskin's name was about to come out. In the past, I'd been less than honest with therapists, especially about my cocaine use, which likely led to my misdiagnosis. I'd mostly seen male psychiatrists, but this time I felt only a woman could truly understand. I scheduled an appointment for the following day, uncertain of what I was hoping for—maybe just a chance to unburden myself and find reassurance that I wasn't losing my grip.

The session was a blur. I shared everything as openly as I have in these pages. My therapist was taken aback, immediately insisting I should check into a psych ward unless I promised to take medication right away. Since psychologists can't prescribe medication, she must've called a doctor. The rest of the afternoon is a haze, but I remember filling the prescription and taking it. Good thing. Around nine that night, two police cars pulled up outside my house. A uniformed officer knocked on my door—the psychologist had called for a wellness check. The officer even counted my pills to confirm I was following my regimen. I was, so they left.

My mistrust of therapists deepened. For years, I'd worried about what might happen if I was truly honest about my thoughts. Sometimes I felt ridiculous, but the evidence seemed all too real to me. Seeking validation, I told my story to a second psychologist—including the fact that the first had called the cops on me. I stated up front. "You are never going to ever convince me that I'm not being surveilled. I want you to help me live with this paranoia whether real or otherwise."

Surprisingly, Carol believed me when I said Lane had followed me for five years; she even described it as "stalking," a term I hadn't used myself at that time. Whether Carol was building trust or truly believed me, I felt vindicated for a few fleeting days.

The second session was just as rewarding, so I scheduled a third. But I never saw Carol again. The "angel" I'd started to trust proved to be a turncoat. Soon after, I got a message labeled "Mousetrap"—the same title as my latest short story. I scoured my emails for the word "Mousetrap": nothing. The last thing I'd told Carol was that I'd bring some of my writing to read. That plan vanished.

I was falling apart. After a week of medication and starting to feel better, I abruptly stopped. The next four months were more the same. My lease expired on December 19th, and I suspect my landlord wasn't sad to see me go.

With nowhere to stay and no invitation for Christmas—nor any subsequent ones—I couldn't go back running to Mama. Miami seemed like my best option. Nearly twenty years after first escaping to Key West, I ended up in Miami again, once more focused on simply getting by.

My initial days there were marked by exhaustion and uncertainty. I bounced between cheap motels, holding onto my few possessions and trying to convince myself things would get better. The city felt at once familiar and alien; the humid air weighed heavily on me. I spent hours wandering different neighborhoods, hoping to find some connection or sense of belonging, but mostly contending with my own unsettled thoughts and persistent loneliness.

Eventually, I realized I needed a change and started making new plans. I remembered Lane's cousin hosted a New Year's gathering every year at their family farm. Though I'd turned down an invite last year, I assumed it was still open. So, I left Miami and drove to Cleveland, Tennessee, arriving in the afternoon without letting anyone know—I wanted my visit to be discreet, hoping to surprise everyone and join the celebration.

Lane's family estate, owned for generations, had a grand entrance that was kept open during daytime for visitors. When I got there, I entered through the gate and parked along the driveway. Approaching the house, a wave of nervousness hit me, but I pressed on, walked to the door and knocked, not knowing what awaited me.

"This is private property. Who are you and what do you want?" a menacing voice thundered behind me.

I did not look back. I panicked and instead turned the knob on the door. It was locked. No other choice. I turned around and saw a smaller man with whiskers that didn't conceal his scowl. A wooden sign on the door behind him read 'Caretaker.'

"I'm a friend of the family. Is Lane Johnson here?" I replied.

"Who did you just say?"

"Lane Johnson."

His disgust was apparent. "Lane Johnson has been dead for fifteen years."

"Oh. I guess I'll go home then." I casually replied and kept my head down and marched to my SUV, opened the door, and jumped in. I heard his angry stammer behind me. Just as I shut the door, the caretaker pounded on the hood. I hoped to simply drive away, and all would be forgotten. Problem. There was only one exit, and my car wasn't facing in that direction. I didn't panic. I hadn't really done anything wrong in my eyes. Hell. I had known the Johnson family since before my mother was born. The caretaker didn't look at it that way. By the time I turned the SUV around in a roundabout, the caretaker was in his truck, and he blocked my path so all I could do was sit in the driver's seat and remain frozen.

I didn't have to wait long. I kid you not. At least eight black and white police cars came roaring up the driveway with lights flashing and sirens blasting. The Johnson's were a prominent family in Cleveland, Tennessee for more than a century, but this was overkill.

I went directly to jail and spent a sleepless New Year's night watching the other inmates receive their commissary including coffee grinds which they all snorted while I remained on the top bunk with my face against the wall and the covers over my head. All night the other eleven prisoners bounced around the room like bunny rabbits and talking the most ridiculous gibberish I'd heard since I was incarcerated in Miami twenty years earlier.

Over the next nineteen days I was so unruly, even by jailhouse standards, they rotated me all over the ward. General population. That didn't work out. Religious section where I got into a fight before they moved me to where all the "crazies" were housed, but when I refused medication, they transferred me to solitary confinement where they took all my clothes including my underwear. I guess they thought I might shove my underwear in my mouth and choke to death. Regular prison garb was replaced with a jacket that went over my head and was so sparse it barely covered my privates.

Long story shirt, and there was a lot of drama, but I don't want to give the blow-by-blow account of my demise like I did in the body of the book. It's the same story again with only different settings and characters. The Johnson's dropped the charges, and my mom drove me away from the courthouse.

My goal is two-fold for "Wrong Side Out," and both are of equal importance. Unfortunately, I can only claim expertise in one. I want people who have acute mental disorders to understand that there is no life without medication. If the patient refuses because of some lame excuse like I don't want to take pills. I explain humbly, "Untreated mental illness is a serious handicap, but a goodhearted abnormal mind on psychiatric medication is like being on steroids. Nobody is on your level or sees the world like you do. Take advantage. Take your f-ing meds."

While there's some exaggeration, it's partly accurate. Without psychiatric medication, I quickly become distrustful and believe the opposite of what I'm told. After months off meds, my thinking becomes highly distorted. On treatment and sober, my mental health stabilizes and no one notices any issues—I appear completely normal.

The main purpose of this book is to help family members and friends better understand what it's like when someone they care about struggles with acute mental illness. During an episode, a person might behave in ways that completely contradict their values, simply because their pain is so overwhelming—even if they believe they're doing everything right. In such distress, they'll do whatever it takes to escape the agony. It feels as though right becomes wrong, and wrong becomes right.

I was released from jail on January 19, 2020—almost exactly six months after I had stopped my medication. At that time, the COVID pandemic was just beginning, and I couldn't make sense of it. My greatest worry was that somehow I had caused it. Ashamed, I isolated myself, knowing I had a long path to recovery ahead. Although I still had a Bipolar diagnosis, it didn't seem important anymore—I didn't even believe it. Instead, I felt the rest of the world was out of touch, not me; I thought I was fine.

For another six months, I mostly avoided medication, only taking it when others insisted. My mom wouldn't let me visit unless I complied, which wasn't a surprise—others didn't want me around either. I was even discharged from the psych ward for refusing medication. But my journey wasn't over yet. Still hoping to prove my stability after years of keeping a journal, I decided to look for work. I received a job offer from a leading real estate firm in Chattanooga, but it came two weeks after my interview, and by then I had moved on. When the company president called while I was already in New Orleans, he was taken aback, especially since I'd seemed so eager to begin anew in Chattanooga.

Living in New Orleans quickly became overwhelming. Fortunately, my financial advisor found me a corporate apartment with a short, three-month lease. It was the so-called "Summer of Love," right during the COVID lockdowns, when New Orleans imposed stricter restrictions than most cities in America. Bourbon Street wasn't just partly shut— it stayed completely closed for weeks or even longer. I struggled to understand what was happening; I felt as though Lane was monitoring me and that everyone was watching my every move. My thoughts raced endlessly, and focusing on anything became nearly impossible.

For some people, that season might have seemed like the Summer of Love. For me, it brought back memories of 1999, when I wandered Miami's streets barefoot. At least this time, unlike twenty years before, I managed to keep my clothes on.

My paranoia and inability to concentrate drove me to search for peace anywhere I could, caring little about where I ended up. I became fixated on finding the ideal job. I looked for work in New Orleans, applied at a Kentucky Fried Chicken in Santa Fe (where I didn't get hired—my impression was I didn't fit the image they wanted), and managed to wait tables in Taos, New Mexico for five days. During that brief stint, I went without food until I escaped Taos and returned once again to New Orleans, which felt unbearable during the continued shutdowns. Live music was absent, and very few restaurants were open.

During this period, my recent schizophrenia diagnosis made me extremely anxious. I visited a doctor in New Orleans, who prescribed Zyprexa and Paxil as requested. Despite this, my mental state was so unstable that sometimes I couldn't even find the pharmacy—or I irrationally suspected the doctor and Lane were having an affair. Everything felt out of control.

When I looked for psychiatrists in New Mexico, I was repeatedly told their schedules were booked. If I needed medication, I'd have to go to the emergency room, which would mean spending at least a few nights in the psych ward—something I wasn't willing to do. My impaired ability to think and focus left me unable to envision any better solution. As I had done many times before, I fled New Orleans in the middle of the night, heading home to my mother. Although I wasn't happy about it, I knew she would help.

On the way, I stopped at Fort Walton Beach, drawn there by nostalgia. One of my family's first vacations had been in Fort Walton Beach. Feeling defeated and desperate, I still believed that Lane Johnson was alive and following me. I had very few options and didn't want to return home, especially at forty-eight. But that's what I was about to do.

To help you understand my mindset, here's why I chose Fort Walton Beach. My family used to vacation in this military town next to Destin, Florida when I was young. We stayed with friends of my parents; the husband had lost his leg in Vietnam, and while recovering in the hospital, he built an intricate model battleship from glue and countless tiny pieces. I watched this one-legged man swim in the ocean—a remarkable sight for my young eyes. The memory was cemented when Doug gave me his battleship. I recall saying that my daughter wouldn't appreciate it; perhaps he had hoped for a son.

But on this day in August 2020, I needed divine intervention. I was looking for anything to emancipate fme from Lane's occupation in my head, and I thought of that childhood family vacation. I thought to myself. I will amputate my leg if that damn Lane stops following me around. Without hesitation, I called out into the GPS. "Fort Walton Beach, Florida."

Looking back, I spent years searching for answers that never fully explained my struggles. Doctors labeled me with various diagnoses—bipolar, mood disorder—but none seemed to fit. Medications brought only fleeting relief or side effects, leaving me wondering if the system was failing me. I realized mental health can't be easily categorized; symptoms and diagnoses often overlap, shifting from one clinician to another, and no label truly captured my condition.

After months of restless driving, I ended up in Fort Walton Beach, unable to find a hotel and weighed down by frustration, especially regarding Lane. Even after twenty years since our engagement and eighteen since her passing, I suspected she'd hidden a camera in my car. I'd always placed Lane above others, never expecting to meet someone who would change my perspective.

From my first step into the Quality Inn, I was drawn to Jenni behind the front desk. Her professionalism and unique vintage-inspired style immediately stood out. Jenni, who is of Jamaican and Indian descent, impressed me with her warm demeanor and distinctive look.

Although I had never dated a Black woman before, I found myself interested in learning more about her background. My interest was obvious—I often found reasons to pass the lobby and chat. Not long after, I started writing a book using the hotel computer, which I eventually published as "Free and Satisfied" in 2025, though Jenni may not know it exists.

Thirteen months after quitting psychiatric medication, I made a reckless choice: deleting everything I'd written over two decades. I even discarded my thumb drive while driving to New Orleans, convinced it was time to let go of my life's work. It wasn't until I needed to earn a living that the loss truly sank in—writing had been my main pursuit, despite the minimal income.

Inspired by Jenni, my first romantic interest in twenty years, I started writing again in Florida. The area felt more open than previous cities I'd lived in, and soon I sought permanent housing. Motivated by the rise of micro poetry on Instagram, I tried my hand at short poems, sharing some with Jenni. She eventually realized my eccentricities, especially after I discussed personal paranoias and Lane's influence, ultimately leading to our falling out.

My paranoia and compulsive tendencies, like calculating equations or reading words backward, persisted. Attempts to seek psychiatric help failed, fueling my irrational beliefs. These struggles strained my relationship with my mom, who remained supportive but firm. She advised me to go to the hospital, making it clear I had to solve these problems myself; no one else could rescue me.

I have been admitted to mental health facilities at least ten times over the last twenty years. Although I never physically resisted intake,

I initially disagreed with the diagnoses. Typically, by the time I was released, my thoughts became more organized.

Yet even then, I felt worse than ever and struggled to make decisions. Since arriving in town, I'd eaten almost every meal at the Red Lobster next door except for one, but couldn't explain why; any attempt to try other places filled me with guilt. I changed my clothes several times a day, searching for a permanent home but hesitant to leave the Quality Inn. My thinking grew so repetitive that I pictured myself living there forever.

A bottle of Woodford Reserve bourbon sat in my room, and strangely, my drinking lessened when I stopped taking medication—mainly because I was focused on controlling my emotions. For the past year, I had fought anger so fierce that my fists would clench and my eyes nearly bulged. After moving to Florida, things deteriorated. Drinking became a daily routine, often starting in the morning.

I took a shot of bourbon, hoping for some clarity. As I paced around the hotel room and looked out the window for guidance, nothing came. The second shot burned as it went down, but now I felt loosened, almost cheerful. I knew I needed to resume my medication but didn't want to go back to the hospital—that felt like surrender. Still, I took a third shot for courage.

As a gentle buzz settled in, my mind was clear enough to consider going to the emergency room. It seemed like the right move, yet I hesitated, worried about driving after three drinks and the possible legal consequences, even though I felt fine. In the end, I called 911 and asked to meet in the Red Lobster parking lot—there was no way I wanted to be picked up at the Quality Inn in front of Jenni, even if it really didn't matter.

It never fails—whenever I'm almost arrested or checked into a mental hospital, I hope for clemency and medication I've relied on for years. After repeated admissions, I know it's not easy.

Nurses ask standard questions about self-harm; I always deny any suicidal thoughts to avoid being hospitalized further. Off medication, I resort to lying and doing whatever I can to stay out of the psych ward.

Even when I lied about drinking and smoking, hospital staff didn't buy it. I'm sure I reeked. Each person asked me the same questions. It went on for hours as they passed me around like a hot potato. Despite my optimism, after a meal, a nurse arrived with a wheelchair—I knew I was going into the mental health ward.

"Really?" I cried out. "You're taking me in there. I just need medication. I'm all right."

"The police just picked you in a parking lot because you couldn't drive. I'm just taking you to the holding area before they move you to general population."

"Think I have a chance of getting out?"

"Just stay relaxed. You'll see the doctor soon."

Inside the psych ward holding area, everyone blended in—same clothes, same tired walk, same mood, same conversation. I just waited for the doctor to arrive; certain I'd be released soon, but time moves slowly in the psych ward. Hours later a burly guy, wearing cowboy boots that clicked with each step, and blue jeans so dark and crisp, it looked like they had been ironed. He didn't look like a psychiatrist compared to usual eggheads I saw. This guy would probably get stoned to death in Harvard Square just because he didn't look the part.

The doctor led me to a small, cluttered, and disorganized office. I guess that many doctors used the same office for different purposes. One of which was a psych interview. The doctor sat in his desk chair and turned around to where I was facing him sitting in an uncomfortable plastic chair. This was intense. Are they going to shine lights in my eyes and see if I sweat?

"I'm Dr. Brown. What brings you in here today. Looks like you were self-admitted," the doctor said in a normal voice.

I looked into his hazel eyes and reddish face, probably from drink, and I discerned a genuine concern from Dr. Brown. I wanted to be as honest as possible. After all, I was already there.

I shook my head in the door's direction. "Everybody out there knows who I am?"

Dr. Brown jerked his head and asked, "Who knows who you are?"

I nodded again as if it was obvious. "Everybody?"

"Out there?" he asked, meaning the psych ward.

I thought he knew it, and I wanted an honest conversation because I was pretty sure I knew what they were doing. CIA again. "Everywhere I go people know who I am."

"Are you from this area? How would they know you?"

"I don't know, but they do." Then I whined, "You know what I'm saying."

The doctor remained puzzled. "I really don't. What are you saying? You seem obviously nervous."

I fidgeted and then snapped my head twice at the door as if the someone would enter. "Yes. I am very anxious. You would be too."

Dr. Brown leaned back his office chair, Besides the cowboy boots he was wearing a yellow button down tucked into his crisp blue jeans. No tie. For a moment we were silent, and then Dr. Brown asked me, "What are you thinking about right now.?"

In the hallway a nurse wearing green scrubs appeared in the window. She was walking by in the hallway.

"Since the nurse is wearing green. I think you are keeping me here to steal money my money."

"What else?" the doctor continued.

"They keep on offering me peanut butter and jelly sandwiches. Why? Are they trying to poison me?"

"No. They're just doing their job. What else? What do you think of my office?"

"There's no pictures."

Dr. Brown looked around and nodded. "I share this office, Mr. Savage."

"I figured."

"I bet you did. And the office being untidy upsets you?"

"Not especially, but you asked me what I was thinking about and I told you."

"I'll ask you again. What are you thinking about right now?"

"Honestly?"

"Yes. Of course."

"I'm afraid you're never going to let me leave."

"What's your diagnosis?"

"They told me I was Bipolar for twenty years. Last doctor diagnosed me with schizophrenia. I don't know. I take Zyprexa. I know it's an antipsychotic but isn't it a mood stabilizer too?"

"Yes. Bipolar patients are on either lithium or Depakote."

My eyes were oiling up I was so upset. "But why did they tell me I was bipolar if I'm not taking Lithium or Depakote?"

"Zyprexa has shown mood stabilization effectiveness as well."

I raised my eyes from the floor. "Tell me the truth. Am I schizophrenic? Just tell me. I want to know. It's very important for me to know. Why don't people understand that? Am I schizophrenic?"

"I don't know if you are schizophrenic, but you are prescribed the correct medication if you are schizophrenic, but I don't believe that's your primary problem."

I'm sure my mouth was agape. "What is my problem then?"

Dr. Brown heartily patted me on the knee and then stood up smiling. "You are going to be just fine. Don't worry. You're not going to be here forever."

"What is it?"

"Mr. Savage. You have a severe case of obsession compulsive disorder. OCD."

"OCD? But nobody's ever said that to me."

"Obvious as day to me. We'll start off on a low level of Prozac and go from there. You'll be out of here in no time."

"I'm not bipolar or schizophrenic?"

"You're not taking lithium or Depakote. Another doctor diagnosed you as schizophrenic or schizo-effective. Your diagnosis of psychosis appears accurate. It was just incomplete."

"OCD? I don't' understand. I've only been talking to you for five minutes if that. I've been doing this for 20 years," I said.

"Feel fortunate. OCD is not easy to deal with, but it's treatable. Trust me. You're going to be a new man in no time. I'm going to take you off Zyprexa and…"

"Off Zypreza? That's the only that has worked in the past."

"We're going to try something different, so you don't end up back here. How does that sound?"

"Sounds wonderful."

"Good. I'm going to start you on Abilify and low dose twenty milligrams of Prozac. Prozac is the best pharmaceutical for treating severe OCD."

I sat very still for a moment. "OCD?" I asked softly.

"Yes sir, Mr. Savage. Now get out of here. Everything is going to be alright," he said almost sounding playful.

I didn't skip out of the room, but I was optimistic. After spending two decades consulting top psychiatrists in hospitals from Northern California to New York City, not one doctor ever dared to tell me I was schizophrenic, even though I suspect they knew. My diagnosis of severe OCD was clear to me now, yet no one—myself included—ever raised it as a possibility.

AFTERWORD

Delivering a diagnosis of schizophrenia is particularly challenging for psychiatrists. The stigma associated with the disorder, coupled with the emotional weight it carries, means that doctors approach these conversations with great care. They worry about how patients will respond, whether it will affect their self-esteem, and if it might discourage them from seeking or continuing treatment. In my experience, despite consulting renowned professionals for years, no one ever directly told me I was schizophrenic. This was likely due to their concerns about my reaction and the difficulties involved in communicating such a complex diagnosis. Ultimately, sharing this kind of news requires a balance between honesty and empathy to ensure that patients feel supported and understood.

Receiving a dual diagnosis felt devastating at first. I was overwhelmed by the question, "Why me?" The relentless, unwanted thoughts swirling in my mind weren't the escape I had hoped for, but I soon realized my experience was not unique. Dr. Brown explained that while some people with severe OCD can function well, others face significant challenges. There is no denying that living in these conditions is difficult.

My life took a positive turn after Dr. Brown diagnosed me with paranoid schizophrenia and severe OCD. In hindsight, the signs of obsessive-compulsive disorder were present from the beginning—especially my persistent fixation on Lane and the impulsiveness that led to my proposal. Both behaviors were clear indicators of OCD that had gone unnoticed for years.

Initially, I was misdiagnosed with bipolar disorder and given medication that didn't address my underlying issues, which had a profound impact on my well-being. Throughout my treatment, clinicians failed to recognize my obsessive-compulsive symptoms, and I was never informed about the possibility of a misdiagnosis. The reality is that psychiatric diagnoses rely on cognitive assessments rather than definitive medical tests, leaving the final decision to the psychiatrist's judgment.

Coming to terms with my diagnosis was a long journey, marked by initial resistance and gradual understanding. I had to address my own misconceptions about mental illness, letting go of the belief that sheer willpower was enough to overcome my struggles. Over time, I learned that seeking help is not a sign of weakness but an essential step toward reclaiming stability and a sense of self.

If I could offer one piece of advice, it would be this: never stop searching for answers. If the first explanation doesn't feel right, keep looking. Don't let stigma or self-doubt convince you that taking medication means you're weak. The struggle is real, regardless of labels, and survival means facing it with courage.

While I may never fully trust what is written in my medical records, I have come to rely on the patterns in my own life. I know that I do better with medication, and I cannot face these challenges alone. That realization has brought me closure—and I hope it can inspire someone else to find a new beginning.

A FINAL LETTER TO MY READERS

If you've made it this far, thank you. Thank you for walking with me through the darkest corridors of my mind, through the chaos, the shame, and the fragile moments of clarity. Writing these pages has been its own kind of therapy, but knowing that someone else might find meaning in them makes the struggle worthwhile.

I don't share my story because I have all the answers. I don't. What I do have is experience, lived, bruised, and unvarnished. If even one part of my journey rings true for you or someone you love, then I've accomplished what I set out to do.

Mental illness is confusing. It hides, it shifts, it gets mislabeled, and too often it convinces us that we're beyond help. But I want you to hear me clearly: you are not beyond help. Whether it's bipolar disorder, schizophrenia, depression, or something that doesn't fit neatly into a definition, there is always hope in treatment, in medication, and in the people who refuse to let you go under.

If you are struggling, don't give up on finding the right care. If someone you love is struggling, don't give up on them. The road is long and uneven, but it is not impassable. I'm still here. You're still here. That's proof enough.

Take care of yourself, take care of each other, and never stop reaching for the better days. They are out there, waiting.

With honesty and gratitude,

Benton Savage